International Federation of Library Associations and Institutions
Fédération Internationale des Associations de Bibliothécaires et des Bibliothèques
Internationaler Verband der bibliothekarischen Vereine und Institutionen
Международная Федерация Библиотечных Ассоциаций и Учреждений

IFLA Publications 45

Newspaper Preservation and Access

Proceedings of the Symposium held in
London, August 12–15, 1987

Volume I

Edited for the Section on Serial Publications
and the Working Group on Newspapers

by Ian P. Gibb

K·G·Saur

München · New York · London · Paris 1988

IFLA Publications
edited by Willem R. H. Koops

Recommended catalog entry:
Newspaper. Preservation and Access:
Proceedings of the Symposium held in
London, August 12–15, 1987;
ed. by Ian P. Gibb.
Volume 1
München, New York, London, Paris: K. G. Saur, 1988
230 p.; 21 cm. –
    (IFLA Publications; 45)
    ISBN 3-598-21775-7

CIP-Titelaufnahme der Deutschen Bibliothek

Newspaper, preservation and access: proceedings of the
symposium held in London, August 12 – 15, 1987 / ed. for the
Sect. on Serial Publ. and the Working Group on Newspapers by
Ian P. Gibb. – München ; London ; New York ; Paris : Saur.
NE: Gibb, Ian P. [Hrsg.]

Vol. 1 (1988)
    (IFLA publications ; 45)
    ISBN 3-598-21775-7
NE: International Federation of Library Associations and Institutions:
    IFLA publications

Druck / Printed by Strauss Offsetdruck GmbH, Hirschberg
Binden / Bound by Buchbinderei Schaumann, Darmstadt
ISBN 3598-21775-7
ISSN 0344-6891 (IFLA Publications)

CONTENTS

Volume 1

Volume 2

FOREWORD

Robert B. HARRIMAN
Chair, IFLA Working Group on Newspapers
and
Mary Sauer PRICE
Chair, IFLA Section on Serial Publications

The International Federation of Library Associations and Institutions (IFLA) Section on Serial Publications has, on several occasions during the past two decades, focused attention on issues related to collections of newspapers in libraries. This work first concentrated on attempts to gather information about policies for collection and retention of newspapers in libraries throughout the world. Surveys to obtain this data were conducted in 1970-71, and again in 1981. In both instances, an ad hoc Working Group on Newspapers was formed by the section to conduct the research. The current Working Group, originally formed in 1981, adopted an expanded agenda of research and activity to supplement the primary survey work. This expanded agenda included discussion leading to the adoption of a recommended definition of a newspaper; survey and research on newspaper microfilming in libraries around the world; the adoption of recommended guidelines for retention of original newspapers after microfilming; and the drafting of international guidelines for cataloguing newspapers.

As work on these and related projects progressed, members of the Working Group were increasingly made aware of the need, first, to gather and make available accurate information about newspaper collections in libraries around the world and, second, to make an attempt to assist librarians who were facing enormous problems in managing and providing access to their own newspaper collections with little knowledge of possible solutions to those problems.

It was out of the latter need that the first plans for an international symposium arose. For those few days in London, at least, the members of the Working Group on Newspapers, especially Ian Gibb, Johan Mannerheim, and Willi Höfig - the three original members of the group formed in 1970 - were able for the first time to share their interest and their concerns with over one hundred librarians, scholars, and information professionals from every continent in a conference setting. We will venture to speak for them in speculating that the experience of these few days was equal to the weeks and months and years spent in isolated research. And we can speak for all the members of the Group in stating that the Symposium focused the many remaining concerns and issues into a full agenda for further study and work. We are now better informed about what our priorities should be and where the greatest needs exist. We are also now much better aware of those people around the world with whom we can work to accomplish our objectives; they are now our friends and colleagues.

Those who were able to be in London for the Symposium found the sessions to be of great benefit. We hope that some of that can be shared with others through the publication of these proceedings. We also hope that the discussion presented here will provoke broader discussion and expanded research, and that body of literature about newspapers in libraries will continue to grow.

We are especially grateful to the United States National Endowment for the Humanities, Office of Preservation and to the Shaw Fund, administered by the British Museum, for their support of the Symposium. In addition, the contributions from many participants' institutions to make their attendance possible was a key factor in providing broad representation. We are also grateful for the support and interest of the exhibitors who participated in the Symposium.

Finally, we want to give special thanks here to the people who are most responsible for this publication. Eve Johansson, Head of the British Library Newspaper Library, was the driving force behind the organization of the symposium. As those of us who have worked with Eve know, her energy is unceasing. Along with Valerie Nurcombe, the conference planner, Eve spent many long hours taking care that all the little details were accounted for. All those who attended the symposium were witness to their organizational skills, attention to detail, concern for the comfort and well-being of the symposium attendees, her remarkable patience and good humour no matter the hour. Along with Eve, we owe a great debt of gratitude to Ian Gibb, who served not only as the rapporteur for the symposium, but also has been the 'éminence grise' of the Working Group on Newspapers; our 'godfather'. And of course a note of recognition is owed to all the members of the Working Group on Newspapers and the Section on Serial Publications who helped to make the Symposium a success. We look forward to working together with all of you in the future. As the papers that follow will prove, there is still much to be done.

EDITOR'S PREFACE

Ian P GIBB

British Library (retired)

The First International Symposium on Newspaper Preservation and Access took place in London from 12 - 15 August 1987 under the auspices of the IFLA Working Group on Newspapers. This volume includes:

- the papers which were presented at the Symposium. These are in general printed in the order in which they were given. They include those given at the Workshop Groups on 14 August, together with reports of those sessions to the full symposium

- introductions to the pre-printed papers, where these introductions were more than a summary of the paper itself

- discussion following the papers as appropriate

- contributions to the session on National Approaches which were either given orally following the programmed papers, or submitted later for inclusion in the Proceedings

- Appendixes covering a Draft Statement of policy on disposals from the IFLA Working Group, a report on the survey of national newspaper collections undertaken by the Group between 1981 and 1983, and lists of participants and exhibitors.

The Editor is grateful to all the speakers for their timely submission of papers and the help that many of them have given in making corrections for publication. The Editor has, without using too heavy a hand, tried to ensure that for publication any significant discrepancies in English usage or technical terminology stemming from translation are as far as possible corrected. Since the Editor is British the spelling is British rather than American where there are differences between the two, e.g. 'cataloguing' rather than 'cataloging' and 'programme' rather than 'program' (except for computer programs); titles are of course left in the original spelling, e.g. United States Newspaper Program. The Editor hopes that any such amendments of terminology or spelling do not inadvertently alter the sense of what the writers of the papers intended and offers his apologies if they do. The credit for the text belongs to the authors, and the faults to the Editor.

Special thanks for help in preparing this publication are due to Eve Johansson, Head of the British Library Newspaper Library, Valerie Nurcombe, the Symposium organiser, and her assistant, Yvonne Cairns. The Proceedings could have appeared without the Editor but could not have done without the hard work that they have put in before, during and after the Symposium.

KEYNOTE ADDRESS

Sir Denis HAMILTON

formerly Editor in Chief of The Times, London,
Trustee of the British Museum, Member of the British Library Board

Fifty years ago this coming week I became a newspaper reporter in the North of
England. After seven years as an amateur warrior I returned to journalism in
London, and from 1950 I spent my life editing or directing newspapers and
chairing the biggest News Agency. I have, in the last 18 years, been a
Trustee of the British Museum and when the British Library was hived off from
the Museum I became an early member of the Board of the Library. I was involved in both sides of the argument for and against the separation, the choice
of site for the new Library, and the cost and scale of the building programme
and its scheduled stages.

The British are a strange race. We should be proud of our courage in difficult days, in going ahead with a building which has been needed for nearly 75
years, and ashamed of the continuing bickering by politicians, academics and
leader writers about its cost. However, I detect a change from scorn, moving
towards pride and, in two or three years' time, we will be claiming to be
almost as bold and noble as the French in their creation of new museums, and
redevelopment of the old, in Paris - all paid for by the State.

There have been many peaks (and troughs) in my life, but my days around the
British Library Boardroom table have a special meaning for me as this immense
project has been born, and survived its difficult childhood. I have, too,
been able to encourage the microfilming programme at Colindale and I am only
sorry that we could not win more space from the Government for an even more
substantial programme for the archive service.

However, the thrust of my work in newspapers has been the problem of publishing great, internationally known newspapers which, though classed as the arch-
etype of the journal of record, had to be economically viable.

Therefore, when I was invited to give this Keynote Address I was not quite
sure whether I was invited to ascend into the pulpit (and no man has prayed
more than I have for miracles), whether I have been asked to go into the dock
or the electric chair (which is a place most people would like to put a newspaper editor into) - as I have had to do so often to defend the antics or
changes in the Press these last few years, to forecast where the Press of much
of the world may be heading, and how the direction it takes will affect the
lives of everyone in this room.

The concept of the journal of record is an old one - the oldest. As a child I
was taught that the <u>Acta Diurna</u>, the daily bulletins issued in Ancient Rome,
were the first newspaper. So, in a sense, they were. The official gazette
was the precursor of the independent newspaper. And if <u>The Times</u> of London
today is still accepted as one of record, it is, nowadays, a paper of only
partial record and its great reputation is due, in part, to its antiquity. It
was first published when the concept of the official gazette and the newspaper

had not yet become entirely differentiated in people's minds. Thus, The Times
still carries:

- The Parliamentary report
- The Law report
- Obituaries
- University, Service and ecclesiastical appointments and
  listing the examination year results at every university
- Court Circular
- Wills
- Birthdays
- Stock Exchange Dealings
  and many columns of Readers' letters whose quality and
  variety is still a unique notice-board of British
  journalism and of British life.

Most of these are a legacy of its eighteenth century origins.

In using the term 'a journal of record' it is important to be clear what kind
of a record is meant, and for whom it is intended.

There is the long-term historian, 50 years hence. He will not turn to newspapers, except for one purpose. Although treaties, laws, etc., may be printed
in extenso in newspapers of record, it is not to newspapers that historians
will turn for treaties, laws, etc., in 50 years' time. They will be found in
more authoritative texts, in book form or stored on computers and discs or
microfilm. Further, a newspaper account of any political event is bound to be
defective beside the word-by-word accounts of Parliaments and Congresses,
official papers, minutes of meetings, politicians' memoirs, all of which will
exist 50 years hence.

What the long-term historian will turn to newspapers for, and then only for a
small item in what actually happened, is mainly to see how the events seemed
to people at the time, how they reacted. For instance, if one takes a couple
of political histories, both of which quote The Times a lot, Dudley Sommer's
"Haldane of Cloan", and Roy Jenkins's "Mr Balfour's Poodle", it will be seen
that it is for opinion more than fact that the paper is cited.   The facts are
taken from books and official records. It is leading articles and letters to
the Editor mainly that are taken from newspapers, though more senior historians today are working on much more detailed and statistical material which
no newspaper could provide and he or she would have to look at special journals, more and more of which are being microfilmed.

However, it is important to remember that there is another kind of historian,
the short-term historian, who is very important in our day. In large numbers
of colleges there is taught a sort of contemporary history, often by quite
able people. These people are seeking to interpret current events to their
students, and they rely greatly upon newspapers. One of these teachers described to me what he considered a newspaper of record to be in terms of contemporary history. 'It was a journal that carried any important event to its
conclusion; there was a riot, for instance, in a particular country, after
investigation it was found to be a riot fomented by a particular political
group, some leading members of this group were imprisoned, after another interval they were sentenced. The newspaper of record will not miss any item of
this chain of events. That is why it is valuable to the contemporary historian.' This concept of completeness I consider to be fundamental to the function of the so-called journal of record.

It is not only the contemporary historian to whom this completeness is necessary. It is necessary to the politician, other journalists and writers, civil servants, businessmen and everyone concerned in public affairs. Such people do not have time to search original records. They need journals of record which they can file away, especially on microfilm, and refer back to in the confident knowledge that all relevant facts, and factors, in a subject with which they have to deal are recorded there. This is the function which a paper in Britain like The Times ought to perform, which a popular paper cannot. It is important, too, that these facts are recorded with selectivity for this is not exercised in official documents, where recording is indiscriminate. Completeness and continuity are, therefore, hallmarks of the journal of record, as is objective selectivity in the choice of what is recorded.

I confess that I do not like the term 'a journal of record' when applied to very many of the great serious journals of the world. To my mind, it is too narrow. It suggests that a newspaper is written not primarily for the next day's readers but to be stuffed away on a shelf in an attic. I am sure that this is not what those who coined the phrase meant. But, I am sure that this is not the effect that its use may have on the journalists who produce the paper.

Mr J C Merrill, of the School of Journalists in Missouri, attempted in his very valuable book "The Elite Press" to define the kind of paper we are talking about. He defines it to some extent by its readership. It is read by the elite of the country where it exists, as well as by the elite outside. And so, he adds to the qualifications of such a paper, cosmopolitanism. This means the maintenance of a high grade staff of foreign correspondents and commentators.

Courage is another quality which he lists. The elite paper is courageous — because it dares to give the readers a serious and heavy portion of news and views. It constantly attempts to lead, not follow, public opinion.

In 1961 the United States magazine, Saturday Review, undertook a mail questionnaire to discover which of 119 American dailies with a circulation of 100,000 or more were most highly rated by members of American schools of journalism. The main criteria used were:

1. Completeness of coverage in foreign and international affairs, business, the arts, science and education;

2. Concern with interpretative pieces, backgrounding articles, and depth news stories;

3. Typographic and general editorial dignity;

4. Lack of sensationalism;

5. Depth and analytical perception of stories;

6. Absence of hysteria, and cultural tone;

7. Thorough and impartial news coverage and serious-minded moral approach to news;

8. Imagination, decency, interest in democratic problems and humanity;

9. Excellent editorial page;

10. Orientation that rises above provincialism and sensationalism.

However, the élite Press as defined by Merrill goes beyond what I would
accept. He includes the serious papers of authoritarian countries, such as
Pravda, Borba and the Spanish ABC among the elite Press, though in 'a separate
category of eliteness.' To my mind, newspapers which accept an Orwellian
approach to the recording of news and history are not newspapers at all. I
prefer Camus's definition of the good journalist who is 'a sort of day to day
historian whose prime concern is the truth'. 'He tried to tell the truth' is
something I would like on my own tombstone.

To sum up, the sort of newspaper I am talking about, whether we call it a
journal of record, the elite Press or any other name we can devise for it, has
these qualities; it has completeness and continuity in its reporting, it is
responsible and courageous in its comment; it is cosmopolitan rather than
local in outlook; it concentrates on the coverage of what is not sensational
or trivial – and it is ruthless in its pursuit of accuracy.

I should say, now, that though much has been written about the duties of the
elite Press, much less attention has been directed to the economic difficulties of running it. Now it is a very common jibe at newspaper proprietors
that they lower standards in order to make profits. I does not seem to occur
to many that by raising standards they may incur losses. I think no-one has
lost more money in running newspapers than I have.

We hear praise for the idealism of those who would run newspapers on a "non-
profit-making basis". Some of those running serious newspapers – incredibly,
there are no less than five each day in London – would be content enough, no
doubt, if they could only run them on a "non-loss-making" basis.

It does not seem to occur to some critics of our industry that the only alternative to running a Press on at least a "break-even" basis is to subsidise it.
And that subsidy means either a very high degree of altruism on the part of an
individual – few such now exist – or the forfeiture of independance either for
dependence on the State or on some agency which is likely, by the nature of
things, to be sinister in terms of a free Press. There are, I know, other
forms of subsidy in Europe – for instance, the levy on advertising, or on
newsprint and distribution – but none that I have so far heard of or can think
of, which are not hazardous to the operation of a free and efficient Press.

In the first place, the standard of editorial staff has to be high. One sup-
reme quality needed is ability to comment with real insight and vigour. The
Leader writers and commentators have to be first-class minds. I have seen it
said that they all have to be University men. In the past this was not always
true. J L Garvin, A P Wadsworth and Sir William Haley had all by-passed the
University. But I doubt whether this could happen today. The proportion of
young men who went to Universities before the war was small. With the development of higher education the likelihood of anyone but a University graduate
qualifying for employment in the elite Press is slight. In fact, he will find
it hard to get a writing job on a national newspaper at all. A paper like The
Times needs half a dozen Leader writers who are not only graduates but graduates of first-class Honours quality, who can also write. Maintaining staff
of this standard is hard, and now more expensive to come by. (Incidentally, I
would plead with my newspaper publisher friends to upgrade the status of
Librarian, who should be a graduate.)

It must have a fully qualified foreign staff. This means keeping something

like 20 highly experienced foreign correspondents en poste throughout the
world. Moreover, there is much more foreign news now than there used to be
and issues are more complex. It relies reciprocally on syndication services
with papers like the New York Times. Above all, it relies on the news agencies. Their role is becoming ever more important (and no great agency will
ever subordinate accuracy to be first with the story). It is no longer possible to pretend that even elite papers can, by themselves, keep all quarters
of the globe covered at all times. I was, for many years, a director and
Chairman of Reuters. Any mistake transmitted by Reuters has to be reported
immediately to the Chief Executive and each member of the Board receives a
monthly list of any inaccuracies. No one is allowed to file in his dispatch
any of his own opinions, though he can quote those of the key figures.
Reuters, incidentally, is constantly increasing the size of its reporting
staff, many of whom are exposed to constant danger.

One of the most expensive items on the budget of the British newspaper is
newsprint. The calls on newsprint of a paper of record are apt to be heavy.
All editors, as we know, are bothered by lack of space. They are constantly
exercising options. These options vary with the style and policy of newspapers. Editors of the elite Press are often faced with very hard options.
How can they pursue important trends while at the same time reporting dramatic
news?

The modern age has placed upon the editor another requirement. He has to
produce a first class business section together with up to date information
and statistical analysis on the money markets. From the point of view of both
costs and reader interest the editor has got to pack all this into a manag-
eable space. It is a hard assignment.

Now I want to look at the situation in other countries, most of which I have
visited in great depth during my career. One of the difficulties here arises
from what I said earlier on - the difficulty of defining papers of record. So
the choice of foreign papers which I am going to make for comparison must be
pretty arbitrary.

I am excluding, for instance, a paper like the Wiener Zeitung in Austria,
which is most certainly a paper of record, because it is subsidised by the
State and, therefore, offers no basis for comparison.

I am excluding Le Monde, which is certainly a leading member of the elite
Press but which has an organisation which is entirely peculiar to itself.

Let us look, however, at a few well-known and serious papers which are listed
as members of the elite Press by Merrill:

> 1. The New York Times
>
> 2. Neue Zürcher Zeitung
>
> 3. Asahi Shimbun
>
> 4. Frankfurter Allgemeine Zeitung
>
> 5. Le Figaro

The five papers I have chosen to look at are not, of course, all identical in
character. Asahi Shimbun, for instance, has a mass circulation of 6m. in the
morning but because of the social and educational situation in Japan, can well
claim to be an elite paper.

The Neue Zürcher Zeitung is specialised in economic and commercial fields.
The Frankfurter Allgemeine Zeitung is owned by a Foundation not primarily
interested in profit. The New York Times has a virtual monopoly of the elite
Press in the United States but is increasingly challenged in this role by the
superb Wall Street Journal, the Washington Post, and that extraordinarily
competent Herald Tribune. Nevertheless, this group of papers does seem to
have a lot in common. Asahi Shimbun has an exceptionally large corps of
Leader writers.

It is impossible not to draw the conclusion that this type of paper fares
better abroad than in Britain. This is because Fleet Street is the most competitive place on earth. We have eleven papers each morning fighting for
survival. The élite papers of many countries have no competition whereas,
there are five quality papers here. If there were fewer one would emerge as
the "outstanding paper of record". I am hopeful that The Times, now it is
moving back into profit, may next year be able to afford the paging to resume
those things it dropped, such as the report of the European Parliament. But I
should like to point out that the financial situation of the paper in the last
four years called for drastic action and I do not disagree, for the present,
with giving more space to features than to some matters of great importance
but very small readership.

We recognise that newspapers have to develope as they go along. Television
has, to some extent, stolen the thunder of the daily Press in the reporting of
spot news. It has, therefore, thrust upon the quality Press the role of
interpreting the last day's doings in far greater depth, and far more rapidly,
than used to be necessary, and there are signs that television will give
longer bulletins.

I come now to my answer to what concerns you so much, whether the substantial
need for investment in microfilming, storage and the requirements of the
market place will change in the next half century. I feel I can absolutely,
unequivocally make this prediction - they will not.

Twenty years ago the two leading publishers in London, Mr Cecil King and Mr
Roy (later, Lord) Thomson, who, between them, owned half the national Press,
said that by today there would be only three or four London morning papers
left; that probably all the six provincial mornings in Glasgow, Edinburgh,
Liverpool, Birmingham, Cardiff, Aberdeen would, with their service of balanced
and accurate regional news, have gone.

Their argument was based on the continued switch to TV of advertising and the
unlikelihood that the printing unions in Britain would ever produce the electronic newspaper, which would be delivered through the letter box while the
readers slept, or use the new printing technology then common in many countries. Their dire predictions were way off course.

The newspaper is mobile. You can read it in the train or the 'plane, on a
beach, on a car journey, or in bed. You can read it next day. The criteria
of the television news bulletin is its graphic quality. The best news broad-
casting is radio, particularly the BBC World Service.

The weekly newspapers thrive on increased advertising and sales and there are
plenty of journalists willing to cut their teeth on the modest items they
report - from funerals to birthday parties. No one here is quite certain
whether one should microfilm the free sheet (which increasingly contains

editorial matter) of which there are now nearly 1,000 in Britain as well as 89
provincial dailes and 850 weeklies, which will in 50 years' time be an absolutely vital record of the day's local news.

Unfortunately, the public now laps up all the scandal going and most proprietors of tabloids spend crazy sums in acquiring material – true or false.
It deeply distresses me. One can be popular without this. Yet I would rather
total freedom than censorship. And in 50 years' time the students and historians will be wondering why society changed overnight, and will want to study
all the tabloids. If one wished to analyse the whole story of Britain and the
Falklands the opinions of the man in the street, especially on such matters as
the sinking of the Belgrano, will require daily reading of The Sun.

I do not forsee any massive change in archive systems for some years. Every
alternative has its problems, storage, cost, and who, as yet, wants a paper's
contents stored on a computer, but the compact disc is a different matter and
may emerge in the next century.

So, ladies and gentlemen of the archive, sleep soundly. Providing there are
no unforeseeable political upheavals, the newspapers will survive at about
their present levels. There will be massive growth of special publications,
most of which will need microfilming, – and how does one deal with the
colossal problem of those TV programmes which must be kept for the record?

As Britain and other countries become more ethnically mixed (Bangladeshi,
Punjabi and the like) ethnic newspapers will become important records of how
these races were absorbed into the total community, and this applies to almost
every country in Europe.

That this conference is being held shows that the progressive forces in archives realise that more co-operation and less duplication inside individual
countries and around the globe is necessary and a central forum was vital to
discuss methods of achieving our ideals.

I therefore congratulate you and your organizers on your initiative in organ-
izing this most important and monumental conference and on the fact that it is
going to be recorded in some way. I am full of admiration for you and extremely proud to have been asked to give the keynote address.

HISTORY AND BIBLIOGRAPHY OF THE PRESS

Dr Hans BOHRMANN

Director, Institut für Zeitungsforschung, Dortmund,
and
Geschäftsführer des Mikrofilmarchivs der deutschsprachigen Presse e.V.

INTRODUCTION BY DR BOHRMANN

It is important to see that the press in the 18th and 19th century and in the days of the 20th century has different roles. We have to take into account the role of the other instruments of mass communication and we have in the 20th century not only the television but also radio, phone and another and other printing media. These media make a difference to the role of the press. In former centuries we have only the press to inform the public. Newspapers are significant for research into the press as part of a modern science of communication in their content and as regards the change that they undergo. I think it is not the task of the history of the press to name all the titles of the newspapers which appeared in one country or another, but to say what are the contents of these newspapers and what are the circumstances in which newspapers could be written, printed and circulated in a specific moment. Only thus can the naive identification of newspaper report with historical reality be avoided.

The first demand for the researcher dealing with the press is based I think on the classical example of the exercise of librarianship namely bibiographic control; this is the first big problem we have. In most cases we do not know how many newspapers appear, what is the circulation and so forth. My paper deals with this problem in the first part, in the second part I list the attempts of German scholars to bring about a complete bibliography of newspapers and the failure of these attempts and in the last part of my paper I make some remarks about a new attempt to establish a good bibliography of German newspapers with the help of the computer with the Zeitschriftendatenbank (periodical data bank) which has been prepared for 12 or 15 years in Berlin.

* * * * * * * * * * * * * * * * * *

Today's meeting is devoted to the relationship between research into the press and library practice. The attempt will be made to define this extremely unclear relationship through comparisons at an international level and, if possible, to improve upon it by formulating realistic objectives. This is also necessary since, in the last few decades, the importance of the press for numerous areas of research has been increasingly recognised. The press is not the object of merely antiquarian interest which amounts to nothing more than the interest of individuals in an exclusively personally experienced past. It is not the task, or at least not the prime task, of the newspaper librarian to look things up and produce copies from newspapers about the birthdays of well-known or unknown contemporaries or the founding dates of singing clubs and charitable societies. Newspapers are significant for research into the press as part of a modern science of communication in their content and as regards

the changes that they undergo. In order to establish these contents one needs
to understand the history of the press which must always be seen in connection
with all media of public communication which existed and were common at any
one period of history.

The history of the press, as press historians of earlier decades did not realise, is not simply a question of a more or less hasty succession of newspaper
publishers, newspaper titles, editors-in-chief and journalists, but rather it
is a question of the contents of the press as a mirror of political, social
and cultural developments. The press is an important source for local
history, but also of social history. When communications scientists research
press structures and examine the structure of the contents according to subjects and themes they are doing preparatory work for a critical evaluation of
the newspaper as a source for many areas of research. To use the newspaper as
a source one must gain a critical distance which can only be achieved by a
sound knowledge of the circumstances under which newspapers could be written,
printed and circulated. Only thus can the naive identification of newspaper
report with historical reality be avoided.

To begin and develop this task, whose enormous size can be judged by looking
at the number of historically established newspaper publishing houses, at all
meaningfully there must be a dialogue between press researchers and newspaper
librarians. The librarians must be able to show which newspapers appeared
where, from when until when, and where they can now be consulted. The researcher needs an overview which is complete and reliable so that he can undertake the choice and evaluation of sources necessary for scientific enquiry
according to his own criteria for deciding what is relevant.

The demand of the researcher is based on the classical example of the exercise
of librarianship, namely the bibliography of monographs. There are national
surveys for this which are of variable quality for some periods and countries,
but which have attained a high level in the industrialised countries of Europe
and North America, a level which partly extends to cover a corresponding knowledge of the countries previously dependent on them either culturally or politically. The mistaken demands made of the newspaper librarian lie in the
fact that monographs and newspapers are not identical or comparable. A newspaper not only has universality and topicality of content in the qualitative
sphere, but also in its regular publication dates (periodicity), which are by
no means limited to six times per week, but, depending on time and place, can
go up to 17 or more times per week, thus presenting a formidable problem for
the librarian. In addition newspapers generally have a particular catchment
area to which their content is limited: a town, a region, in rare cases a
whole country, and they are easily comprehensible within this town or region;
but outside this catchment area they cannot be circulated, or they can be only
with difficulty, or only in a completely different edition than the one circulated in the place of publication. The librarian therefore has a hard task
to identify unambiguously the object which is a newspaper and to grasp it.
Most newspaper collections are for this reason not complete but have small or
large gaps. The numbers lost during both world wars have only increased these
gaps in Europe.

But the newspaper also has other properties which are problematic for the
librarian and which make it different from the monograph. Newspapers have a
tendency to change their titles and subtitles from time to time to fit in with
new political circumstances and new social relations. They sometimes even
hide themselves completely, then appear as an exile publication somewhere
else, create secondary publications, assimilate other newspapers which circulate with completely different titles but with the same or largely the same

contents. Newspapers gain supplements, which disappear again without the
editor devoting so much as a line to it. Sometimes these supplements become
papers in their own right and self-sufficient papers continue to appear as
supplements to a newspaper.

In order to recognise clearly all these factors important in establishing the
source of a newspaper, the librarian needs insight into the whole series and
even this autopsy may not offer him the final key, for he also needs, for the
complete bibliographic understanding of his object, quite distinct from monographs, a series of data to do with press history which will, for example,
allow him to recognise gaps in publication as being caused by censorship, and
so on. The librarian must have the paper in front of him, he must not rely on
oral or written accounts from publishers or editors, who frequently are not so
clear themselves as to the facts. How many newspapers have there been which
have celebrated jubilees on the wrong day? And further: the need to consult
external data is true for the present, but it is even more necessary for the
past, for the criteria used today in the bibliographic descriptions of newspapers were not applied so rigorously in previous centuries. In the early
days of the press newspapers had no titles. Later these were of baroque form
and length, so that they could only be used at all for the purposes of bibliography in shortened form. Shortened titles were frequently only quotation
titles, which did not correspond at all with the actual title formulations.
There is for example a politically significant Berlin newspaper, the Vossische
Zeitung 1721-1934, which only actually bore the generally used title Vossische
Zeitung in 1904, the title referring to the newspaper's owner in the 18th
century, the publisher Voss. The rest of the time it had a quite different
title. But for the press researcher it is an entity which can be divided only
with difficulty. It forms a unit and if the librarian wants to make the unit
bibliographically visible, if he wants to practise serious newspaper bibliography, he is forced to overlook a whole host of his methods learned in a long
professional training. All the systems of rules for the recording of titles
which I know are based on the norm of the monograph. One exception is the
periodical magazines which have appeared numerously and in many forms over the
years. These were understood as being close to the series and therefore again
appeared to be related to the monograph. This genealogy does not apply to the
newspaper. Newspaper bibliography can only be begun properly when one takes a
decisive step at this point and defines newspapers as a branch of the publishing media which is quite distinct and therefore also requires its own
rules to tie it down bibliographically.

The history, collection and bibliography of newspapers are inter-dependent.
They are also a precondition for the serious use of newspapers as a source for
research in various subjects.

This realisation has only been arrived at slowly. It did not only depend on a
development of the historical consciousness which only occurred in the course
of the nineteenth century, but also the newspaper medium had to develop to its
highest level of achievement as publishing. It had to become a means of information for all, or at least for large circles of the population as a whole.
The periodic news sheets of the 17th century only partly performed this function and, in as far as they did, this fact was analysed in a pedagogic and
moralistic way rather than an empiric-sociological one. Here too there had to
be a specific development in research in order to comprehend the newspaper as
an object.

I can distinguish four attempts which were undertaken in Germany to get to
grips with the newspaper bibliographically.

The first attempt goes back to the then Strasbourg Professor of History,
Martin Spahn. Spahn gave a lecture to the International Congress of Historical Sciences on 12 August 1908 in Berlin entitled "Die Presse als Quelle der
neuesten Geschichte und ihre gegenwärtigen Benutzungsmöglichkeiten" (The press
as a source of the most recent history and the current possibilities for
exploiting it). In the lecture he made use of the experience that he and his
pupils in Strasbourg had built up in their historical work with newspapers.
He wanted to show that the newspaper conveys extremely valuable information
which can give rise to historically significant insights which would not be
gained from other sources like, for example, diplomatic records. Martin Spahn
was on the one hand criticising the understanding of historical science which
was generally recognised. This conception, in the tradition of Ranke, was to
see political history as the acts of sovereign states, and it therefore sought
the expression of these actions in government records and the private papers
of the protagonists. Spahn wanted also to describe the assimilation of government actions by the bourgeois public and their struggles. He also wanted
to grasp the day by day effects of that lofty sphere of politics which historical science normally describes. This meant drawing up and analysing discussion in bourgeois society by means of newspaper announcements and comment-
aries. For this he needed large comprehensive collections of newspapers which
simply did not exist in Germany. Therefore, and this was the second thrust of
Spahn's Berlin lecture, he proposed a national newspaper museum, i.e. a newspaper library, which should collect all newspapers of importance as historical
sources.

It was a good moment to make such a suggestion, for after Germany was united
politically in 1871 under Prussian leadership, the idea of establishing a
national library had received new impetus. The national library would collect
all German language literature, while the state libraries of the individual
German states had only ever collected the literature of their own catchment
areas. Newspapers had played an increasingly important role since the March
revolution of 1848. But a central collecting point was lacking, and in the
German library planned for Leipzig, which was started in 1911 and on which
work began at the beginning of the First World War, an overall collecting
place for newspapers could have been put into action. Spahn joined in this
discussion. No success was, however, granted him. The Leipzig German library
did not become the central newspaper collecting place. Financial reasons, for
example the considerable amount of storage space necessary, were always advanced against it.

The second move to further the collecting and bibliography of newspapers in
order to advance on the one hand the history of the press and on the other
hand the use of the newspaper as an historic source came from the International Committee of Historical Sciences, an international federation of historians. At the annual meeting of the Committee in May 1929 in Venice, Malcolm
Carroll (USA) proposed the creation of an international bibliography of the
press from similar viewpoints. Suitable experts should be approached in as
many countries as possible who might be prepared and in a position to create a
national bibliography according to the rules which an international Commission
would lay down. The historians' Committee would act as editors of the whole
and guarantee the unity of the product by doing some final editing.

This impulse came from the official face of historical science. It therefore
had a better chance of success than the plans of an outsider to the field such
as Martin Spahn. Nevertheless the realisation of the initiatives progressed
only very slowly. Two years later, at a meeting in Rome, Wilhelm Mommsen, who
was also, as secretary to the international historians' Committee, responsible
for the progress of this bibliography, was able to give an interim report:

'the Commission is of the opinion that a bibliography of the press must
be as comprehensive as possible and should serve all historical enquiry
... It is however clear that a comprehensive bibliography with a listing of all newspapers of the last few decades is impossible on technical grounds. The bibliography should be as comprehensive as possible
up to the first appearance of the cheap daily papers. For later
periods there must be a selection which should be as varied as possible
and must if possible include all separate papers which are of more than
just local interest, in general not those papers which basically depend
on the printing of correspondence ... The Commission has provisionally
decided on the following outline for the form of the bibliography.
Each national bibliography should contain: [1] Summary of the history
of the newspaper in the various countries, length 2-12 sides. The
latter length only for those countries with complex press
relationships [2]. A bibliography of literature about the history of
the newspaper business and the history of individual papers [3].
Selection for the period for which a comprehensive bibliography is not
possible ... For the newspapers listed should be given: name, place of
publication, first year of publication and frequency (weekly, daily,
etc. ...). Also political direction, and any changes therein, the
nature of the paper, e.g. if of importance for trade. Listing of chief
editors ... perhaps also of owners who have played a significant
historical role or who have laid the foundations for the politcal
meaning of the paper concerned. Naming of those libraries where
complete editions of the paper concerned may be found. Precise
verification of the completeness of the individual editions is
necessary for this.'

Acting upon this suggestion was facilitated in Germany by the fact that in the
20's a new university discipline, namely newspaper studies/newspaper science,
had been established. Wilhelm Mommsen approached newspaper scientists and
asked for a bibliography of the press to be realised. He gave a report on
this subject at the founding meeting of the German "Conference of Newspaper
Scientists" at the beginning of January 1930 in Berlin. Hans-Georg Klose
wrote in his investigation of newsaper science in Cologne:
'For the formulation of a planned bibliography of newspapers ... a
commission was chosen, consisting of Professors Dovifat, d'Ester and
von Ekhardt, library directors Schulz and Kirchner and the Cologne
assistant Wohler.'(p.261)
Emil Dovifat was director of the German Institute for Newspaper Studies in
Berlin, the largest establishment of this kind in Germany; Karl d'Ester was a
professor at the University of Munich and head of the Institute for Newspaper
Science there; Hans von Eckhardt was a professor at and director of the Institute for Newspaper Studies in Heidelberg; Professor Dr Joachim Kirchner,
library director in Frankfurt, had just qualified as a lecturer by writing a
general picture of the history of the German newspaper and was in the process
of finishing a comprehensive bibliography of newspapers in the 17th and 18th
centuries which had formed the basis of his work on newspaper history; finally
Dr Erich Schulz, director of the Dortmund Stadtbibliothek (town library) and
founder and first head of the Dortmund Institute for Newspaper Research (founded 1926), and who was elected leader of the (German) Commission for Newspaper
Science.

Work progressed only slowly, although there was no shortage of ideas. As
early as 10th January Joachim Kirchner produced a wide-ranging plan of how the
bibliographic work might be organised. Karl d'Ester followed suit in the same
month. Emil Dovifat also took part; he sent in the plan of his collaborator,
Dr Hans Traub, on 14th January 1930. Like Joachim Kirchner, Karl d'Ester

suggested a division of the bibliographic task according to historical periods, although he wanted to treat intellectual papers as a separate case. On the basis of his bibliographic experience with newspaper bibliography he made adequate funding of the project, in particular the idea of calling in foreign collaborators for a fee, into a precondition.

Hans Traub wanted to pursue another course. He suggested a topographic division into geographical units because then the enquiries to be made by collaborators at libraries and archives containing newspapers would be practically and methodologically facilitated, since the helpers would already know about their own local areas.

> 'With a topographic structure the whole project would be given a systematic procedural method, from state to province to town libraries. Penetration of private collections as well as the larger libraries in a clearly defined area would be facilitated. The quickest way of finding the location of a newspaper is to start with the area where it had an influence, this is certainly quicker than looking in a certain period at all areas.'

The exclusion of the intellectual press Traub also felt to be correct. In the autumn of 1930 Erich Schulz summarised his ideas in a memorandum for the international historians commission. He followed the suggestions of Kirchner and d'Ester, but did not go into the possibilities of financing such a project. In the records which have been preserved Schulz's memorandum is the last discussion to do with the bibliographic project. What followed were tactical evasions. On 15 February 1931 Hans Traub sent Erich Schulz a request:

> 'For the first time an attempt should be made to establish the most important holdings of newsapers, approx 2,400 titles, by means of a questionnaire to all German libraries ... In the attached list you will find the most important Westphalian newspaper titles about which the German libraries should be questioned. Local papers, intellectual papers, papers filled purely with advertisements, and magazines are excluded from the questionnaire. The geographic boundaries are based on what today constitutes Westphalia. ... May we ask you today just to read through the list once and let us know from your experience whether we have forgotten any important papers and which titles these appeared under.'

This request, it appears from the later correspondence, was answered promptly from Dortmund with corrections and suggestions for the inclusion of new titles. Traub's letter was the herald of his location index of important German newspaper holdings, which was published in 1933. When Schulz recognised that the Berlin project was progressing while his own bibliographic plans had foundered he decided in favour of a boycott. The holdings of the Dortmund Institute are not contained in Traub's catalogue, but the crucial thing was that the entire initiative for Germany of the international historians' Committee did not proceed any further. The planned bibliography, prepared for as it was by Wilhelm Mommsen with much care and energy, was never achieved. Erich Schulz maintained a complete silence, not only towards Wilhelm Mommsen, but also towards his colleagues on the commission, for example Karl d'Ester. The initiative of the international historians' Committee admittedly also only developed positively in exceptional cases in other countries. The reports in the bulletin of the International Committee of Historical Sciences, which appeared until 1939, testify to this. As I learned from Wilhelm Mommsen in 1964/65, he handed over the bibliographic material on the press which he received in his capacity as secretary of the international historian's Committee to the Austrian National Library, Vienna, in about 1934. The National Socialists did not regard him as reliable, and the director of the Vienna library, Dr Heigl, was to take over Mommsen's duties. Heigl apparently, before the start of the Second World War sent all the plans to the then secretary of the international historians' Committee, Professor L'Héritier (Paris). Publications did not ensue. It is doubtful whether the material was ready for publication, even for individual areas.

For Switzerland and Liechtenstein Fritz Blaser published his bibliography of the Swiss press in 1956/58. This sprang from the initiative of the international historians' Committee. But Blaser had contradicted basic rules of international newspaper bibliography, for example in the arrangement of the newspapers which he did according to title and not place of publication.

The second attempt to create a German press bibliography from the initiative of the international historian's Committee had thus failed. But the location catalogue produced by Traub in this connection provided a practical means of finding important German newspapers. But its significance was seriously affected by the moving about and destruction of newspaper holdings and then also by the division of Germany during and after the Second World War. The details today rarely correspond with actual holdings. In addition Traub limited himself to holdings which had been preserved; he did not produce a complete bibliography. Thus some important titles, of which there were no issues present in the libraries approached, were not listed at all.

For all these reasons it was not surprising that in the 50's, when research was slowly beginning again, a third attempt was started, this time in Bremen. The man responsible was Dr Hans Jessen who had emerged in the 30's as a literate newspaper librarian and now began work on a location catalogue of the German press. This catalogue was meant to achieve two things. It was meant to be on the one hand a complete bibliography of all newspapers which had appeared in the German language, and it was also meant to give the locations where issues of these newspapers, of at least some years, had been preserved. Libraries, archives and also private archives at home and abroad were investigated. This intensive searching of foreign libraries and archives served the double purpose of comparing war losses through evidence from abroad and in particular of advancing the bibliography of 17th century newspapers which became a particular strength of the Bremen project, also under Jessen's successors Lutz Mackensen and Elger Blühm.

The Bremen project for a complete catalogue has also not been finished. Its achievement both as a complete catalogue and as a finding catalogue is limited, although it is certainly the largest list of newspaper titles with locations in the Federal Republic. On the basis of and in connection with the Bremen catalogue two important newspaper bibliographical works arose. Else Bogel and Elger Blühm have since published a three volume bibliography of the German press of the 17th century and Gert Hagelweide, using analysis of the catalogue and the additional help of his own investigations on several bibliographical journeys to newspaper libraries in the Federal Republic and the DDR, published his location index of important newspaper holdings (1974). Blühm/-Bogel have, by means of a strict utilisation of all available sources, described in bibliographic detail the extant newspapers of the 17th century. Bibliography and location index coincide here. Hagelwide, in his bibliographic plan ranging from the 17th to the 20th century, also laid emphasis on the evidence of holdings, while the purely bibliographic viewpoint took second place.

To supplement the Bremen catalogue, which had covered newspapers appearing in Germany and in the German language, a location index of foreign periodicals and magazines in libraries of the Federal Republic was built up by the Staatsbibliothek Preussischer Kulturbesitz (West Berlin). This was published to mark the end of the first phase of editorial work (1975). This index, which was only ever thought of as a location index, has been continuously updated and will now be put into the periodicals data base which is being prepared in the Staatsbibliothek Preussischer Kulturbesitz (West Berlin) with Federal Republic research resources. The periodicals data base is the first sign of a fourth attempt to create a bibliography of newspapers in Germany. Originally developed to give the locations of specialist research periodicals, the periodicals data base is built on the decentralised registering of holdings by research libraries, especially the university libraries, and state and municipal libraries which are participants. Newspapers have come into their own as an additional field of work in the last few years because a whole series of the libraries collaborating on the periodicals data base have also added newspapers to the bibliographic holdings. Connected to this fact the suggestion to bring the bibliographic material of the Bremen location catalogue into the periodicals data base was considered. A close investigation showed, however, that the Bremen data were not suitable for this. But since, in the last few years, newspapers, sometimes in the form of microfilm, had played an ever increasing part in the lending service of research libraries, the question of the relationship between the periodicals data base and newspapers could not be avoided. There is now the prospect that, in future, beginning with films of newspapers to hand in libraries, the daily press will also be contained in the periodicals data base.

This is a long term project and nobody can say today when one will be able to look up the most important newspapers in the periodicals data base. But in view of the large scale of the task of listing newspapers bibliographically, the earlier projects that I have described were in every case doomed to failure in that the tried to make good, in the shortest possible time, what had been neglected over decades. The seed of failure was present from the outset of these projec s. Because the libraries are so scattered and in view of the fact that the o ly copy of a newspaper is sometimes to be found in archives, or even a priva e newspaper publisher's archives, it is clear that this task extends beyond libraries. Progress can only be achieved by recognising this state of affairs and by manipulating data. The periodicals data base has at its disposal the latest technology, the lists are published every six months in microform so that they can be used straight away for bibliographic checking and for the management of inter-library loan, and it is controlled by a balanced system of decentralised and central responsibility.

Assuming that, in the course of the next few years and decades, the periodicals data base system will create a German newspaper bibliography that will become ever more complete, and which can also be printed separately, it is to be expected that the writing of newspaper history will undergo changes in form and intensity. Newspaper history to date has found expression in locally and regionally limited accounts, for example in the multi-volume works of Salomon and of Koszyk an Lindemann. More general accounts had to base themselves on selective or not so selective individual studies or on the general accounts to be found in seco dary literature. The secondary literature is heavily based on journalistic judgements. These can only be questioned by historical scientists when the conditions for an investigation of the whole field based on the division of labour have been produced through the production of a reliable bibliography.

REFERENCES

1   Sources: Exchange of letters with Professor Dr Wilhelm Mommsen, Marburg, about the international newspaper bibliography of the International Historians' Commission, 1929–1934, from the author's own archive.

     Estate of Dr Erich Schulz, Dortmund, Institut für Zeitungsforschung.

2   Periodicals: Bulletin of the International Committee of Historical Sciences, Paris, Presses Universitaires de France; especially Vol.VI, pt.1, no.22, March 1934 (Richtlinien für die historische Bibliographie der Presse, pp.3–13), and Vol.II, pt.1–5, no.6–10, 1929/30 (Commission pour la Bibliographie rétrospective de la Presse, pp.427–441).

3   Monographs and essays
    Blaser, Fritz, (editor) 'Bibliographie der schweizer Presse mit Einschluss des Fürstentums Liechtenstein'. Basel, Birkhäuser, 1956/58. 2 volumes.

    Blühm, Elger, and Else Bogel, 'Die deutschen Zeitungen des 17. Jahrhunderts. Ein Bestandsverzeichnis'. Bremen, Schünemann, 1971. 2 volumes. Suppl. v. III, Munich (etc.), Saur, 1985.

    Hagelweide, Gert, 'Deutsche Zeitungsbestände in Bibliotheken und Archiven'. Düsseldorf, Droste, 1974.

    Höfig, Willi, 'Besonderheiten der Formalkatalogisierung von Zeitungen', in: Höfig, Willi, and Ubbens, Wilbert, (editors.), 'Zeitungen in Bibliotheken'. Berlin, Deutsches Bibliotheksinstitut, 1986. pp.106– .

    Jessen, Hans, 'Das Zitieren von Zeitungen in wissenschaftlichen Arbeiten', in: Zeitungswissenschaft, Jg.17, 1942. pp.316–325.

    Kilger, Otto, 'Das pflichtmässige Sammeln von Tageszeitungen in Deutschland'. Leipzig, Harrassowitz, 1938.

    Kirchner, Joachim, 'Bibliographie der Zeitschriften des deutschen Sprachgebietes bis 1900'. Under general editorship of Hans Jessen. Stuttgart, Hiersemann, 1969–1977. 3 volumes.

    Klose, Hans-Georg, 'Presseausstellung und Zeitungswissenschaft', in: Bruch, Rüdiger vom, and Roegels, Otto B, (editors) 'Von der Zeitungskunde zur Publizistik'. Frankfurt-am-Main, Haag und Herchen, 1986. pp.197–233.

    Klose, Hans-Georg, 'Zeitungswissenschaft in Köln'. Doctoral thesis, 1986.

    Koszyk, Kurt, 'Geschichte der deutschen Presse. Vol.1 by Margot Lindemann. Berlin, Colloquium, 1966–1986. 4 volumes.

    Salomon, Ludwig, 'Geschichte des deutschen Zeitungswesens'. Oldenburg, Leipzig, Schule, 1900–1906. 3 volumes.

    Spahn, Martin, 'Die Presse als Quelle der neuesten Geschichte und ihre gegenwartigen Benutzungsmöglichkeiten', in: 'Internationale Wochenschrift für Wissenschaft, Kunst und Technik', Gr.2, 1908, no.37–38, pp.1163–1170, 1201–1211. (Vortrag vor dem Internationalen Kongress für historische Wissenschaften, 12 August 1908 in Berlin).

Süle, Gisela, 'Gutachten zum Standortkatalog der deutschsprachigen Presse',
(Bremen), in: Höfig, Willi, and Ubbens, Wilbert, (editors), 'Zeitungen in
Bibliotheken'. Berlin, Deutsches Bibliotheksinstitut, 1986. pp.187- .

Traub, Hans, 'Standortsverzeichnis wichtiger deutscher Zeitungen'. Leipzig,
Hiersemann 1933.

Winckler, Martin, 'Standortsverzeichnis ausländischer Zeitungen und
Illustrier en in Bibliotheken und Instituten der Bundesrepublik
Deutschland und Berlin (West)'. Munich, SAZI, Pullach, Verlag
Dokumentation, 1975.

Zeitschriften-Datenbank (ZDB). Benutzerhinweise, bearb. vom Deutschen
Bibliotheksinstitut und der Staatsbibliothek Preussischer Kulturbesitz
Berlin (West). Wiesbaden, Harrassowitz, 16. Gesamtausdruck, Herbst 1986.

APPENDIX

THE MICROFILM ARCHIVES OF THE GERMAN LANGUAGE PRESS, DORTMUND

The Microfilm Archives of the German Language Press is a non-profit making
organisation founded in 1965 by libraries and archives with a particular interest in the collection and use of newspapers. Amongst the founding members
were the Deutsche Bibliothek (German Library), Frankfurt am Main, as the major
deposit library in the Federal Republic of Germany, the Bibliothek des Deutschen Bundestages (Library of the Bundestag), Bonn, the Bundesarchiv (Federal
archives), Koblenz, the Institut fur Auslandsbeziehungen (Institute for
Foreign Relations), Stuttgart, which has a large collection of German language
newspapers published outside Germany, the Gesamtdeutsche Institut (German
Institute), Bonn, which collects newspapers from the German Democratic Republic and the Institut fur Zeitungsforschung (Institute for Newspaper Research),
Dortmund. The offices of the Microfilm Archives are also in Dortmund.

The main task of he Microfilm Archives [MFA] is to produce microfilm copies
of newspapers which then become available to members of the organisation
wanting to complete existing collections or to acquire new material. This
ensures both the preservation of newspapers and access to them for purposes of
research. As important as the preservation of newspapers per se is - from a
historical and cultural point of view - it cannot be denied that newspaper
collections in almost all libraries and archives are incomplete and that the
loan of newspapers with their unwieldy format and poor wood pulp paper results
in their disintegration.

Film allows a library to acquire as complete a collection of newspapers as is
possible by the integration of materials from several different archives. By
using film individual articles or whole pages can easily be restored to original size and copied. Furthermore film has the additional advantage of being
easy to send on inter-library loan.

The MFA publishes   catalogue ("Bestandsverzeichnis", 1st ed., Dortmund, 1967/

7th ed., Dortmund, 1987, in print) which provides a bibliography of the original microfilm copies held by the MFA. This catalogue is available from the MFA office in Dortmund. Duplicate microfilms can also be ordered from there. The MFA supplies microfilms on a fully customised 35m diazo film reel or on 65.5m direct copy silverhalide film. If a publication is not available on film, the MFA office will help track down the original paper version and where possible will assist with the provision of a microfilm copy.

(Discussion of Dr Bohrmann's paper is included with that of the following papers by Dr Harris and Dr Black and is summarized at the end of Dr Black's paper.)

Dr Michael HARRIS

Lecturer, Department of Extra-Mural Studies, University of London

INTRODUCTION BY Dr HARRIS

In my paper what I have tried to do is to identify some general elements in
the bibliography and history of the English press which had some relevance
across a fairly broad geographical and chronological front. This is an attempt
on my part to acknowledge the international flavour of this conference. However, as I have mentioned already my own research has been focused on what are
essentially London-based publications in the 18th and 19th centuries and in
particular on the commercial structures of the newspaper business, so that is
my starting point, and I might mention in passing that one of the functional
ambiguities in t e general picture of the history of the English press is the
relationship between the metropolitan and the provincial output.

In the phases of newspaper development in this country London is always at the
centre of the picture but it is nonetheless true that the intricate patterns
of newspaper publication nationally have yet to be effectively described. My
comments here are therefore going to be Anglo-centred and are going to relate
to the history and bibliography of newspapers as constituted in this country.

I do not want to be at all structuralist, I barely want to mention a newspaper
by name; in other words, I simply want to bring together some ideas about the
newspaper as a problem and to identify what that problem is.

It seems to me th-t the problem of newspapers is not just the conventional
problem of scale and dispersal. It is not just a question of those physical
difficulties, though goodness knows those difficulties are great enough. The
British Library holdings stretch for, to me at least, an unknown mileage of
shelf space and weigh an unknown tonnage. My own sense of the bulk of the
British Library collection is when I actually got trapped in the stacks of the
North Library looking at Burney volumes when there was a power cut and all
the lights went out and I thought my last moment had come, surrounded by acres
of moribund newspapers but I escaped from that plight.

There is then the problem of bulk and I do not want to deal with that and I do
not want to deal w th the problem of there being holes in the collection. It
is very interestin how when you get close to the British Library collection
that it evaporates in some sense. There are for example large numbers of
newspapers represented by single copies. I am thinking in particular of American newspapers of the 1860's and 70's which are just one-offs. There is that
problem, and there is also the problem of wastage and general loss. Even the
most important 18th century newspapers run out of steam in the British Library
collection or can do. Papers such as The Craftsman, the most important paper
of the first half of the century, which actually disappears after 1740 although publication continued week in, week out for another 40 or 50 years. So
these problems are conventional problems of the collection of newspapers and

the British Library, and the British Museum before it, has been struggling for
well over a century to sort out and control its own collection, to actually
establish what it has got and to describe what it has got and the problem is
at least in hand.

The British Library of course as you will know from your own experience is
also engaged in initiating a national process of listing newspapers locating
holdings and where possible filming those holdings so that they can be maintained at a central point. The NEWSPLAN project is I think one of the most
useful and interesting innovations that we have presently in hand. Now this
programme is largely self justifying. Conservation is the name of that particular game and I think there is a general agreement that there is a profound
value in this and need for it. It is in fact crucial to preserve the materials, there is no doubt about that. However this is not the drift of what I
have to say. What I want to try and indicate is an equally substantial and in
some ways a less tractable problem which I have tried to indicate in my paper
and which I would like to develop briefly now.

This problem is the consistant and general failure to locate newspapers as
well as the massive and equally elusive categories of serials and periodicals
as an object of study. In my paper I refer to the lack of an institutional
base for newspaper history. Now whether or not such an institution can or
should be created, its absence can be taken as a metaphor for the absence of a
methodology, perhaps even as I heard it described recently, a theory with a
small 't' which can be used for the organisation and development of research
into newspaper history.

Obviously there are a lot of people who use newspapers. If you go to Colindale and look in the reading room it is always full of people and there are
always a great number of people working on the press in its historical form.
None the less although lots of people are working on newspapers and through
newspapers the results seem to me very fragmented, almost in some cases incom-
patible and the reason for this is partly at least, and this is my hypothesis,
that the main lines of research remain rooted in the powerful and established
disciplines within which newspapers are not effectively located -these are the
disciplines of history, of literature, of social science. Each of these, even
when directly concerned with newspaper history identifies a set of preoccup-
ations, which it seems to me subordinate and marginalise the press as an institution, as an engine, even as a printed artefact. Now that is my contention:
whether I can substantiate it or not is another matter but I will try and do
so as briefly as I can. Before I do that I would like to say that as often as
not interest in the newspaper, the historical newspaper, starts from its acknowledged value as a source of information. If you go to Colindale on any
given day the majority of people using the newspapers are using them as a
source of information, they are not interested in the newspapers themselves.
The value of the newspaper as a record I think cannot be denied; however, the
tendency to view the newspaper as little more than a collection of discrete
items to be judiciously extracted and deployed across a variety of historically oriented investigations seems to me to conspire with the marginalising
tendency. In this approach to the newspaper as historical record the recurrent use of reflective metaphor, the newspaper as 'a mirror of society', for
example, and indeed the use of the term 'mirror' in the titles of newspapers
presents and constructs a passive one-dimensional image for the press. This
is sharply at odds with the interactional reality. The reference in my paper
to various internal and external pressures is partly an attempt to indicate
the multiple personae of the newspaper and in a way to suggest its position at
the centre of a vortex of activity, commercial, literary, political and so on.
This approach to the newspaper as a passive entity is only one of the problems.

Clearly I do not have time to demonstrate very fully how work on the history of the newspaper based in the established disciplines can distort as well as describe but I can perhaps give one example from the field of history to try and indicate what I am getting at. The majority of historians who have attacked the press have done so through an interest in politics. In this context the primary concern has been with the ways in which politicians have sought to manipulate or were in turn manipulated by the press. It is clear enough that this is an important theme in newspaper history, approaching the vital but difficult area of public opinion: what public opinion was, how it worked, how it manifested itself and what the role of the press was in that context. Even so, in isolating the single issue, politics, the whole character, the whole framework for establishing the character of and development of the press can be distorted. In this setting subsidies become crucial, correspondence between politicians and journalists is given heavy emphasis, stages in the process of party attachment and detachment become central, in other words political configurations gradually assume a predominant interest and are used to define the structures of newspaper history itself, hence the constant and morbid emphasis on the career, for example, of John Wilkes. Now this insidious process within the field of history, seems to me evident in the interesting but ultimately unsatisfactory work running in a line from Arthur Aspinall to Stephen Koss. Unsatisfactory, that is, in terms of newspaper history. That is a critique that I would make for studies of the newspaper from a historical base, the political over-emphasis. It seems to me it is possible also to see studies of the newspaper which have a literary base as equally partial.

I want briefly to pursue the problem of the marginalisation or non-location of the newspaper within the discipline to which it seems potentially at least, most closely related, namely bibliography. Bibliography clearly has a strong library base, that is where it came from, and therefore it has a particular relevance, I think, to us, and yet if you look at the study of bibliography one has to ask oneself: where is the history of the newspaper? Scholars in the field of bibliography have never been very comfortable with newspapers. The reasons for this are complex but have to do, I think, with the status of the newspaper as a sub-literary product. There is this amazing judgement about the nature and importance of the newspaper embodied in the absence of an effective range of studies of its history which is really status based. Bibliographers are also deterred, I think, by the essential instability of the newspaper's text. They cannot deal with a text which is always the same, always different. The newspaper rolls on through time in a way which makes it peculiarly difficult for a bibliographer who is used to, in a sense, identifying a single entity and focussing on it, to find a methodology which will work. It seems to me, therefore, that bibliographers have defined newspapers as ephemara, pushed them to the margins and allowed eccentric individuals like Stanley Morrison to engage with the problem, but it has never been in any sense a central element in that activity.

One can see the physical manifestations of this problem in the organisation of newspapers in the British Museum/British Library itself, I am trying to link here bibliography and the library. At the beginning of this century the bulk of the newspaper collection was removed from the Bloomsbury site. It was removed to the waste land of North London, to Colindale. It remains there, lost in the mists of obscurity, and the decision has been taken that it should remain there. When the new building is constructed newspapers are to remain out on a limb. The original move was not just a matter of storage. Obviously storage was important. But also involved in that move, in that separation, in

that dislocation of printed materials, there was a judgement and the judgement
was about importance, value or lack of importance and lack of value. I would
suggest that the continuing separation, linked to a low priority within the
general structures of the Library and the Museum, has meaning as well as function.

However, I would pass from that to a slightly more positive note in saying
that within the field of bibliography this sort of long term evasion is being
reconsidered. In his Panizzi lectures of 1986, Professor Don Mackenzie has
laid out a new agenda. He proposes, firstly that there should be a redefin-
ition of what consititutes a text. Don Mackenzie's position is that we should
be able to find a way of handling things like, film, video, on-screen electronic material. Bibliography in other words, has got to adapt itself to modern circumstances if it is to survive as a form of discipline. Don Mackenzie
had some very interesting things to say in this lecture about the relationship
even between landscape and bibliography, how in fact the configuration of
areas can have textual and bibliographical meaning. The second point that he
makes in his lectures, which is a sound one I think, is that bibliographers
have got to accept a methodology which will locate the text within the networks of action and reaction, which bear on its construction and use. This is
what he calls the sociology of texts. Now it seems to me that this flexible
model could actually accommodate the newspaper as well as the more recent
forms of non-print technology, and should provide a kind of impetus, a kind of
focus for engagement with newspaper history.

One practical extension to the forms of bibliography which have already taken
place and which is in line with Mackenzie's proposals is the emergence of book
trade history. This is a reasonably undefined area of research, embracing the
creation, production, distribution and consumption of printed material at a
pragmatic level. It is a setting in which newspaper history should be
central, this is not yet the case. The current project to produce the
'History of the Book in Britain', a multi volume enterprise which is now just
on the point of being set up, fails, I think, dismally to acknowledge the
central position of the newspaper. In book trade history how can the study of
printing and bookselling be undertaken without some notion of the fact that in
that setting, one of the organising principles, around which the entire business is constructed is the production of newspaper and related material. I
shall be speaking on that subject at the Bibliographical Society meeting in
October 1987, so it is not something that I need explore here, but to put
these comment in another way, I would simply say that the failure to establish
an effective conceptual framework for newspaper history has not only distorted
the history of the press itself, but has also thrown a large segment of cultural and economic history into disorder.

In conclusion, I would suggest that the mechanical processes of bibliography,
description, enumeration, are moving forward in terms of newspapers steadily.
Although this is the case the general understanding of the newspaper press in
an historical setting remains relatively static. The two enterprises should
be inter-connected. The construction, description and organisation of newspaper collections needs to be informed by a realistic sense of the history of
the press. Whatever the technology, mistakes in ordering material are very
difficult to correct without starting again. I would therefore suggest that
the library system itself should have a direct interest in the struggle to
establish an identity for the newspaper as a focus for systematic investigation. What this means in practice may be worth discussing. Meanwhile, the
task seems to be largely one of consiousness raising, and perhaps I could
mention in this context two gestures in that direction, one the seminar on
newspaper and periodical history organised at the Institute of Historical

Research in the University of London, to which anybody is welcome to attend;
it is held three or four times each term during the academic year. The second
is the Journal of Newspaper and Periodical History, and to which subscriptions
and papers wou d be welcome.

* * * * * * * * * * * * * * * * * *

1. INTRODUCTION

These notes offer an outline sketch of some of the issues which are central to
the construction of the history of the English newspaper press. Although the
focus is on England and in particular on those papers published during the
eighteenth century the intention is to provide a starting point for consideration of output across a broader front. Newspaper history is becoming an
international p eoccupation. Progress has been more rapid in some countries,
France and Germany for example, than in others. However, there are indicat-
ions that in all societies in which print has represented a major cultural
force, an understanding of the workings of the newspaper press through time is
seen as a matter of considerable importance. The mechanisms by which newspapers relate to the societies in which they are produced and circulated vary
widely according to both period and geographical location. Nonetheless a
range of overlapping characteristics can be identified which suggest the possibility of, as well as the need for, the construction of an integrating framework within which the international study of newspaper history can be located.
The remarks which follow are intended as a modest contribution to the debates
which need to be initiated about differences and similarities across sectors
of the world's press.

2. THE DEVELOPMENT OF NEWSPAPER HISTORY

2.1. Background

The initial interest in newspaper history in this country which appeared in
the mid-nineteenth century can, to some extent, be associated with the growing
importance and strength of the English press itself. The timing of the emergence of the newspaper as a major influence within English society is a matter
of some dispute. However, a combination of circumstances in the mid-nineteenth century, not least the massive increase in output, gave a boost to the
notion of the press as the 'fourth estate' and to the general expression of a
belief in its power as an engine of social improvement. In this setting the
idea of newspaper history as a legitimate area of investigation took root. At
the same time the middle decades of the nineteenth century also saw the construction of a national newspaper archive at the British Museum around which
such studies could be located. To some extent the interest in newspaper history was prefigured by the process of collecting. Newspapers had from the
middle of the seventeenth century combined a high degree of ephemerality with
an acknowledged status as a component of the historical record. The production by newspaper publishers from the 1640s of annual indexes and title pages
to be bound up with collected copies was part of a general recognition that
newspaper content offered a durable account of events and opinions. The accumulation of files for reference in the English coffee houses or in such large
scale private collections as those of George Thomason in the seventeenth and
Charles Burney in the eighteenth century, pointed irresistibly towards the
need for some sort of national newspaper repository. The intractable problems

of space and cost alone meant that comprehensive collecting could only be
undertaken on an institutional basis. Through an initially haphazard process
of gift and purchase the British Museum reluctantly assumed the responsibility. Arrangements with the Stamp Tax Office in the 1820s and later the law of
copyright secured a comprehensive supply of newspapers from across the United
Kingdom, supplemented by increasing numbers of colonial papers as well as a
selection from the United States, Europe and other parts of the world. Consequently, from mid-century the rapidly expanding English press, whose output
was secured in a carefully monitored national collection, became a clear target for historical research. It was in this period and against this background that the earliest newspaper directories as well as the first general
histories of the English press were produced.

Although this represented an early start, the subsequent development of newspaper history in England was both slow and erratic. The underlying reasons
for this are complex but the major problems can be isolated within two main
areas.

2.1. The character of the materials

The British Library collection illustrates clearly the intractable nature of
the newspaper as an object for study. On one hand, however great the efforts
at the retrospective filling of gaps, the wastage of material means that the
historian is frequently confronted by blank space. As might be expected, the
rate of survival of papers published in the seventeenth century is extremly
erratic. However, all periods suffer from wastage. In the eighteenth century
for example, even such major London papers as the Champion and the Craftsman
exist only in highly defective runs. More often this problem is focussed in
the lower levels of output and the cut-price publications of the eighteenth
and nineteenth centuries are particularly hard to find. Newspapers published
in the London region after the repeal of the "taxes on knowledge" often escaped even the contemporary compilers of directories and have left no other
trace than a casual reference to a title in an unrelated source. On the other
hand, the sheer weight of material in certain parts of all periods, but most
strikingly from the mid-nineteenth century onwards, make comprehensive, individual investigation almost impossibly time-consuming. How, for example, can
the history of eighteenth century journalism be written when life is too short
to read more than a fraction of the surviving files? Both problems are agg-
ravated by the dispersal of holdings across the country but perhaps most importantly by the lack of comprehensive bibliographical control. The main collections of English newspapers are accessible by way of individual catalogues
developed, in the case of the British Library, over a long period. However,
even here there are difficulties. For example, the Burney Collection of Newspapers is still only available by way of the collector's own manuscript list.
The exclusion of newspapers (and periodicals) from the machine readable
"Eighteenth Century Short Title Catalogue" reflects the way in which problems
of time and money have consistently interrupted the developing control of
these materials. Nonetheless, the British Library, as well as being engaged
in a continuing struggle to develop its own cataloguing system, is and has
been a focus for work in the locating and describing of newspaper holdings
which are scattered across the country. The "British Union Catalogue of Periodicals" remains the best finding list for scholars, while current projects
such as the "Bibliography of British Newspapers" and NEWSPLAN are producing a
great deal of new information. It remains true that detailed bibliographical
analysis of English newspapers is patchy and limited by theme or period.
Historians of the English press have usually found it necessary to assume the
role of bibliographer and to compile their own lists of newspapers.

The materials also present serious problems of definition. Although the pragmatic combination of frequency of publication, style of format, and currency of content offers a reasonable starting point, it is seldom possible to isolate the newspaper and the material it contains from the noisy background against which it has been produced. In the seventeenth century the confusion of forms is considerable. George Thomason's collection of newspapers, newsbooks and related material displays a bewildering range. The major bibliographical project based at Yale University which is compiling a comprehensive list of materials published between 1641 and 1700 has necessarily to use the broader terms of "serial" and "periodical" to describe an area of output within which the newspaper remains submerged. Such problems of identification continue in later periods. Publications produced in London during the eighteenth century with the deliberate intention of confusing their status and ephemeral material at the end of the newspaper range in the nineteenth and twentieth centuries (ships' newspapers, estate newspapers, typescript serials and occasional publications of all sorts) blur the boundaries between forms and make comprehensive historical assessment highly problematic. On the other hand, the miscellaneous content of the newspaper offers its own ambiguities. Material published separately has been absorbed by or thrown off from the newspaper press creating a vortex of output within which separate identification is particularly difficult. Advertising and fiction, for example, are among the components of newspaper content which appear in separate serial forms while throughout the eighteenth century political controversy rambled through newspapers, pamphlets, serial publications and books. The instability of newspaper content has to be accommodated within newspaper history if a realistic perspective is to be established.

2.3. The framework for research

The second major problem to be identified alongside the inherent difficulty of the materials is the lack of focus for the study of newspaper history. In England this area of research has never had an institutional base. The newspaper business itself, though dominated over a long period by traditional attitudes and practices, has not shown much effective interest in the history of its own development. The continued initiation of journalists through an apprenticeship system has meant that the network of centres concerned with the training of personnel, within which newspaper history can be located, has not emerged here as it has in the USA. Library schools are equally limited in number and range of interests. Within the structures of higher education departments of communication, with their heavy emphasis on contemporary issues, sometimes offer support for research. However, only the University of Wales has a department within which the history of the press forms an identifiable component. As a result newspaper history is highly fragmented. Individuals have been inclined to launch themselves into the blank spaces of the subject as a venture. Bibliographies without point and histories without substance are, unfortunately, too often the result of an independent excursion into the field. At the same time, scholars from the disciplines of history, literature and the social sciences have attacked the subject from very different starting points and it is often difficult to see how the resulting material can be integrated into a coherent picture of the history of the English press. If newspaper history in this country is to be established within an effective academic framework it may be through association with the rapidly developing field of book trade history. Although this is currently itself a free floating area of research, the focus on the printed materials and concern with the processes of production and distribution as well as readership suggest a natural affinity with newspaper history. Whether this will lead towards the development of an institutional centre for the exploration of such mutual interests remains to be seen.

The problems identified in outline above represent some of the practical constraints on the practice of newspaper history. As has been suggested they are bound up with the difficulties of historical analysis which arise out of the diverse character of the newspaper itself. How is the historian of the press to accommodate such a kaleidoscope of variables? Shifts in the dominance of forms defined by frequency of publication; differing commercial structures for daily, tri-weekly and weekly newspapers; the fluctuating relationship at all levels between papers published in London and those produced in the English provinces and beyond. These are among the elements of newspaper history which have to be kept in sight and which require a strong sense of balance. However, perhaps the most striking problem of historical analysis lies in the dual character of the newspaper as both a commercial enterprise and as a medium of communication.

3.   PRESSURES ON THE PRESS

In the second part of this short paper a few ideas will be offered on the way in which the highly miscellaneous material relating to the history of the English press can be held together within a general picture. The approach to be adopted is based on the identification of the shifting and closely interwoven pressures, both internal and external, shared by all sections of the newspaper press. The comments mainly relate to the eighteenth century, a period which, partly as a result of lack of bibliographical information, is heavily under-researched.

3.1. Internal Pressures

(a) **Ownership.** Changes in the pattern of ownership with the accompanying impact on organisation and content are crucial components of any historical analysis of the press. Although the structures of the seventeenth century need further investigation it seems that control of most newspapers remained in the hands of the printer. Offering regularity of income and employment, such publications fitted easily into the economy of the printing office. This continued to provide the conventional base for the provincial publications spreading out from London after 1695 and the printer remained a key figure in the conduct of the metropolitan publications of the eighteenth century. However, the force of the newspaper as a medium of communication increasingly attracted the attention of outside interest groups. On the one hand politicians became involved in setting up or buying into London newspapers, overseeing, or at least financing, some of the routine processes of publication and distribution. On the other, the more extensive and probably more important intervention of groups of booksellers, attracted mainly by the value of the newspaper as an advertising medium, led to the virtual take-over of the London press by mid-century. The emergence of this first newspaper establishment operating a variably effective oversight of the major London papers had several long term results. The injection of capital which they gave to the business produced a greater stability in titles and provided the opportunity for an increase in the level of staffing. Offsetting this, the newspapers remained a subordinate element within the trade and the booksellers' interest in commercial stability probably discouraged change in the nature of the London papers. The booksellers and politicians both worked to exclude those whom they identified as interlopers and this in itself had major repercussions on the structure of the press.

(b) **Finance.** Part of any explanation for the form and character of the English newspapers must lie in an assessment of the financial pressures bearing on the processes of production and distribution. The basic costs have to be balanced against the variable sources of income which befit such publications afloat within a highly competitive market. During the eighteenth century income from sales was restricted by constraints of technology, distribution and, to some extent, demand. At the same time, price levels were fixed, at the lower end by the exigencies of taxation and at the upper by public acceptability. Offsetting costs and producing a modest profit from this source alone was therefore only achievable through papers with wide catchment areas and reasonably slow production schedules. In the case of the London dailies and to some extent of the tri-weeklies of the eighteenth century, sales income could barely cover and usually fell short of costs. From the seventeenth century advertising had provided a component of newspaper income and during the eighteenth became a vital prop for the most successful metropolitan publications. This introduces the highly contentious issue of the relationship of financial influence to editorial policy which dominates current debates around the freedom of the press and comes into sharp focus after 1855. Although the provincial weeklies of the eighteenth century were not entirely reliant on advertising revenue, the crucial importance of local contact locked the printers into the prevailing economic system in which advertiser and newspaper-owner shared a variety of commercial interests. In London, where the market was more diffuse, the overlap between advertisers and propietors in the persons of the bookselling shareholders created an equal identity of concern. Finances were a defining element in the conduct of the English press, operating at a variety of levels and influencing aspects of both organisation and content.

3.2. External Pressures

(a) **Political intervention.** The emphasis which has been placed by some historians on this area of newspaper history reflects a preoccupation with the activities of the political interest group with which sectors of the London press were closely associated from the Queen Anne period onwards. The peaks and troughs of political involvement have in this context become the major reference points in the history of the newspaper press. The more general attempts to fit the newspaper into a political structure in which the emphasis is either on change or continuity are equally liable to produce distortions. While allowing for controversy over the extent to which the press engaged extra-parliamentary individuals and groups during the eighteenth century, the broader impact of political intervention is clear enough. Legal action helped to define the range of acceptable content while the taxes on advertising and newsprint, introduced in 1712 and systematically increased thereafter, served to limit the range of purchase. At the same time the deployment of political money in the form of salaries and subsidies could influence the structure of output and offset or supplement some of the market forces which determined commercial success or failure.

(b) **Readership.** The pressure exerted on the English newspaper through the demand and taste of its readers, actual and potential, is particularly difficult to assess. The problem has to be confronted in relation to the shaping of newspaper content but the solutions inevitably remain speculative. The number and identity of newspaper readers in any historical period is itself extremely difficult to pin down. In the eighteenth century the existence of occasional detailed estimates of circulation level and the grand totals of the Stamp Tax returns provide only a generalised outline. However, in spite of the lack of precision it is possible, at least, to offer an explanation of the way in which newspaper content was mediated within English society. Individual publications stood at the centre of overlapping networks of purchasers, supplied through an intricate distribution system made up of hawkers, newsmen, agents, booksellers, Post Office clerks, politicians and personal contacts. Casual access was extended in most urban centres through a miscellaneous collection of public houses and by such devices as shared purchase. As a reactive medium, lacking a large-scale editorial staff, most of the newspapers of this period relied heavily on input from readers, whether in the form of essays, poems, information and news, or advertisements and notices. This material was vetted, printed and then recirculated through the distribution system to generate new responses. In this way circuits of communication were established in which the newspapers acted as conductors of material flowing within English society. Setting this process in motion was one primary objective of the newspaper proprietor of the eighteenth century and injecting material into the system for commercial or political reasons could produce observable results. The operation and use of the communication circuit is perhaps clearest in the field of advertising. However, its actions can also be demonstrated in relation to national politics. Comment and information published in the leading opposition papers of the Walpole period was used to stimulate local pressure groups to lobby MPs on a variety of issues. The texts of the resulting addresses and petitions were in turn supplied to the newspapers and published, providing a stimulus for a further round of local action. The development of the newspaper from the end of the eighteenth century as an almost inevitable component of pressure group activity reflected a role already well established in a more generalised setting. Questions about the influence of newspapers on readers have to accommodate those about the influence of readers on newspapers. The mechanism requires a great deal more systematic investigation before the parameters of mutual involvement can be established but its importance in any assessment of the role of the newspaper in English society is clear enough.

4. CONCLUSION

These elements of ownership, finance, political intervention and readership contact have to be integrated within any study of the history of the English press. The position of the newspaper shifted over time and the balance between the formative pressures varied considerably. In the nineteenth century, for example, the scale of production and the range of output increased dramatically. As England underwent a protracted if erratic industrialisation, the emergence of new social and political groupings created an active environment for an extension of newspaper publication. On the production side, technological innovation impinged directly on the internal organisation of the press. The introduction of railway distribution, the replacement of the hand press by a variety of steam powered machines and the harnessing of the telegraph to the process of newsgathering all helped to streamline the industry. The newspaper assumed for the first time during this period a degree of commercial self-sufficiency. At the same time the tax repeals of mid-century themselves led directly to an increase in the scale of output, the comprehensive development of the local press and the introduction of new forms of management. However, although much as been made of the qualitative changes of the nineteenth century, particularly in the series of political studies in which the creation of a "free press" is part of the hidden agenda, the underlying forces shaping the English publications remained constant. The balance between the commercial enterprise and the medium of communication continued to generate pressures which had to be reconciled within the newspaper business as they still do within newspaper history.

(Discussion of Dr Harris's paper is included with that of the papers by Dr Bohrmann and Dr Black, and is summarized at the end of Dr Black's paper).

Dr Jeremy BLACK

Lecturer, Department of History, University of Durham

INTRODUCTION BY Dr BLACK

I would like to make several reflections upon what we have heard so far with
relation to what possibly is needed in the microfilming of newspapers. I want
first to take up a point that Sir Denis Hamilton made in the first paper: that
if you spent all your time reading the journals of record and ignored the
popular press or what we would now call in Britain the tabloid press, you
might find it very difficult to understand the politics of the last few years.
Now this is not a new phenomenon; one of the greatest problems for historians
of the English press in the 18th century is that the papers that have largely
survived have been the stamped press, the papers in other words that paid tax,
and were of the more expensive part of the market, whereas the papers that
were cheaper (and in addition the papers that were unstamped), have had a very
poor survival rate. As a result we have a skewed and inaccurate portrayal of
the British press of that period. Now if one notices what the prime stress at
the present moment is, either on microfilming by the microfilming companies or
in terms of library purchase by the libraries, one notices that the newspapers
that are purchased and copied are overwhelmingly those of the quality end of
the market. I believe this is going to cause considerable problems to future
researchers.

I also take note of the comment that was made this morning about free sheets.
Now obviously one cannot microfilm 1000 free sheets. It is ridiculous and
nobody would buy 1000, which is possibly more to the point, but again one has
to bear in mind that newspapers set out themselves to serve a variety of purposes and will be of use for a variety of purposes by future researchers. One
of the obvious points of the free sheets is not only are they an important
part of the newspaper production at the present moment, but they also provide
a crucial source of evidence through advertising, which is after all their
prime content, on issues of public concern from the commercial point of view.
In some areas 1 have noticed recently an enormous expansion in advertisements
for bottled water, responding to worries that have been aroused over the quality of the British water supply. If you just simply studied that from the
point of view of editorial comment you would miss such a development.

Now this leads me to a more wide ranging point about newspaper history which
may or may not be controversial, and which obviously is applicable more for
some countries than others. History is largely a product, in a mass sense,
over the last 100 years. During that period it has been dominated by people
whose intellectual traditions are relatively clear in many countries. Most
historians have been secular in their assumptions, most of them have been
liberal or left of centre in their politics, most of them have adopted a teleological perspective, what in Britain we would call 'Whig history'. Now as Dr
Harris very correctly pointed out, historians have therefore plundered the
press for material that supports their assumptions and have purchased copies

of past newspapers, reels of microfilm, etc., that fit into these perspectives. They have overwhelmingly concentrated on the press as a political source of commentary. Now clearly, by country and by region, the importance of
politics varies but it is certainly appropriate to point out that far less
scholarly endeavour has been devoted to non-political aspects of newspapers
than to their political aspects. This has not only gravely distorted in my
view scholarly work on newspapers, it has also gravely distorted the library
holdings of newspapers. I look, for example, at a University library like my
own, which cannot afford to subscribe to enormous microfilm projects and one
finds that what they have bought has overwhelmingly been radical newspapers
from the past. So that if one looks at the 19th Century and if one looks at
the European scene one sees virtually no interest in monarchical newspapers,
catholic newspapers, newspapers that were anything other than to the left.
This I suppose is just part and parcel of the general historical world at the
moment, but if we are to look ahead I think it is quite conceivable that in
100 years the people who will be going into libraries and looking for the
microfilms of past newspapers, will be possibly more interested in the non-
political side of the press, particularly in popular culture, which is an
issue that is becoming much more important in the agenda of historians at the
moment. And secondly that when they do consider politics they may have a more
diffuse understanding of past politics, they may have more diffuse interests,
and if they go into libraries and simply find microfilms of newspapers that
fitted certain political agenda in the past, then they are in danger of being
disappointed. So what I, in other words, am saying is that it would be a
great pity if people in 200 years would be in the same position that we are
to-day when we look back at the 18th century press; we have very good holdings
of some of the major London papers of the high quality level, we have very few
equivalents of the 'Sun's' of those days. We are in danger however, of rep-
licating this situation anew.

So far the papers have shown that there are different ways in which one can
look at the role of the press in the past, there are different ways in which
one can look at the commercial interest of newspapers, and clearly matters
vary by particular country on questions such as censorship. What I think they
do mean is that in the context of limited financial provision which after all
are the constraints which all libraries operate under, it is far better, if
you are going to buy the microfilms of 10 newspapers, that you do not buy 10
quality newspapers. It is far better that you try for a range that is socio-
logically more astute than simply concentrating on the quality press, because
after all it is ridiculous for history to just be a matter for the interest of
the middle class intellectuals.

* * * * * * * * * * * * * * * * * *

This paper will concentrate on the social and political implications of the
development of the press. Based on the author's personal research on the
eighteenth century British press, it is nevertheless hoped that it will be of
value to those interested in other periods. However, the specific political,
social, economic and cultural circumstances of Britain in that period mean
that conclusions based on that period are not necessarily appropriate for
other societies.

In 1774 Voltaire received the sort of sycophantic letter he was well accust-
omed to.
        'It is to you principally that the human spirit owes its triumph in
        surmounting and destroying that ignorance, fanaticism and false

politics have placed in its path. Your writings have revealed to
rulers their true interests. You have showed them that the more a
people is enlightened, the more it is tranquil and faithful to its
obligations.'
The letter, sent by King Gustavus III of Sweden, brought news of a new Swedish
edict strengthening the freedom of the press. It expressed a common view,
held both in the eighteenth century and subsequently, that the extension of
this freedom was related to the freeing of the human spirit, was indeed one
definition of it. It has been common to adopt a perspective on the culture of
print that is in accordance with progressive interpretations of history.

It is first necessary to define what a newspaper is. The impact of the press
is fatally intertwined with the impact of print. There is no clear definition
of newspapers that can enable a ready distinction to be drawn between the two.
It is necessary to adopt a flexible approach to the problem of defining newspapers. There are several possible bases for differentiating between newspapers and other periodicals, including frequency of appearance, size, content
and payment of duty. Joseph Frank defined a newspaper as being printed,
appearing at regular and frequent intervals and concentrating on current
events. That might appear a reasonable definition and yet journals that are
widely accepted as newspapers did and do not devote themselves to current
affairs only. Items that are characteristic of magazines, past and present,
can and could be found in abundance in newspapers. The distinction between
the two is more one of size and frequency than of content. Essay-sheets,
journals devoted to a single essay and bereft usually of news and advertisements, are not regarded by some as newspapers. Rae Blanchard argued that
Richard Steele's tri-weekly paper the Reader, a Whig propaganda sheet of 1714,
which was printed on stamped paper of newspaper half-sheet size, was not a
newspaper for this reason. However, as with magazines, there is a continuum,
not a sharp break, in the case of essay-sheets. Any rigid definition of the
press ignores its fluid nature, with regard to format, content and frequency
of publication. The common goal of newspapers was and is to find readers.
The Country Spectator pointed out in 1792, 'To find readers is the first
object with every man, who offers his labours to the Public.'

Any definition of a newspaper must thus be a working one, but this makes it
harder to differentiate the press from other printed works when judging its
impact. There is little doubt of the general received wisdom on the impact of
print. Its role in subverting established beliefs and institutions is generally taken. Elizabeth Eisenstein has recently claimed that :
    'the drive to tap new markets, which differentiated the profit-seeking
    printer from the manuscript book dealer was not neutral with regard to
    censorship. It also worked against elitism and favoured democratic as
    well as heterodox trends. Printers reinforced opposition to theolo-
    gians and priests who veiled gospel truths and sought to withhold
    sacred truths from the profane.'
In short, print sapped the foundations of the old order and helped to usher in
the new.

It has been common to adopt a perspective on the culture of print that is in
accordance with progressive interpretations of history. This perspective
draws on untested assumptions concerning the efficacy of print and is apt to
neglect the vast amount of material produced that in no way sought to sap the
old order. Some of the greatest producers of printed material in seventeenth
and eighteenth century Europe were the governments and churches of the era.
Print was the medium used for ordinances and edicts, regulations and injunc-
tions. It was an obvious characteristic of what Marc Raeff has termed the
'Well-Ordered Police States' of the period that they issued a mass of adminis-

trative regulations and that these appeared in print. The same is clearly true today both of societies that are regarded as democratic and those that are seen as totalitarian. Thus the printing press represented a tremendous technological advance for the state, enabling it to extend the audience for its views, possibly crucially so given the disruption in certain countries of the relationship between state and church in the early—modern period. As the nature and strength of so—called absolutist states is increasingly questioned by historians, it is possible that we may well end up with an interpretation that sees print as a source of the expansion of state potential rather than a subverter. In particular, print helped to extend the range and depth of governmental penetration of society.

In questioning the historical impact of the newspaper press, it is necessary to ask whether it promoted change. One source of the exaggeration of the impact of print is that of assuming that change is synonymous with challenge, that societies contained no internal dynamic. It is erroneous to speak of old and new orders as if they were defined as well as opposing entities. There was no homogeneous unchanging ancien régime either in Britain or in continental Europe. Any assumption of a consistent ideological programme is open to question. This is most clearly seen in the case of religion. The idea of ancien régime Church—States, of stable ideological regimes challenged by radical printed material, is undercut by the reality of doctrinal and ecclesiastical rivalry within as well as between churches. Thus the old order was no static entity, and change was an integral feature of it, rather than an external threat. Such a suggestion poses a further query as to how best to consider critical printed remarks. Should they be seen as part of a debate with the old order, as so much for example of the literature of social manners was? There was little by way of radical political or social comment in the eighteenth—century British press. It also raises the question as to how far change in the past should be seen as a matter of style and sensibility, rather than substance, insofar as the two can be separated. Thus the issue of the impact of the press is fatally intertwined with the evaluation of change itself.

One sphere in which change definitely occurred was the growth of the press. To take eighteenth—century Britain, though it is singularly difficult to assess the significance of the press, one clear dramatic change was the growth of the press. There was an expansion both in the quantity and in the variety of types of newspapers produced. The lapsing of the Licensing Act in 1695 was followed by an immediate growth in the London press. There had been several licensed newspapers in 1689—94, besides the Gazette, but nothing comparable in number to the spate of new titles thereafter. A day after the Act lapsed on 3 May 1695 Richard Baldwin recommenced his Historical Account and three days later the Flying Post appeared. The following month saw the appearance of the first tri—weekly the Post Boy. Contemporaries were in no doubt of the growth of the press. The first number of the Old Post—Master, a tri—weekly that appeared in 1696, noted, 'so many news papers (or so called) are daily published, that it would seem needless to trouble the world with more.' In addition, different types of papers appeared in this period. The first successful daily paper, the Daily Courant, began publication in March 1702. Though the earliest extant copy of a provincial paper, the Bristol Post—Boy, dates from 1704, it is probable that the first provincial paper was the Norwich Post, starting in 1701 and followed by the Bristol paper a year later. The number of papers grew until the first major blow, the first Stamp Act of 1712, put several out of business. However, there was no permanent decline. The Wednesday's Journal commented in 1717, 'We see so many Pretenders to Journals starting up every day.' Two years later, the St James's Weekly Journal noted, 'At present both city, town and country, are over-flow'd every

day with an inundation of news-papers.' Oedipus: or the Postman Remounted, a
good instance of the more exotic names chosen by many papers, started in 1730,
'There is almost every day new papers coming out, as well as old ones continued and improved.'

These comments represent a sense of continuous activity and expansion in the
press. Due to the large number of newspapers that ceased publication, a topic
that has attracted little attention, the rise in the number of titles was more
modest, but it nevertheless existed. The Stamp Tax returns for 1712 and 1714
both list 12 London newspapers. In 1746 and 1760 the number of titles was
approximately the same, but by 1770 there were at least five dailies, eight
tri-weeklies and four weeklies printed in the capital. In 1783 London possessed nine dailies and ten bi- or tri-weeklies. By 1790 the figures were 13
morning, 1 evening, 7 tri-weekly and 2 bi-weekly papers: by early 1792 the
number of dailies had risen to 14 and by the end of the year 16. In 1811 the
total of papers in all categories published in London was 52, a number swelled
by Sunday newspapers, the first of which the British Gazette and Sunday
Monitor was started in about 1779, and all of which were illegal due to sabb-
atarian legislation. A comparable expansion occurred in the English provincial
and in the Scottish press. In 1723 there were about 24 provincial newspapers
in existence, in 1753 32, in 1760 35, in 1782 about 50 and in 1808 over 100.

The rise in the number of titles was matched by a rise in the number of copies
sold. In 1713 the latter has been estimated as 2,400,000. The figures for
newspaper stamps issued in 1750, 1760 and 1775 were 7.3, 9.4 and 12.6 million
respectively. The annual sale of London papers in 1780 has been estimated as
16.6 million. Seven million stamps were issued for London papers in 1801, 9
million for provincial. As the population of England and Wales was approximately 5.5 million in 1695, of Britain 7.75 million in 1750 and 10.7 million
in 1801, this represented a substantial increase in per capita sales.

Similar developments can be plotted in other countries for other periods, and
indeed the trend towards growth continued in Britain after 1800. The difficulty comes in assessing the significance of such episodes of growth. It is
all too easy to extrapolate from the culture of print, to assume that this
culture defines and in turn inspires national activity. However, the evidence
underlying such assumptions is very limited. The growth of the press is not
in itself an argument for its influence in promoting change. The assessment
of production figures, whether of newspapers, books, or pig iron, is fraught
with difficulties. There is for example no evidence that the rise in sales
leads to a comparable per capita rise in newspaper readership. Evidence about
readership is not the same thing as evidence about volume of copies printed.
In the case of eighteenth-century Britain contemporary estimates both of the
number of readers in the country and of the number of readers per individual
paper varied widely. Addison claimed twenty readers to every paper as a
'modest computation', a figure supported for later in the century by Paterson,
but others gave figures such as 5 and 40. It is necessary to caution against
the use of this multiplier that has been made by some scholars and was indeed
made by several contemporaries, such as Paterson. Simply to multiply the
number of papers read by the multiplier and assume that this represents even
approximately the total readership of the press is fallacious. Instead it is
clear that some people read more than one paper. This is obvious in the case
of some subscribers. Thomas Pelham of Stanmer, spending the summer of 1726 at
his Sussex seat, received more than one paper from London. The complaints
that were made about the overloading of coffee-houses with too many papers and
of readers sated with news suggest that at least in that milieu one is dealing
with individuals reading many newspapers.

Such points are fairly simple to establish. For the historian the more difficult question is that of the effect of the growth of the press. In general
this has been approached from a political angle, the press seen as constituting a central part of what John Brewer has termed the alternative structure
of politics. This reflects the historiography of the press. The Freedom of
the Press is one of the essential components of the liberal inheritance, both
Anglo-American and in continental Europe, its virtues proclaimed, rather than
analysed, in tome after tome, both constitutional and popular. The process by
which this Freedom was achieved was treated as a heroic struggle by historians
of a liberal disposition the world over. The excellent works that set out the
judicial bases of government regulations and the causes célèbres by which
these were challenged were imbued with support for the liberty of the press as
a definition and cause of civilized society. There was and has been since
little attempt within the liberal traditions to appreciate the ministerial
points of view, the motives that led governments to take action and the difficulties they faced. Current liberal intellectual suppositions are scarcely
favourable to the problems that press freedoms can pose for governments and
societies. If the heroes of today are no longer the liberal judges and law-
yers of the eighteenth century, such as Camden and Erskine, they are instead
enterprising and radical classless newspaper printers.

The historical function of the press within the liberal tradition has been
that of opponent of tyranny, subverter of fanaticism, spreader of liberalism.
This analysis corresponds with and has been fortified by the study of newspapers by Whiggish historians. Radical newspapers have been considered, their
conservative rivals dismissed. This approach is of dubious validity on two
grounds. First, it exaggerates the role of politics in the press. The 'low-
brow' content of newspapers was important and has been neglected. Second, it
adopts a partisan stance on the matter. The appropriateness of the first
point varies by time and area, but, in general, it could be fairly suggested
that historians considering the political impact of the press have concentrated on its political effectiveness and on those newspapers that took a
marked political slant and were held to be of political significance. This
approach, though valid in itself, has, arguably, led to a misplaced direction
of scholarly activity. To take the case of eighteenth-century Britain, it
tends to be forgotten that most newspapers, particularly in the provinces,
were apolitical, that the profit motive, rather than political conviction,
dominated production, that the heavily politicised essay sheets sold very few
copies, far less than those of the generally non-political Advertisers, and
that the rise of the magazines appears to have led to a general drift in much
of the press away from the dominance of political news and towards a more
varied product that included a lot of magazine-type material.

A similar point could be made with regard to the twentieth-century British
press. Commentators frequently condemn what they term as trivial. Such content is almost invariably non-political material, the modern equivalent of
'tea-tables and gossip', as material suitable for a newspaper. As with the
stress on a progressive political interpretation of the press, this is an
effect of the nineteenth-century historiographical tradition of work on the
press, one might almost say hagiographical, which established an agenda for
study that is still with us today. The definition of newspapers worthy for
study as high-brow and preponderantly political has had a major influence. Of
the two London opposition newspapers of the late 1720s, the Craftsman and
Fog's Weekly Journal, the vast bulk of scholarly attention has been devoted to
the former and singularly little to the latter, despite the fact that their
circulation appears to have been about the same, with possibly the greater
figure being enjoyed by the latter. The portentous pretentious lengthy essays
that characterised the Craftsman have enjoyed more favour with newspaper hist-

orians than the witty often irreverent idiom perfected by Nathaniel Mist with
his use of short punchy items. It was Mists's style that was to be most infl-
uential in terms of the British press. His preference for punchy abbreviated
items rather than lengthy essays was to be taken up by the London Evening Post
and to become the staple of the British press, a format suitable for both news
and comment. In contrast the lengthy essay, regularly occupying a quarter of
each issue, that characterised the Craftsman became less significant, increasingly relegated to low-circulation essay papers. The essay was a form ideally
suited for lengthy comment, indeed it stemmed in part from the literature of
social manners, but it proved of limited appeal in the second half of the
eighteenth century as shorter items preponderated and the range of news,
political and otherwise, increased, at the expense of comment.

Newspapers existed for the transmission of news as much as vehicles for political expression. Possibly the preference shown by historians towards newspapers such as the Craftsman, Monitor and North Briton reflects not only an
interest in the 'progressive' press, but also a greater concern with the press
as a vehicle for political comment than as a means for the provision of news,
both political and non-political. News is essentially a transitory product
often of limited contemporary significance and historical interest, to those
historians who adopt a teleological perspective. Thus the prime concern of
newspapers, both in the past and in the present, the speedy provision of accurate news, is of limited interest to historians who quarry the press and to
those who consider its wider impact. This is yet another of the areas where
the historian's general perspective is unhelpful, as it tends to underrate the
need to consider the press as an industry with its own interests and problems,
the latter centring on the speedy provision of news and production of newspapers rather than on more intangible socio-political goals. En passant it is
important to note that in democratic societies newspapers are a competitive
product and that the historical stress on the confrontation between the press
and established authority is often misplaced, as for most newspapers the prime
challenge was their counterparts. Clearly different criteria pertain in the
case of newspapers that were and are subsidised by political groups and those
that derive their support simply from the market. However, to take the case
of eighteenth-century Britain, more newspapers collapsed as a result of commercial competition than as a consequence of governmental action. In general,
in the past, state action against the press has been episodic and often poorly
enforced, a necessary consequence of the small-scale and often dispersed
nature of production that predominated until comparatively recently, while
competition from other newspapers has been a continuous feature.

Accepting that many newspapers were commercial products whose rationale was
not political, though in certain circumstances the political nature of individual titles could make them more attractive as commercial products, it is
nevertheless important to consider the political impact of the press. Clearly
a whole host of factors has to be considered at this point. The nature of a
given society and its political culture, the role and contemporary definition
of public opinion, the existence and strength of other media, ranging from
sermons to cable television, and the political commitment and degree of unity
of the church are all important. All these variables must affect the discussion of the impact of the press, a discussion that is further complicated by
the absence of any obvious methodology for assessing the issue.

Clearly the impact of the press varies. The popular dissemination of a concept is in no way equivalent to the development of opinion that might persuade
or pressure a government into altering its policy. Part of the problem that
occurs when the impact of the press is discussed stems from a failure to distinguish adequately between these differing forms of political action.

The impact of public opinion is often exaggerated. In general terms it can be suggested that it is too easy to stress the direct effect of public opinion, however expressed, on governmental policy. It is too easy to note newspaper calls for a change in government policy, to observe a subsequent change and to regard it as consequent upon this press pressure. First the openness of the political system to outside pressures is not necessarily the best way of treating the role of the political press: that is to say, those newspapers that discussed politics and advocated particular policies, rather than simply reporting without comment or not reporting at all. For in many senses the press and the amorphous pressures, interests and opinions understood by the term public opinion were an integral part of the political system, however much they may have lacked constitutional expressions of their role and any formal political definition of their importance. There has been no society in which the press has ever been formally a fourth estate, but to understand its role it is not necessary to imagine it as requiring constitutional definition or as divorced from the other components of the political system. Thus, calls from newspapers for a change of policy are often no more than the expression in one form of already defined views that are simultaneously being expressed elsewhere, rather than the products of an autonomous agency in some ways both part of and yet separate from political society.

This analysis inevitably lessens the influence that is attributed to the press. By appreciating that the press is usually but one agency calling for a change of policies, and that it is commonly divided in intentions, it is poss- ible to discern the limited role of newspapers in terms of their direct polit- ical impact. This can be seen in terms of eighteenth-century British polit- ical behaviour. It is indeed possible to point to episodes of high-political history when the press appears to have had a considerable impact: the agita- tion over Spanish depredations in 1738-9 helped to limit the British govern- ment's diplomatic options and thus to lead to war with Spain. The agitation over the Jewish Naturalization Act in 1753 led to a reversal of policy. It was generally believed that popular opinion affected policy. Commenting on the decision of the peaceably inclined British ministry to present an aggress- ive memorandum in 1769, the French envoy Balailhe de Frances placed the blame on the role of 'opinion vulgaire' in British policy. He claimed that the Crown, the government, Parliament and national interests were all subordinated to the popular will, and that popular prejudices served as the rule of conduct. He had already suggested that Britain was sliding towards the cond- ition of being a democratic anarchy and was to claim that ministerial weakness played a role in British unwillingness to abandon the Falklands. In 1768 the Secretary of State for the Southern Department, the Earl of Shelburne, told the Sardinian envoy that the government might be forced to war by public dis- quiet over Corsica, and that the nation was so enraged that if a minor incid- ent occurred between the two states, Britain would be forced to declare war. In 1787 the French foreign minister Montmorin feared that William Pitt wished to fight France in order to maintain his 'credit and influence in the H. of Commons and with the nation at large.'

Such comments relating either to the press specifically or to public opinion in general can be multiplied. They must however be placed in perspective. First it is necessary to note that a characteristic of all governments is to resist pressure that affects their autonomy of decision-making. The London Evening Post noted this in an article published on 11 January 1757.
    'There is no one Point that we have labour'd more, than to convince the
    Publick, that there is no Foundation, for the grievous Complaints made
    by some who take themselves to be Great Men, of illegal and
    unconstitutional Freedom taken with them, and of increasing the Spirit

of Insolence, as they call it, which prevails among the Mass of the
People. All this proceeds upon the Principle, that Great Men have a
Title to Power, without any Account; and that Authority is in them an
inherent Prerogative, to which implicit Obedience becomes a Duty. But
our Constitution speaks another Language; it informs us, that Power is
delegated in Trust for the Benefit of the People; and that if Authority
be not exerted for the Publick Good, it ceases to be legal Authority.'
The author's political observation was more appropriate than his constitutional outrage. The Old Corps Whigs who dominated British politics in the reigns
of George I and II were no more willing to accept the views of 'the Mass of
the People' than the attempt of George III and his upstart Scottish favourite,
the Earl of Bute, to work within the political system in order to produce a
new government. If the principal theme of British politics over the last few
centuries, indeed one might suggest a principal theme of world politics, has
been the reluctance of those who have wielded political power to accept the
political, social, cultural and economic consequences of democracy, democratic
constitutions and democratic ideology, then it is not surprising that popular
opinion, however defined, has been less effective than some might assume.

Such a theme should not be adopted without some hesitation. Just as newspapers have held various political opinions, so the principal political
struggles have often been between those who wield power rather than between
the powerful and the underprivileged. Popular opinion is rarely uniform and
consistent. Modern British politics could be approached in terms of pro- and
anti-Establishment forces and their supporting newspapers. It could equally
be suggested that the various political groups each represent Establishments
and that British politics is a matter of particular middle-class groups, each
with supporting papers, competing to win working-class support in order to
gain electoral victory. The newspapers thus serve to articulate political
groupings rather than to challenge an obvious Establishment.

Nevertheless, the press clearly possessed and possesses influence. Querying
the specific influence of newspapers in particular political conjunctures does
not mean that it is necessary to argue that the press had no influence under
any circumstances. Instead, it is possible to suggest that the prime significance of the press, in common with the rest of the culture of print, has been
as an educating rather than a campaigning medium, in particular by the facilities it has provided for the provision of a variety of opinions; in short
that the press is a source of pluralism. This is obviously only the case in
societies that have permitted the development of a critical press. In these
societies newspapers, by providing a variety of information and opinion,
played an important role in the political education of the population, for
they probably encouraged the habit of conceiving of politics in adversarial
terms.

It is at this point necessary to note that the effectiveness of the press in
this sphere is difficult to judge. When modern advertising agencies with vast
resources find it difficult to assess the impact of particular campaigns, it
is scarcely surprising if historians find it impossible to establish the widely diffused effects of the very existence of the press. A whole range of
factors affected the latter. Some are obvious. Literacy, however much obvia-
ted by the reading aloud of newspapers in oral societies, is important. Cost
is another factor, though clearly newspapers can be read as a result of comm-
unal expenditure. Newspaper-purchasing patterns have varied considerably. In
western Europe in the present day the vast bulk of sales are made to individuals, purchasing them from points of sale or having them delivered. In
early-eighteenth-century Britain a large percentage of the sales appears to
have been made to commercial concerns, where they were subsequently read free

by customers who had paid for the service. The reading of these papers in
public places probably encouraged a habit of publicly discussing the news.
Furthermore, it was possible in the eighteenth century to rent newspapers from
hawkers in the street.

Cost and literacy both act as prohibitive factors, affecting the total possible readership. Furthermore, it is of course rarely profitable for an industry to exist so that it taps all available demand. Newspapers have historically competed with other products as much as each other, magazines in eighteenth-century Britain prefiguring the subsequent challenge of radio and television. More intangible are factors that affected the impact of the press
among those who could and/or did consume the product. There have always been
those among potential consumers who doubted the value of the product. In an
interesting essay 'On the Authenticity of News' written by a pseudonymous
contributor, Philalethes, and published in Lloyd's Evening Post, a London tri-
weekly newspaper, in its issue of 1 January 1762 it was claimed,
> 'There is a vulgar opinion which prevails with the lower class of men,
> and which Sir Francis Wronghead adopts in the Journey to London, That
> there is little or no credit to be given to News Papers ... the
> canaille, or mob, are like Sir Francis, apt to swim on the surface of
> things, having but narrow and bounded prospects, and seeing things in a
> partial light. For certainly it will be granted, even by the meanest
> capacity, that if there were not ten to one more truths, in the News,
> than falsehoods, they would never be read; and though, by mistake,
> design, for want of information, or, what is worse, from wrong
> information, two or three falsehoods may have crept into a Paper, this
> is no cause whereby to invalidate the truth of the whole; nor would a
> whole nation flock in crowds to places of intelligence to read the
> Papers, if they did not expect, at least, ten truths for one falsehood.
> To be willingly imposed upon, and to lose their time and money into the
> bargain, can never be the standard ...'

Doubts concerning accuracy may have led some to be sceptical about the value
of the news, but it is possible that a more significant limitation of the
impact of the press was a lack of interest in the product or an unwillingness
to heed opinion that did not please readers. The latter was no different from
unwillingness of successive governments to heed critical comment.

To a certain extent the eighteenth-century British press was marginal with
respect to the interests and views of the bulk of the population. Arguably
this reflected the failure to develop the inexpensive press. Unstamped newspapers were squeezed out of existence by an Act of Parliament in 1743, the
cut-price London papers of the second quarter of the eighteenth century disappeared for reasons that are obscure. The press in that period was largely
read by upper and middle-class consumers, a readership it shared with books
and magazines, a contrast to the much larger, but less exalted readership of
chapbooks and ballad sheets. In an interesting recent article Susan Pedersen
has suggested that the strength of popular literature lay in its ability to
amuse. Instruction was clearly for a different social bracket. Thus rather
than assuming that the press as some sort of external force moulded society,
one can present it as heavily influenced by its readers, necessarily so in its
commercial and competitive context. When the market was socially restricted,
as in the eighteenth century, the press tended to approximate to a certain
style. The subsequent expansion of the market did not lead to a moulding of
readership patterns. Instead the press diversified to meet differing demands.

If the direct and indirect influence of the press is probably weaker than has
been often assumed, it is nevertheless appropriate to consider why certain
societies have deemed it necessary to control or seek to control the press.

From the liberal perspective this is generally presented in a negative light, because there has been no attempt to grasp the social and political cost of press freedom. Indeed, the modern cult of the 'open society' has further enhanced the already strong nineteenth-century tradition of judging all restrictions on press freedom as dangerous as well as negative. Whereas exceptions used to be made in the cases of sensitive areas of foreign policy, matters of national security and periods of warfare, the recent history of the British and American press suggests that self-restraint or censorship in these areas is no longer regarded as appropriate by much of the press. Furthermore, the political response to episodes where censorship has been applied suggests that these views are shared by sizeable sections of the political community, albeit usually those who are freed by the luxury of opposition from the necessity of considering consequences.

As a result the views of societies that have sought and seek to apply censorship have been largely ignored. Possibly this reflects the limited understanding within the Anglo-American liberal tradition of the precariousness of government and the fragility of stability. The assumption that a beneficial democratic consensus can be created and that those who dissent can be persuaded to accept the rules of the political game is a comforting one and a view that leaves room for the development of an active press. It is however one that is outside the past and present experiences of many societies. Frequently the press serves for the creation of dangerous expectations or the expression of hostile views that threaten stability. An obvious example is the publication of material that by defining racial and/or religious and/or linguistic identity helps to inculcate hostility and create disorder. This instance would be accepted within the liberal tradition, but less tolerance would be extended to the view that the expression of nationalist sentiment can be dangerous. Where however states represent an amalgam of differing groups then the expression of such views can pose a particular threat, and this to governments, such as modern India, Russia and Spain, of widely varying political persuasions. Again the publication of radical views can be seen as dangerous. Thus the Hungarian newspaper Bécsi Magyar Kurir supported the French Revolution. Its editor Sándor Szacsvay published and analyzed several of the French cahiers, reported accurately and in detail the events of 4 August 1789, the storming of the Bastille, printed several imaginary discussions concerning France and published the only Hungarian translation of the Déclaration des Droits de l'homme et du citoyen. Eventually action was taken against Szacsvay.

It is often difficult for modern readers to appreciate the rationale behind censorship, or to see it as anything other than a sinister force. This arguably has led to a misunderstanding of the treatment of newspapers by many governments in the past. A pessimistic interpretation of human nature could lead to a feeling that the press would naturally tend to express dangerous views that were acceptable to and in turn fortified negative elements of public opinion. The pro-government London paper the Senator declared in its issue of 16 February 1728,

> 'The natural Malevolence of Mankind, their Idleness, their Curiosity, their Misfortunes, nay even their Prosperity, do all most naturally incline them to listen after scandal of all kinds. The abuse of Power is undoubtedly of all Morcels the most delicious ... The author of the Medley was a writer of the utmost Politeness, and was for that reason little read, and less admired; while the Examiner who knew no Decency or distinction was the Darling of the Rabble.'

Ministerial papers regularly harped on the malevolent nature of the opposition press. The Honest True Briton, a London newspaper, declared in its first

issue, that of 21 February 1724, that the reader
'may depend upon having, in the course of these papers, an impartial,
unbiased way of writing, neither courting friends nor making enemies;
the placing things in false lights shall be avoided, which seems to
have been the greatest art, and only merit, of some writers, with whom
(whether they speak of private persons or of publick) the character of
no man is safe; but scandal and calumny are dealt about like dirt,
without regard to things or persons, either sacred or civil.'
Commenting on reports of the war in India against Tippoo Sahib, the World
declared in its issue of 31 May 1791, ' "No news is good news!" But the
OPPOSITION reverse this totally. When there is no intelligence, they immediately spread abroad "the spirit of misfortune". Thus TIPPOO SULTAN is to cut
off Lord Cornwallis.'

These comments could be dismissed as the partisan remarks of specific journals, but they reflected also the experience of eighteenth-century governments. Through their system of postal interception the British government
knew that the envoys of hostile foreign powers sought to influence the press.
At a time when Jacobitism was a significant ideological and political challenge, the expression of Jacobite material in the press was clearly dangerous.
In the 1790s the French government sought to influence the opposition British
press. Within Britain there were not only opposition elements willing to
employ violence to overthrow the government. There was also in a more general
sense opposition activity that lacked guidelines as to what behaviour was
legitimate. Furthermore, complicating the response to opposition activity,
was the fact that in the political culture of the age the position, indeed
legitimacy, of opposition was distinctly uncertain.

Prudentially there were reasons for governments to resort to censorship. It
was necessary to deny foreign powers the opportunity to recruit domestic
assistance. In 1732 the British government was asked for funds to set up a
newspaper that would exacerbate French domestic difficulties. Nothing came of
the proposal, but such ideas were a significant threat. Furthermore, the
press could affect the view of a state held by other powers. In October 1753
Frederick the Great pressed his envoy in London, Michell, to ascertain whether
the British government would pay peace-time subsidies, whether Parliament
would support them and, if so, whether Parliament would find the nation disposed to pay. He added,
'Comme les gazettes publiques annoncent des émeutes qu'il avait eu dans
différentes provinces de l'Angleterre touchant l'élection des membres
du nouveau Parlement, et qu'on proposerait, à la prochaine séance de
celui qu'on congédierait, la révocation de l'acte de naturalisation des
juifs, l'abolition de l'entretien des troupes trop nombreuses, la
liberté des élections des membres du Parlement et la suppression de
plusieurs taxes trop à charge au peuple, je fais à la vérité peu de cas
de pareilles nouvelles, cependant je serai bien aisé que vous
m'éclaircissiez sur ces objets, et que vous me mandiez tout
naturellement la vraie situation des affaires présentes de l'Angleterre
par rapport à son interieur.' [26.10.53, x (1883) 138-9].
British ministers were aware that foreign states, bereft of reliable information on the domestic circumstances of Britain, placed a lot of weight on the
British press. It was therefore in their interest to censor the press.

The willingness of newspapers to report whatever news they received and the
difficulty of checking reports were further irritants. The press was dominated by foreign news which it was difficult to check, but which was of great
importance given the role of the debate over foreign policy in domestic politics. The scepticism of Ayre's Sunday London Gazette in its issue of 7 April

1793 was unusual,

> 'At all times when the country is involved in a war, flying reports are
> to be received with doubts, and credited with caution, but certainly
> much more so when the official accounts of one side only are to be
> procured. This being our case at present, we feel the greatest
> surprise at more not having been fabricated than at the daily inven-
> tions and contradictions which float in the political hemisphere.
> Whatever may be our wishes for the conclusion of a war, (and no man
> deprecates the idea of the human race being set on to butcher one
> another more than we) yet we cannot give belief, where our judgment
> tells us the assertions are not founded in probability, and therefore,
> although we consider it a duty to state the current report, let it
> proceed from whatever channel it may, we cannot do so without guarding
> our readers against too much confidence.'

If it is accepted that there might be a point in censoring the press, that the
free expression of news and/or opinion might be regarded as harmful for social
and/or political reasons, then it is possible to regard the history of the
press in a different light. Different societies and governmental systems
adopt and have adopted various strategies in dealing with the issue. By
avoiding the seductive trap of both dismissing their problems and their solutions out of hand, it is possible to begin a more valuable enquiry, one that
proceeds pragmatically by examining the difficulties that faced particular
governments in specific circumstances. Thus, aside from the challenge of
establishing a methodology to assess the impact of the press, it is also necessary to devise one that would permit a more accurate judgment of censorship.
Unless the purposes that lay behind regulation of the press are appreciated,
it is difficult to assess its success. Thus, a suggestion that the censorship
of the period 1714-50 in Britain was essentially inspired by the Jacobite
threat and the existence of Jacobite newspapers leads to the possible conclusion that the situation eased in the following 40 years because the threat had
diminished. In this perspective the controversies over the press in 1763-74
reflect in part the ministerial defence of an established system (if that is
not too grand a term) of regulation that was no longer greatly required, and
the relative success enjoyed by those who pressed against regulations may stem
in part from the lessened stress on defending the system. The perceived need
had altered faster than the legal situation.

If specificity is to be the key both to assessing impact and considering judgment, then it is likely that a more accurate but more disparate picture of the
political history of the press will emerge. In some ways however the challenge of assessing the social impact is greater. In the case of political
impact the issues are clear even though the methodology may not be. The
extent and nature of political news can be established, judicial and governmental records of censorship exist, and an examination of political correspondence permits an investigation of the extent to which newspapers are considered or ignored. The situation is very different in the case of social
issues. The extent of social news and comment is open to debate and there is
no obvious way in which impact can be established, or the press differentiated
from other aspects of print.

To take the example of the eighteenth-century British press there was no
shortage of suggestions for changes in social policy. For example, the
Middlesex Journal in its issue of 21 October 1783 complained about the number
of prostitutes on the streets of London and their shocking obscenities, and
proposed that they should be both taxed and restricted to certain streets. On
19 June 1795 the London Packet claimed that 'private avarice and monopoly'
were to blame for the rise in food prices and called for government action

against them. 'A Travrllee'[sic] writing in the <u>General Advertiser and
Morning Intelligencer</u> of 16 August 1777 noted,
>'It is with the utmost pleasaure that you give admittance, in your
>sensible and impartial paper, to every complaint that affects the
>public. It ought, and you have most judiciously made it the business
>of your paper, to hold up in exposure whatever is rendered obnoxious or
>hurtful by crime or malice ... I set out from a celebrated inn
>yesterday morning, in the Brightelmstone stage, on my way to France,
>but we had not proceeded half the way before the company at large
>determined to leave the coach, as the behaviour of the driver was
>really intolerable; he stopt at every alehouse, and got himself dead
>drunk before we had been two hours on our journy; he abused every
>gentleman in the coach, and at several times had well night overset us
>by mere drunkenness and inattention.'

If calls for specific action can be treated in the same light as comparable
political demands, it is by no means clear how to assess the general consequences of the provision of regular printed comment and news. Clearly this
represented in part an addition to or replacement of already existing means of
disseminating both, usually summarised by the term oral culture. If the press
offered information, <u>The Bee and Sketchley's Weekly Advertiser</u>, a Bristol
paper, providing for example in its issue of 16 December 1777 accounts of
Virginia and Nova Scotia, it is by no means clear what use was made of this
information and how far it supplemented existing sources. There were suggestions that the press provided topics for thought. 'Papyrus Cursor' writing in
the <u>St James's Chronicle</u> of 11 December 1766 claimed that,
>'if most of the fine Gentlemen about Town would be as candid and
>ingenious as myself: they too would freely confess, that the Figure
>they make in Company is entirely owing to the Occurrences of the Day,
>with occasional Essays, and Literary Articles in the public papers.'

Though the agenda of conversation and the scope of opinion may have been set
by newspapers it is as persuasive to argue that no such process took place,
that the impact of newspapers was lessened by their very variety and by alternative media and that it is necessary to be cautious in assessing the impact
of the press. Newspapers certainly enabled the challenging of existing views
and the questioning of authority by those who wielded no more power than that
of the pen. In its issue of 25 September 1773 the <u>Westminster Journal</u> commented,
>'Philanthropy is witness to the large number of letters which we lately
>published, the subject predestination, or the searching into the secret
>decrees of the omnipotent God. This one was sure he was right, and
>that other was sure he was right. This brought texts of scripture to
>prove he could not err, and that to convince his readers that he was on
>the indubitable side of the question. And what did all this amount to,
>more than to demonstrate that the thoughts of men are vain.'

Thus, the press permitted the expression of opinion by many even if its impact
may have been limited. It allowed those outside the usual sphere of political
activity to express views. This did not necessarily have the significance
that some have assumed, though its effect is intangible.

In conclusion it is possible that more attention should be devoted to the
views of those who were sceptical about the value of the press. Criticisms do
not need to be taken at their face value, but they should be noted. On 6
March 1789 the <u>London Packet</u> stated,
>'The liberty of the press, and freedom of opinion, have ever been
>esteemed the two grand bulwarks of the British constitution; when
>however the one is suffered to degenerate into libellous

licentiousness, and the other into desperate faction, they become the most dangerous innovations on public peace and security - Yet who are more ready to raise the cry in support of these valuable privileges than those who disgrace them by the grossest abuse? As a pickpocket is always the first to cry stop thief!'

Alternatively one can note a private letter from Charles Dibdin Junior proprietor of Sadler's Wells, sent in 1813 to the clergyman Edward Nares, 'There really is an impudence in the press of this age that does the country more disservice in disorganising the people than all the democratic leaders can do, I think; and I'm afraid it is sowing the seeds of a commotion that our children or grandchildren will feel the dire effects of.' [G Cecil White (ed), "A Versatile Professor. Reminiscences of the Rev. Edward Nares, DD" (London, 1903) p177].

By suggesting that the press should not be regarded as a benefit, and by calling for more work on the specific, rather than general impact of the press one necessarily argues in favour of more work on newspaper history. In place of the often simplistic explanations of the past, beneficial growth and general impact, a more complex analysis is necessary and this requires more work on the subject. The press of the past should neither be quarried for convenient examples nor have its role and impact taken for granted. Instead it is necessary to devote more attention to the subject in order to achieve a more accurate grasp of its significance.

BIBLIOGRAPHY

Altick, R D, 'The English Common Reader'. Chicago, 1957.

Aspinall, A, 'Politics and the Press c1780-1850'. London, 1949.

Bailyn, B, and Hench, S B, (editors) 'The Press and the American Revolution'. Worcester, Mass, 1980.

Black, J M, (editor) 'Britain in the Age of Walpole'. London, 1984.

Black, J M, 'the English Press in the Eighteenth Century'. London, 1987.

Bond, D H, and McLeod, W R, (editors) 'Newsletters to Newspapers: Eighteenth-Century Journalism'. Morgantown, 1977.

Bond, R P, (editor) 'Studies in the Early English Periodical'. Chapel Hill, 1957.

Bond, R P, 'Growth and Change in the Early English Press'. Lawrence, Kansas, 1969.

Botein, S, Censor, J, and Ritvo, H, 'The Periodical Press in eighteenth-century English and French Society: a cross cultural approach', in: Comparative Studies in Society and History, Vol.3, 1981, pp.464-90.

Brewer, J, 'Party Ideology and Popular Politics at the Accession of George III'. Cambridge, 1976.

Christie, I, 'Myth and Reality in Late-Eighteenth-Century British Politics and other papers'. London, 1970.

Craig, M E, 'The Scottish Periodical Press 1750-89'. Edinburgh, 1931.

Cranfield, G A, 'The Development of the Provincial Newspaper, 1700-1760'. Oxford, 1962.

Cranfield, G A, 'The Press and Society'. London, 1978.

Haig, B L, 'The Gazetteer'. Carbondale, Illinois, 1960.

Hanson, L, 'Government and the Press 1695-1763'. Oxford, 1936.

Harris, M, (editor) 'The Press in English Society from the Seventeenth to the Nineteenth Centuries'. London, 1986.

Klaits, J, 'Printed Propaganda under Louis XIV: Absolute Monarchy and Public Opinion'. Princeton, 1976.

Looney, J J, 'Advertising and Society in England, 1720-1820 : A statistical analysis, of Yorkshire newspaper advertisments.' PhD thesis, Princeton, 1983.

McKendrick, N, Brewer, J, and Plumb, J H, 'The Birth of a Consumer Society'. London, 1982.

Money, J, 'Experience and Identity. Birmingham and the West Midlands 1760-1800'. Manchester, 1977.

Munter, B, 'History of Irish Newspapers'. Cambridge, 1967.

Peters, M, 'Pitt and Popularity: The Patriot Minister and London Opinion during the Seven Years' War'. Oxford, 1980.

Rea, R, 'The English Press in Politics 1760-1774'. Lincoln, Nebraska, 1962.

Read, D, 'Press and People, 1790-1850: Opinion in Three English Cities'. London, 1961.

Retat, P, (editor) 'Le journalisme d'Ancien Régime'. Lyons, 1983.

Siebert, F S, 'Freedom of the Press in England 1476-1776'. Urbana, 1965.

Tucoo-Chala, S, 'Presse et Vérité sous l'Ancien Régime', in: Revue du Nord 66 1984.

Werkmeister, L, 'The London Daily Press 1772-1792'. Lincoln, Nebraska, 1963.

DISCUSSION OF THE PAPERS BY DR BOHRMANN, DR HARRIS AND DR BLACK

Q.   Ian Gibb, British Library, Retired

I agree with much of what Dr Harris said about the lack of status of newspapers conditioning their treatment both in libraries and by bibliographers.
However, as a librarian who has had to deal with problems of resource allocation, I think one of the problems is to know how far we can go in libraries
to satisfy the needs of researchers without doing their research for them.   In
other words where do libraries stop?   Their provision of information about
what newspapers are held and where is a good point to stop and leave it to the
bibliographers and historians to take up the research from there.

A.   Dr Harris

Yes there is a lot in that.   Certainly the practical realities of life in
libraries do subvert some of the comments I was making.   However, it does seem
to me that libraries are a little passive in their response to what happens
around them.   There are libraries at Universities and National Libraries,
which could without massive expenditure, support in some way, the process of
the investigation, around which the organisation of their collection can be
placed.   I am not quite sure how this can work.   It always seems to me that
the distinction within Universities between the academic departments and the
library is a very mysterious one.   I came across this recently in relation to
the BBC, which is a very active organisation with the most striking and dramatic press cuttings collection probably in the world,   and yet their library,
which is making up those collections, is inert, it responds.   Therefore there
are no judgements made within the library about what ought to be taken and cut
because the demand is not forthcoming from outside.   Now it seems to me that
there is a role perhaps which is a slightly more active one.   The same might
be true in a historical sense in some of the libraries around the country
which are concerned with newspapers.   But I do take the point very strongly
that financial considerations and considerations of time and staffing are
paramount and have to be.

Q.   Eve Johansson, British Library

I would be interested to know which countries and which national libraries in
the opinion of Dr Bohrmann and of the countries represented here have achieved
the most in this direction.

A.   Dr Bohrmann

I am not sure that I am the right speaker to answer your question.   I have
experience in the Federal Republic of Germany and I think I can say something
about some countries around the Federal Republic.   In Germany we have failed
in establishing such a framework for constructing a bibliography up to now,
such as I saw in the United States; in France and in Great Britain there are
bibliographic projects, not for the whole country but for parts of them, and
there we have good bibliographies.   We have then the problems Dr Harris
described, with the one number or two numbers you will find in some libararies
or in archives.   But in Germany we are not yet at this stage of bibliographic
identification of all the papers appearing since the 17th century.

A. Dr Black

I think it surely fair to observe that it is a major problem of institutions
in the world today, that as the scale of activity increases and their internal
sophistication and organisation increases so they become less able to take
advice from outside. I think that this is obviously a very major problem that
academics encounter with dealing with both libraries and archives. One is
particularly these days told that in the context of cuts it is impossible to
consider things, but it seems to me that often existing programmes are kept in
being not because they fulfill any academic purpose whatsoever, but simply
because they have become a part of the establishment: they have an agreed
budget, they have an established staff, and therefore, they should keep going.
I hasten to add universities are exactly the same. I teach in a history department. It is only in the last year that we have started to examine critically things that we have been doing in teaching terms for about twenty years,
so in no way am I wishing to castigate libraries and imply that the blame is
not found elsewhere in the system. But I think that it is fair to say that
one notes with mounting irritation the way in which established programmes are
kept in being in things like purchasing, for example, when they quite obviously are foolish. One sees this most obviously in the context actually of books
not newspapers, that once a subscription is taken out to a series or a periodical it is often maintained, even if that periodical or that series is judged
by the people who use it to be not particularly effective. There is, for example, at the present moment one English language journal for the history of
France, which is not a terribly good one and is acknowledged not to be a terribly good one. Another one has been launched this year by the Oxford University Press. The new one whose existing quality judged on its papers so far is
very high, is finding it very difficult to establish itself, because libraries
simply say we have already got one French history journal we do not need
another one.

Q. Mr Mannerheim, Royal Library, Stockholm

I think that if you want the libraries to do bibliographic work, it is certainly a problem of funds as Mr Gibb said. But I think that there is a possibility that we could do something, and that is if you connect it somehow with
other activities of the library. If you can link it, for instance, to microfilming, I think that the libraries could contribute something in this
respect, because if you want to make a high standard microfilm you have to
make thorough investigations of the newspapers, how they were published, which
was their publishing pattern, you have to go into the problem of editions and
so on; microfilming is the golden opportunity for libraries to do something
in this respect, and one where the researchers could help us.

I would also mention another problem in this respect, and that is the difference between retrospective microfilming or retrospective bibliography and
current bibliography because with retrospective bibliography there are many
difficulties in actually establishing what happened. There, we librarians
often go over the limit for our task and we need to leave it to the researchers to do the digging. For current bibliography, it is very easy to make a
good description because we can ask the publishers how their newspapers are
constructed and we should record that in the service of future research.

A. Dr Harris

Can I make a point? I think that the microfilming point is a good one but I
think any kind of bibliographical listing and descriptive enterprise is going

to be one which involves historical analysis. I do not think that you can do
the one without the other and I have in mind here the very interesting project
based in Yale University in America for the listing and the description of all
the newspapers, newsbooks and serials published in this country between 1641
and 1700, which is presently in hand. Compiling such a list, is incredibly
complicated, because all those publications shift about in a quite striking
way, so that a publication can change its title and change back again in the
course of a matter of a few months. The people who have been working on this
have produced a very interesting publication which is one of the special publications of the Bibliographical Society and which is in fact historical. In
other words their work has spun off material which is essentially in the
broadest sense bibliographical historical, and it seems to me that these two
enterprises go together. There should be some system, I think very much in
line with what Mr Mannerheim was saying, of making it possible for people who
are working on the one to do the other, but at the same time to record what
they are doing within a broader framework.

Statement. Ms Penny Griffith, National Library of New Zealand

I would just like to pick up Mr Gibb's point which he made about the cut off
point between librarian's responsibility and scholar's interest, if you like.
I believe that at a national level we have a very great responsibility to
create national bibliographic records for newspapers, and I know that in New
Zealand we are very bad at that, because I believe that without bibliographic
records you can neither have microfilming programmes, collection development
policies, preservation programmes or any means of controlling this vast mass
of material to which we all need access for information for various reasons.

Q.   Mr Mannerheim

I think that what Dr Black is really saying is that what we need for the future is a complete microfilming programme, full of current and retrospective
newspapers. But we librarians, we cannot achieve that. Only you, the scholars can achieve that by pointing that out so loudly that the authorities do
understand it.

A.   Dr Black

Oh yes, but the in the second half of the paper I did say that in the context
of constraints it is necessary not simply to concentrate on the quality press.
If one could only afford 3 microfilms of London papers at the present moment,
I would not buy the _Times_, the _Guardian_ and the _Telegraph_, because I think
that would be ridiculous.

Q.   Mr Mannerheim

This question really divides into two: one is what should be microfilmed,
(that is a national programme of microfilming), and the other is the question
of acquisition by different libraries, I think this second question might be
important to you, but we think that we have instruments like inter-library
lending and things like that which might help a bit and which might make this
question less serious.

A.   Dr Harris

The question of selectivity is a very continuously active one. In the 19th
century when Panizzi was trying to put together what is now the British Library collection he wanted to collect everything. He felt that everything had

to be collected bacause there is no basis for including or excluding particular publications - you need everything. The Trustees of the Museum refused
to do this. He would dash into meetings with an armload of newspapers and
would say 'we must buy these newspapers because they exist'. The Trustees
would say 'no, we haven't got room for them, we haven't got the money, we do
not need them'. Now, it seems to me that there are no grounds for selection.
Unfortunately if you apply any criteria at all at any given moment it is not
going to be adequate for the purpose of future generations. Dr Black's point
is about the political emphasis, the collection of radical newspapers on
microfilm for example, which has inevitably a distorting effect on the process
of research. I do not see how it could have been got around; if you are
going to have a selective process it is going to be one way or another. Personally I would prefer the radical ones because they satisfy the criteria of
low key output which it is harder to find, so I would think that was probably
a good choice from that point of view.

But I think one of the issues of the moment is the free newspapers. There are
a thousand free newspapers. The British Library has the utmost difficulty in
identifying those newspapers, let alone getting an adequate supply of them on
a regular basis. So the whole business of total collecting is a very vexed
and difficult one, and I would just say that I have the utmost sympathy with
people who are trying to make decisions on the basis of no information.

A.   Dr Black

One other point from the teaching point of view. Library acquisitions are a
problem because, in many countries at the present moment universities are
trying to increasingly push undergraduate students not towards written papers
but towards dissertation work. (At masters level or for postgraduates newspapers are clearly a tremendously valuable source). This is largely, in fact,
because there is no problem in reading them. I know that sounds a silly
reason, but in fact if you have got to set up somebody to do a dissertation in
two months or so, you cannot afford to spend four weeks of getting them used
to the handwriting of the 18th or 19th century. So newspapers are a tremendously valuable source for teaching under-graduates. One of the things that I
find very difficult, because I do try to get the students to use newspapers
for this purpose, is that a lot of microfilm companies, for obvious reasons
(I am not in any way criticising them), want to sell you massive runs that you
cannot afford. That is understandable if after all your biggest customer is a
national library since that is what a national library wants, but in fact from
the teaching point of view you want as many individual reels from different
titles can be acquired by your University library, and that is very, very
difficult actually to set up. But I do believe that newspapers are useful not
only from the research point of view but also from the teaching point of view
and I think they will become increasingly valuable from the teaching point of
view.

This brings up one other problem. You say that a researcher can rely or seek
to use inter-library loan facilities; that is absolutely right. But at the
level of a student who is not doing postgraduate research that is impossible.
The cost of inter-library loan facilities in Britain is already high and we
are now reaching a very dangerous position in which new bibliographical tools,
such as the "Eighteenth Century Short Title Catalogue", produced by the British Library, are not available in British Universities because they cannot
afford the annual subscription, to be on-line to them. I have however been
told by various microfilm companies that some universities will buy everything that they print it does not matter what it is; the state of the art for
them is obviously very sophisticated. I am a worried that a lot of present

developments are very much geared, for obvious reasons, to the very major
libraries, but at the lesser libraries it is a bigger problem. My personal
view has always been that the wrong place to put the British Library was London. You have an extraordinary attitude among people in some National Libraries that they are not really aware of the practical problems of using their
resources for teaching and such like matters, and the fact that you set up
sophisticated bibliographical projects is hopeless if the institutions that
are designed to purchase them cannot afford to; that, I think, is a very major
problem which is going to get worse.

Q.   Ian Gibb

Could I differentiate between some of the points which Dr Black has made? I
fully agree with him that what you need in teaching is a range of material. I
think one has got to distinguish two things: first of all Dr Black quite
rightly says that commercial firms making microfilm have to have a market
because they are commercial and therefore they choose the things which will
sell in large numbers which tend to be the papers of record. That means that
the market is primarily national libraries or national plans for coverage in
different countries. In this country, the British library, together with the
other libraries in the country that we are trying to involve in NEWSPLAN, have
to pick up the residue and they do that largely by devoting money for preservation functions. They are not looking at this commercially, but once a microfilm has been made for preservation purposes a copy can be of course sold.
That should enable a wider range of material to be available. But then of
course you come back to the second problem which is to differentiate between
the resources of the national library and the resources of university and
other libraries, I could not disagree with you that resources in national
libraries are becoming less, but they are much more severely limited in universities. One has to acknowledge that and say that the first priority must be
to ensure that <u>nationally</u> something is done. If the worst comes to the worst,
researchers may have to travel, if their library cannot afford the funds to
buy the microfilm that they want, but at least that is better than having
nothing. I think we have to be able to differentiate these problems before we
put all library purchases into the same boat.

Additional comment by Dr Harris

Can I just add one thing about selective microfilming? That is that I have
been particularly interested recently in local newspapers in London in the
19th century, and these are forms of material which it is economically not
viable to microfilm under any circumstances at all. It seems to me there is
this serious danger if you place the emphasis on commercial links between
microfilm organisations and libraries you have always got the discontinuity
of objective and there are going to be certain categories of material that
slip through and I think that is a problem. If you are in London, it is all
right as Dr Black says, because that is where the British library is, but if
you are somewhere else then you really are stuck, because if the stuff is not
on film you cannot look at it and as far as you are concerned it does not
exist. One of the reasons why newspaper history in this country is so erratic
is that some of the best studies of newspapers as such have been based in
provincial centres where people who are academics have found a subject which
they can deal with and so they have produced histories of the provincial press
or the press in Northumberland or wherever it happens to be and so the picture
is peculiarly eccentric because of the dispersal of materials in that way.
The <u>commercial</u> microfilm process aggravates that to some extent it seems to me
and is a problem.

A.   Dr Black

It is also the case that some of the major libraries follow curious policies,
I remember putting in an inter-library loan request for microfilms held in
Cambridge, which is a copyright library, and Cambridge replied that it did not
lend periodicals through inter-library loan and that it included 18th century
newspapers under that, which seems to me an extraordinary view. The fact is
that sometimes there are no problems at all in borrowing; the British Library's Document Supply Centre at Boston Spa is very good at lending things. I
have borrowed things easily from some other libraries, but each library follows it own policy and there is no standard policy in Britain which means that
you cannot know that simply because an institution buys something that you
will be able to look at it somewhere else.

Q.   Thomas Bourke, New York Public Library, (for Dr Black)

Your field is based on the eighteenth century press and you have alluded to
the dominance of what you reffered to as 'Whig history'. In the second third
of the 19th century when Disraeli was coming to prominence in expounding his
theories of Tory Democracy, he once pointed out that he could understand the
Tory and he could understand the Radical, but a weak democratic aristocrat he
could not understand and made the accusation that the effects of Whiggery on
Britain had been French wars, Dutch finance and the Venetian constitution. Do
you think that you can date the decline in the influence of Whig history in
the British press in the 19th century?

A.   Dr Black

That is a very good question though I am not sure that I can produce a very
good answer to it. I think that when we usually use the phrase 'Whig history'
we are referring to the views of historians and I would say that Whig history,
although it has been criticised by a number of scholars on both sides of the
Atlantic, is still with us today. As far as the press of the 19th century is
concerned, I would say firstly look at Lucy Brown's book on the Victorian
newspapers. I think it is fair to say that there was a variety of views advanced in the newspapers of the 19th century on all sorts of issues, ranging
from land reform, political rights in Ireland to Bulgarian atrocities. The
worrying thing is not so much the newspapers of the period, which as I have
said were very varied, but the problem is rather what the historian does looking at the past. Let me give you another example, the French Revolutionary
Press. With the Revolution in France the press became very, very active
indeed and remained so for a certain number of years. Now it is only in recent years that a number of scholars such as the American Jeremy Popkin or the
Australian W J Murray, have drawn attention to the fact that a lot of those
newspapers produced in the 1790's were actually Royalist and Conservative - a
very large number indeed and that most of these had to be closed down at the
end of the decade. Now the point is that, if you read most historical works
on the French Revolution produced by scholars both French and non-French, when
they look at newspapers they overwhelmingly are talking about Radical papers,
but there is no evidence at all that these newspapers necessarily had a greater circulation or importance - they just fit in with the historian's perspective. Really one of the major problems that Popkin and Murray faced (and they
were really very innovative in this field), was actually just establishing the
bibliographical history of these newspapers, of the ones they were looking at
because so little work had been done on them. All I am saying, as I have said
at the very end of my paper, is precisely that if you look in the past you see
a more complex picture, therefore we need to do more work on newspapers, both

on their politics and on their non-politics. The simplistic view that the press is always on the side of liberalism, always on the side of radicalism (which I am sure nobody in this room holds) is a view you will find in a lot of history books. If you take that view, if you do as John Brewer does and use the press from which to extrapolate what he terms an alternative structure of politics, then you are going to go badly wrong; also you do not really need to read any newspapers because if you believe that the press is always a radical/liberal force then why bother to read any newspapers. It is only if you are aware that there really was a debate in the past that different views were advanced on a wide variety of issues it is only then that it becomes important to read them and I do not think that it is any accident. I think Dr Harris is right, the existing state in Britain is a mess as far as press history is concerned, but one of the reasons is because so many historians do not believe that it is necessary to do press history because they know that the press has always been liberal and radical, so why bother to do it?

Q. Mr Mannerheim

What about retrospective indexing? I think it is not possible to index whole papers and I think it is impossible to undertake this for the 19th century especially. You can make indexes for the revolutionary press in 1848, for instance, for the purpose of research on economic and political reforms and so on but I think it is not possible to construct indexes like the index of the New York Times, as you do not have enough funds and not enough personnel to construct them.

A. Dr Harris

Indexing is a highly desirable notion and it would be very nice if everything was indexed, and I think of the project to index all 18th century newspapers which is based at the University of Texas. It got as far as the year 1700 and then the whole thing broke down, so if anybody is interested in 1700 there is a good index! Yes, there are a lot of projects, retrospective indexing projects in hand, with some interesting material. I was saying to one of members of this group that the latest issue of the British Library Newspaper Library Newsletter contains a very full and interesting account of a number of projects of that kind which are in hand. Certainly I remember hearing somebody from Scotland talking about the indexing of a Scottish Newspaper in which a group of manic depressives have been hired under a job creation scheme to index the paper; I do not know how far that has actually got, or what the human cost of the process actually was. But I think really inevitably one needs a form of technology where by scanning the printed page, indexing is possible mechanically. That is a process which is way off in the future, but when that happens then I think the indexing of newspapers would be very valuably and usefully done. I find, for example, that the indexes to the early years of The Times, The London Times, 1785 - 89, which has been undertaken recently is a really wonderful help and aid to various kinds of investigation, because they have indexed everything, advertisements as well as news, editorial as well as miscellaneous bits of information that appear at random points, poems and so on. In principle everyone would like everything indexed, although it would rather take the savour out of research perhaps, but the process is too complex at the moment.

A. Dr Black

Yes I agree with Dr Harris that the possiblity of linking up scanning devices to computers and doing it all mechanically would be very attractive, but at the present moment it is obviously too expensive. Technology does not yet fully exist though actually one can see how the technology could exist, so it is not likely to be as far off in the future as one might imagine, but how much these indexes would be used is obviously something which libraries would have to consider very seriously before purchasing them. The problem is also that you would have to have an indexing method that was not going to be present in a printed out form but would be present in the computer so that you could then key in questions because that would have the attraction that if subsequently you had different methods of approach you could key into the data already in the computer. I think the dangerous thing would be if one printed out the material and then a class of researchers, librarians, scholars for whatever purpose wanted to use the material and did not find it suitable. I suppose most of the catalogues of the future are in fact going to be on computer and those would be more flexible than current cataloging methods but obviously the cost would be enormous and, as you quite rightly say, this is a powerful constraint.

I think I might just make a reflection. The point I made might have sounded a bit silly, but the point I have made about one of the great appeals of newspapers being that they are easy to read is actually going to become more and more important as palaeographical skills diminish. They are obviously going to be not only a way of looking at the past, but for many people the only way of looking at the past in the pre-photograph, pre-visual image, age and in that context I think that one is performing a tremendous service in purchasing and storing microfilm material. I often wonder, looking at some of the manuscript collections that are acquired; they would obviously be extraordinarily useful to scholars working per se on that topic, but they demand a certain degree of knowledge of the handwriting, at the very least, of the period and I think therefore do not always have the pedagogic value that newspapers have.

Q.   Andrew Phillips, British Library

I wonder if I can ask a supplementary question to the topic on indexing we were just addressing. There are a few and limited indexes available such as you have mentioned, the New York Times and The Times and although indexing to-day's Times in London is very different from indexing to-days Daily Mirror or Sun newspaper, or some of the other national newspapers, it has occurred to me whether any studies have been made of the overlap of indexed material between a newspaper of record, to use one of the terms Sir Denis used, and perhaps, if I could put it this way, a newspaper of lesser record but nonetheless recording some similar items on Sweden, or Sri Lanka or whatever, during that period. Have any studies been made as to how much a major and authoritative index to a major newspaper can provide something of a key to the coverage of other newspapers published during the same time scale?

A.   Dr Harris

Personally I have no idea but I would imagine very little. Of course the main themes are shared between the newspapers there is no doubt about that. In a sense one's interest as an investigator is in points of difference. I do not think you can actually have an accumulated body of information by which you can say 'well the Times has got it we do not need to look at the Sun', but on the other hand it is fair to say that you can pick up an issue in relation to the Times you can hope, at least, to find it in another publication. I have not actually tried any sort of cross search of that sort, but I would think the results of it would be fairly modest. I think that you have got to index everything or not.

A. Dr Black

I can tell you one very small example, a very small example, that the surveys
that are produced by the Nuffield people on British Elections include always a
detailed examination of the press coverage and the sort of things they look at
are, for example, on a given day or for a given speech, how many of the newspapers put that in lead position and that actually can be very interesting. I
have very recently read a book on the press coverage of the 1983 General
Election, and it was very interesting to see that for a large number of British newspapers the election was not the most important item. Obviously that
has to be demonstrated statistically; you cannot just produce that as an
impression. One thing of course from the indexing point of view is that to
know for example, to take a French context that _Figaro_ and _Libération_ have
both put in an editorial about Mr Chirac does not mean that it is the same
item. I am not particularly knowledgeable on indexing but it is obviously a
major problem with using indexing simply on a statistical machine basis that
one has to be careful not to push statistics too far; you cannot take away
the human element of using it. But as a finding tool they are invaluable.

One of the aspects of indexing which is very important from a finding tool
point of view is that there are different conventions in different countries,
different periods, and different newspapers, as to the organisation of newspapers, their internal organisation by issue. Now in the modern world newspapers are relatively well organised, if you look, for example, at most Western European newspapers, the financial news will always be in a certain section, the weather will always be in a certain section so will the crossword, so
will the editorial. It is unfortunately the case that there are many situations in the past, where it is fair to say that the organisation or method is
not apparent or is not consistent, or the headlining system is, for obvious
reasons in some cases, so primitive that you have to read the entire newspaper
to find its view or its report on what happened that week. Now in such a
context the use of a machine finding system is extraordinarily useful I would
imagine, but at the present moment one just has to sit there and read the
whole newspaper, which becomes a considerable problem by the early 19th
century because the increase of the newspapers' size of issue means that it is
very difficult to scan on microfilm and it is also difficult to scan holding
the original. It is easy for people to draw attention to the problems of
microfilm use of newspapers, there are many problems with holding the original
copies of enormous scale particularly when they have been bound, as was too
obviously often the case, into very heavy books, many physically too heavy to
handle.

Q. Graham Cranfield, British Library, Newspaper Library

I am sure that anybody working in a public service area dealing with newspapers will be well aware that one of the major problems, perhaps _the_ major
problem, for readers is that when they come into the newspaper library they
have some idea of what they want but no idea of how to identify where precisely it is in the particular newspaper they are after, or even in which group of
newspapers. Now, as far as indexes are concerned the national newspapers are
generally only tackled on a commercial basis. Certainly the Newspaper Library
has never attempted to index its own collections, it has always been accepted
as totally outside of our remit, although we do, where we can collect media
cuttings collection. We have two major cuttings collection the Daily Express
obituary file and part of the Chatham House collection. What we have done is
to try and find out what local indexing has been going on in the country.
Now, there are obviously a lot of local intiatives that have been taking place
over many years in local centres. They have been operating mainly individ-

ually according to their own thesaurus, their own vocabularies, that they have built up, and with not a lot of communication between them. What we have been trying to do very recently is to try and find out where those indexes are, the scope of them, what newspapers they cover and so on and try and codify that information. Where such an index has been published and is available to us we obviously try to purchase it, but for the most part they tend to be not in that kind of format. I would be interested to know whether that is a similar pattern in other countries or whether other solutions have been found.

A.   Mr Mannerheim

I think that this is a very interesting development taking place here in the U.K. and I think really as the previous speaker that indexing and press cutt-ings are part of the same issue really. There are actually many retrospective indexes in the form of press cuttings, but the question is, do we take care of those collections? Are we concious of them? Can we lead researchers to them? Are national libraries considered if some local library does not have any space any more or if a big newspaper collapses and throws away its press cuttings?

A.   Dr Harris

It is certainly true that press cuttings collections are extremely important. The Francis Place papers in the British Library for example, are a multi-volume press cutting service which Francis Place undertook for his interest in social reform, but his selection of material of course is peculiar to his own interests and it is therefore an eccentric item in its own right. But the newspaper, the current newspapers, that are producing their own cuttings coll-ections are very full and very thorough indeed. Now I know that the British Library is actively engaged in sorting out material which was taken over from the Daily Express. And this is a massive collection. I have not seen it but I gather its a kind of gigantic million item thing, and a member of staff at Colindale is more or less full time at the moment trying to sort it out and get it into a form where it can actually be used. So there is, yes, a great deal of valuable material to be found in such collections, but they can be partial and they can be problematic in the sense that any index which is based on just working principles is evidently going to be eccentric, so I think there is a problem with it that way.

A.   Dr Black

One does not want to load the already groaning shelves of libraries or arch-ives, but one obvious form of material which it would be very valuable to have in conjunction with modern contemporary newspaper collections would be a more sophisticated attempt to grab hold of the papers of advertising companies when they go bankrupt or before they throw them away. Of course a very major development in Western Europe in archival terms, since the war has been the development of business archives, in other words not just leaving it up to the individual bank or company, but the attempt to ensure that major or even some-times minor companies keep this sort of material.

But obviously if we are going to ask questions in 70 years' time about the success for example of the British Government's, but it could equally be the American or Swedish Government's attempts to use newspapers and television on its AIDS programme which is just the same as Proctor and Gamble trying to sell soap powder, it would be very useful if you could link the material, but obv-iously this requires co-operation of the archival service, with some attempt to ensure that those institutions or companies which have press sections retain their papers. The great problem in Britain, has been that the institutions in the commercial world that have retained their papers are the greatest industrial firms and also the financial firms. Those that have least retained their papers are the very institutions that would fit in with work on the press. It is only in very recent times that people will have been aware of the tremendous amount of material that is being destroyed. The problem that the archivist will tell you is coming along is that the present bulk of material deposited is so great that it is impossible to hold it. The British Government destroys, not because it wishes to keep the Russians in the dark or to keep the British press in the dark, over 97% of the material that it accumulates in a paper form every year. It has to. There is no way that you could hope to keep most of this material which is obviously things like correspondence dealing with people's income tax.

Now the problem that libraries, it seems to me, face once they start moving into the newspaper world is very similar to the problems that archives have been having for a very long time, is how on earth can you define things when you are looking at contemporary material. You would have to fill quarries of material every year with the sort of paper that modern government and modern corporate organisations create. I wonder how much co-operation there is between libraries and archives on a national scale on matters of a common interest. I am not aware that archivists have much knowledge of or much interest in what national libraries are doing on a non-manuscript basis.

Q. Dr Ashin Das Gupta, National Library of India

May I draw your attention to something about newspapers which as a student of history I would always like to know, before I handle it or as I handle it. It is, what is the newspaper like. It is a document for the historian with a very strong slant of its own. Will· the library help the historian or the student in introducing this particular document. Now let me explain this in this manner. What the newspaper does not tell you is something equally important as what it _is_ telling you. There is the question of ownership. There is the question of the newspaper's affiliations. There is the question of how much the newspaper allows its news presentation to be influenced by considerations of this kind. Is the library justified in going into this field at all? At times we are asked questions at our library, where we have to go into this. People come in and ask for extreme left wing radical newspapers of the 1960's, so we have to make a judgement, only we have not yet put this on paper. We guide the researcher to the particular channels, but the question remains will the scholars and the librarians come together to do it? There is the enormous problem of having to do this on contemporary newspapers as, if the National Library in Calcutta describes, let us say, one great National Daily as capitalist and right wing, we will be taken to court. So we are not going to do that but what we are thinking of, if we can do it, is to keep profile cards of newspapers where our panel of academic experts will help us in describing at least those newspapers which definitely belong to history, even if it is history of the 1960's.

A. Dr Harris

Well the idea of a descriptive finding list is a very interesting one. In the 19th century the directories of newspapers attempted to categorise the materials. They would say a conservative and family newspaper, or a newspaper with radical tendencies. Unfortunately such categorisations are subjective and liable actually to distort the reality. My feeling about the question is that this is exactly what I was talking about, that there needs to be this conjunction of scholars and librarians but whether the result of their activity

would be to categorise the newspapers according to some sort of political
system, I would rather doubt. It seems to me the job is more neutral (I am
not sure if that is the right word) than that suggests. I have sympathy with
those people who have asked me 'where can I find material on this or on that'
and I am obliged to give them an answer as far as I know one, but I do not
feel the answer itself is worth enshrining somewhere so that other people can
go and look at it. I think the issue is too problematic; I would think that
it could not be done, except in the most generalised terms in which case it
would probably be not worth doing.

A.   Mr Mannerheim

Well I just want to mention that we actually list the political colour of
Swedish newspapers, but it might be only possible in our country because we
are not judging them. We are using their own descriptions which they used on
themselves by the time and we have a special source for that that is a joint
price lists for advertising because in those price lists newspapers give a
political categorization of themselves and this we publish. That means that
the researcher has to know something to be able to evaluate this description,
because a left liberal of the 1920's might be something different from a left
liberal of the 40's. You have to put it in the right context.

A.   Dr Black

That is excellent. One of the problems though is the perversity of people.
In Britain just about everybody claims to be a liberal at the moment. Mrs
Thatcher claims that she is a liberal and so does just about everybody else.
In the late 18th century in Britain, nobody claimed to be a Tory. It was
quite remarkable how everybody claimed to be a Whig, so I think that you are
right that there are in some countries possibilities from using what the
papers say. But in Britain certainly the perversity of politicians has gone
over into a lot of the political newspapers and this general perversity makes
it very difficult to use the language that they themselves use. Even at this
present moment what you would mean in Britain today by a Conservative is a
very difficult issue.   Political labelling is very hard in this country, I
suspect because we have a single vote system, not proportional representation, therefore we have a small number of political parties, and each political party contains within it a whole series of different strains of opinion,
ideology and action; it is therefore often very difficult to sort out continuity in terms of intellectual development or idealogical development over the
newspaper spectrum.

Q.   Mme E Delauney, Bibliothèque Nationale, Paris

I think we have, for that kind of question, in France the Annuelle de la
Presse and for the last hundred years at least it gives a sort of classification of the newspapers and of the contents of the newspapers, for example, if
it is Liberal or radical. Is it partial or is it not partial? It is difficult to say but you still can have an idea of what newspapers stand for or not.

Q.   Mr W Ubbens

Most of the newspapers in the Federal Republic of Germany claim they are independant and you must have good information about the companies to see what
this independence is dependant on. It is not the work of the librarian to
judge what is independant and what is liberal independant, socialist independant and so on. The researcher has to use the newspaper to read in and to make
other investigations about this problem and then you can form a catalogue with

this indexing. But I think this is not a problem of one judging in 1987. In 50 years the scientific community will have other points of view and I am sure that political arguments are other ones, and the conclusion is another one and I think the progress of science is another thing than the progress of librar- ies. The library has to preserve the material and to catalogue the material and the researcher has to read it, develop theories and come to conclusions etc. They are, perhaps, two sides of one coin, but not the same.

A. Dr Harris

Yes the classification of newspapers has to be done in some mechanical way that you can observe without difficulty, size and price for example. There are of course ways in which the mechanical process of description can coincide with politics. I am thinking in this case of the bibliography of unstamped newspapers in the 1820's and 30's, a list which Joel Wiener produced some time ago and which does conveniently encapsulate information about the range of publications mostly of a radical nature, large numbers of which were produced in that period. So it is possible but you have to have some pragmatic guide in order to be able to isolate and identify this sort of material in a clear way. I think the general view of liberal or conservative newspapers is use- less as a form of guide.

Q. Mr Mannerheim

But we have no real answer to the question put by Dr Das Gupta.

A. Dr Black

I certainly think that he is correct to draw attention to the fact that if you label a modern paper as something, although 99% of papers will not mind, it is exactly the sort of thing that could cause embarrassment in some circumstan- ces. I think that that is true.

Comment. Mr Kenneth Tillman, University Microfilms International, USA

I just have a comment since you have not heard from a commercial microfilm publisher I thought I would just make a couple of comments maybe to provide a little bit of insight. Dr Black's comment earlier about the importance of the lesser elite newspapers, maybe the tabloids of the day, in their value maybe in 50 years from now to historians and researcher, I thought that was a good point. There doesn't from a commercial point of view seem to be that great a demand to-day and our horizon unfortunately is 5 to 10 years. But I think you are right and that information needs to be preserved. Our focus, like Mr Gibb mentioned, is on the more popular and intellectual; we talked about the middle class and their use of the New York Times, the London Times and other such publications. That is where our focus is primarily. However, we are concerned about the other end of the market as well and our primary concern is meeting the greatest market demand. However, we do work with publishers. There are two different approaches that we use: one is we will invest in photographing and indexing newspapers that we can sell many copies of and recoup our investment and make a profit. On the other hand the newspapers that we can sell very few copies of we will include in our programme and that usually is the result of the publishers working with us because they want to preserve their newspaper, so we have another aspect to our programme whereby publishers will help support the investment that we have to make in photog- raphing their newspaper. Our attempt in that case is barely to break even and if we can sell a copy or two so much the better. Another comment about retro- spective indexing. Right now we index approximately 18 newspapers on a current basis. One publisher that we were working with wanted us to do some retrospective indexing. We provided an estimate on the cost and in this particular case we were looking at our costs to index this newspaper for the years, I think, '80 and '81, of about $75,000 a year to do the kind of indexing that we do which includes a short abstract. The publisher was interested. They had the money but, decided that they could use it in a more profitable area. But we do our best and I just wanted to provide a little insight from a commercial point of view.

USES OF THE PRESS:
current and research use of retrospective holdings

THE NEWSPAPER ARCHIVIST

Dennis GRIFFITHS

Former Director of Development, Express Newspapers, London

1. INTRODUCTION

It has been said that while historians using the press are legion, historians of the press are few ...

For the newspaper historian, difficulties are encountered in using the archives of British newspapers; and even for an archivist looking at his own newspaper there can be a distinct lack of material, especially if the newspaper in question has undergone various office moves. Unfortunately, with these moves, there has, invariably, been a "weeding out" of material. In Fleet Street, space has been at a premium.

During my final years at Express Newspapers, as Research and Development Director, I was in the strange but delightful position of peering into the technological future of the company — including the use of space satellites — and, simultaneously, looking back to the foundation of the group.

For almost a century, the keystone of the group had been The Daily Express, founded by Arthur Pearson in April 1904, but its stablemate, The Evening Standard, had a much longer pedigree, having been launched on 21 May 1827; and it was only this Spring that the paper celebrated its 50,000th issue, as London's oldest evening title.

In researching the history of The Standard, I assumed that its origins lay in the early nineteenth century. This was soon to be proved wrong, for there emerged a story of a dedicated Protestant family of printers and publishers which stretched back to the time of Oliver Cromwell, as it was then that the founder of the dynasty, Richard Baldwin, was born.

For the next 200 years, the Baldwin family was to be a major force in the publishing of newspapers in this country; and from humble origins near St Paul's Cathedral, the business moved to Fleet Street; New Bridge Street, where The Standard was launched; and finally to St Bride Street, the site of the present offices. During these two centuries, the family was involved in every major issue in the fight for the freedom of the press; and from the early days of Richard and Anne Baldwin, innovators in newspaper publication, to Henry, founder of The St James's Chronicle, to his son Charles, who started The Standard, and finally to Edward of The Morning Herald, there was the utmost dedication.

Throughout those years, the best writers had been attracted: Defoe, Dryden and Purcell in the early eighteenth century; Addison and Steele with Mrs Baldwin on The Tatler and The Spectator; the "phalanx of first class wits" on The St James's Chronicle — Boswell, Burke, Colman, Cowper, Garrick, Goldsmith, Sheridan and Thornton — and Maginn with his acerbic writings in the first issues of The Standard.

Politically, the papers were always in the forefront; and, on The Standard, from the first editorship of Giffard to that of Mudford at the close of the nineteenth century, there was a constant involvement with the Tory leaders: Wellington, Peel, Disraeli and Salisbury - all endeavoured to influence the editorial columns. Gradually, though, the policy of the paper changed until, under Mudford, it pursued a brand of Conservative independence.

Salisbury, a one-time leader writer on the paper, could even inform Queen Victoria, when he was Prime Minister:
> 'We have no influence with the paper by which we could keep it from any line of writing or tone of policy that we disapproved. Occasionally it will put in what it is asked to put in: but that is very rare. The paper is quite independent: but we have to bear the blame of its proceedings.'

And for much of that time, through the influence of James Johnstone, its new owner, the paper was extremely successful and the chief rival to The Times.

The Standard was first published at 2pm on Monday 21 May 1827, realizing the hopes of Arbuthnott, Wellington and Peel and their fellow Old Tory supporters.

As Charles Baldwin was later to reveal:
> 'I was not willing to risk the continuance of my old and valued journal [The St James's Chronicle]; I preferred the heavier risk of establishing at my own expense and hazard, a Daily Evening Paper to be conducted on the same principles and by the same editor. I also engaged the assistance of Dr Maggin and other celebrated writers.

> 'The choice of a name then claimed our attention. The object was to make a stand against the inroad of principle; contrary to our Constitution in Church and State; a very appropriate motto was chosen by Dr Giffard (the Editor):
>> Signifer, statue signum,
>> Hic optime manebimus

>> Plant here The Standard.
>> Here we shall best remain.

> 'and on the 21st May, 1827, The Standard was reared, hauled as a rallying point and was speedily followed by the raising of Standards in the Provincial and Colonial Conservative Press. Even foreign newspapers have adopted the name.'

2. THE RESEARCH

My initial reaction in commencing the research was to examine the material in The Evening Standard library. The result was most disappointing; just two brown envelopes with a half-dozen faded press cuttings and memoranda. Of correspondence, there was none pre-1960, and the files of the paper only ran for the past few years with an outdated microfilm unit, and no pre-1939 films.

While this "research" was taking place, I was also involved in trying to find a home for the millions of Evening Standard press cuttings now surplus to requirements. For in 1981, the Evening Standard offices were at long last being moved into those of the Daily Express in Fleet Street, some 300 yards away. The result was that there was now a spare press cuttings library, as

both The Standard and The Express were to use the Express library. Gordon
Phillips, The Times archivist, wrote at the time of his concern that these
cuttings could be lost, and suggested that they could form part of a National
Press Archive. I can assure you that I agreed completely with Gordon's sent-
iments. For 12 months we stored these surplus cuttings, at considerable cost,
in a West London warehouse. The size of the warehouse was as large as a foot-
ball pitch, and there must have been more than 600 cabinets in storage.
During this period I contacted the Newspaper Library and every English university offering them the cuttings gratis. The Newspaper Library and two universities specializing in media studies, would have been delighted to have accepted the cuttings but when they realized the size of the operation and the
probable cost of re-classification and storage they reluctantly had to decline. The cuttings were then, unfortunately, destroyed, but not before key
files – including those of the Abdication of Edward VIII – had been saved.
The burning of those cuttings was not an act of which we were proud.

We were, however, far more successful with The Evening Standard picture
library. Here were some six million pictures from the 1920s to 1981, and it
was a collection especially strong in pre-war London. With the efforts of
Richard Hewlett, Head of BBC Data, and David Lee, the Chief Librarian of the
BBC Hulton Picture Library, we were able to amalgamate the collection to provide a new base of more than 12 million pictures, with the possibility of their
being updated on a regular basis from the Express files.

Tests were also undertaken with Datasolve, so that on four computer co-
ordinates one was able to reach almost any category. For instance, the
keying-in of :   CHARLES – HORSE – FALL – POLO
would then throw up two captions referring to Prince Charles's mishaps on the
polo field. Here was the base of a far-reaching photographic archive, an
archive which could be accessed via satellite on a world-wide basis, the first
major step towards a possible national press/media collection.

For far too long, national newspapers – with the notable exception of The
Times – have religiously guarded their indexes. They have seldom been willing
to share their secrets with the general public or national libraries.

In recent years the libraries of The Daily Sketch and The Sunday Citizen have
disappeared without trace, while the last heard of The Daily Herald cuttings
was that they were gathering dust in a garage near King's Cross Station.
        'Press librarians, for a variety of reasons, work completely in a self-
        imposed isolation, and there is no central organization on the alert to
        save libraries from destruction when newspapers are forced to
        amalgamate, vacate premises or close down.'
There are in Britain two post-graduate Centres for Journalism Studies, at
University College, Cardiff and, possibly the more important, The City University, London. Here at City, each year, more than 500 graduates apply for
just 24 places on the one-year diploma course. With the advantage of being
able to draw on top-name journalists from Fleet Street and the magazine world,
plus leading politicians and business people as lecturers, the staff at City
are able to provide students with an excellent background to current affairs.

But even though an increasing amount of research is being undertaken, there is
a distinct lack of newspaper library facilities. Given the appropriate Government grant – or even private money – here could be a heaven-sent opportunity to establish an Institute of Press Studies.

With the vast amount of data being keyed each day into the ocmputers of national newspapers and, then, a few hours later, unceremoniously dumped, it

would be a relatively easy matter to capture this information for all time.
At Wolverhampton, The Express and Star is making big strides in this area, but
it is very much the front runner.

I would suggest that there is now a need for the setting-up of a proper national press archive, run in conjunction with academics, librarians, The Newspaper Society and the Newspaper Publishers' Association. If such an archive
had existed these past 150 years my research would have been so much easier,
but, probably not as satisfying ...

3. EARLY DAYS

Without doubt, for any student of the early days of printing and the press in
Great Britain the two founts of knowledge are the Stationers' Company, near St
Paul's and St Bride Printing Library, off Fleet Street. To work with the
actual Apprentices' Register Book 1666 - 1727 at Stationer's Hall brings into
proper perspective the long history of printing in Great Britain. And it was
there that I came upon the first references to the Baldwin family, when
Richard, the son of Thomas, a hempdresser, from High Wycombe, Bucks, was bound
at the age of fourteen from August 1668 for seven years to George Eversden, a
printer, specialising in the publication and sale of theological works. From
such small beginnings was to grow a newspaper empire ... Mention is also made
in these registers, in later years, of Henry Baldwin, founder of The St
James's Chronicle, and his son, Charles, of Standard fame, both of whom were
to become Masters of the Stationer's Company.

Secondary works covering this period include those of Maxted, Plomer, Dunton,
Rosenberg and Richard and Marjorie Bond's researches into the Minutes Books of
The St James's Chronicle. The minute books, discovered only 25 years ago,
were sold to the Manuscripts Department of the University of North Carolina
Library. Contained in three volumes they detail more than 550 meetings held
between 15 May 1761 and 9 August 1815. The great pity is that these were
allowed to leave Great Britain: they really should be forming a key sector in
a British Press Archive.

We are fortunate, though, that an excellent run of The St James's Chronicle
from 14 March 1761, exists in the City of London Reference Library - and here
one is able to examine the newspaper and not the microfilm. As a newspaper
man, and not only as an archivist, it is far more satisfying and rewarding to
examine the actual paper, to feel the texture of the newsprint and to look at
the pressmanship. None of this is possible with microfilm. So, in this
sense, I would opt every time to work with the original. One sour note,
though, about the City of London Reference Library: until some 18 months ago
one was able to examine files of The Times, Financial Times and other publications. Now, "because of lack of space", these papers are available only on
microfilm.

Although, as indicated, no records of early correspondence existed in The
Standard Library, through the aegis of Professor Aspinall's work I was led to
letters from Dr Stanley Lees Giffard, the editor, offering the services of his
newspaper to Peel and Wellington. During all this time, the late Professor
Stephen Koss, and his great works, proved of immense help. Not only did he
check the early research, offering his advice, but proffered suggestions in
other areas.

One such area was to bring me into contact with the present Earl of Halsbury,
the distinguished Chancellor of Brunel University. At a full-day meeting, he

was able to provide information on his great-grandfather, Stanley Lees
Giffard, and, more importantly, was able to give a first-hand account of talks
with his grandfather, the first Earl of Halsbury, Lord Chancellor of England.
As a young man, the first Earl, then Hardinge Giffard, had worked on the paper
as a sub-editor. Here was a remarkable direct link with the first days of The
Standard, including an eye-witness account of The Chartist Demonstration on 10
May 1848 :

> '... I came across a big policeman, twice as big as myself, who was
> being sent with a message to Fergus O'Connor, the head of the movement,
> and I went with him. He said, I suppose with some irony, "I suppose,
> Sir, you are protecting me" '

Apart from these direct references, the files of The Standard from day one
were to prove invaluable. And here I was fortunate in having the "freedom of
the shelves" of the Newspaper Library in Colindale.

Of the many fascinating incidents of this time, recorded in the paper, one was
to stand out: the duel between the Duke of Wellington, then Prime Minister,
and the Earl of Winchilsea, on Saturday 21 March 1829. It arose out of a
letter from Winchilsea published in The Standard in which he accused Wellington of supporting Catholic Emancipation. Some 18 letters were to pass between
the combatants before the duel; and all were later published in the paper
along with the Earl's fulsome apology. As the Duke was to say some months
later: 'The truth is that the duel with Lord Winchilsea was as much part of
the Roman Catholick question, and it was necessary to undertake it ... as was
to do everything else that I could do to attain the object which I had in
view.'

Many other characters were to grace the pages of The Standard in those early
days, but none more colourful than Dr William Maginn, immortalized by
Thackeray as the Captain Shandon of Pendennis. One critic noted of Maginn:
"He would write a leader in The Standard one evening, answer it is The True
Sun the following day and abuse both in John Bull on the ensuing Sunday."
Thackeray, his close friend, has left a vivid account of his meeting with the
Doctor in Fleet Prison, from whence Maginn would provide copy for The Stand-
ard. But probably the best passage in the book is the visit to The Standard
offices, one of the most quoted and descriptive passages in all newspaper
literature:

> ' "Look at that, Penn," Warrington said. "There she is – the great
> engine – she never sleeps. She has her ambassadors in every quarter of
> the world – her couriers upon every road. Her officers march with
> armies, and her envoys walk into statemen's cabinets. They are
> ubiquitous. Yonder journal has an agent, at this minute, giving bribes
> at Madrid; and another inspecting the price of potatoes in Covent
> Garden. Look! here comes the Foreign Express galloping in. They will
> be able to give news to Downing Street tomorrow: funds will rise or
> fall, fortunes will be made or lost; Lord B will get up, and holding
> the paper in his hand, and seeing the noble Marquis in his place, will
> make a great speech; and Mr Doolan will be called away from his supper
> at the Back Kitchen; for he is foreign sub-editor, and sees the mail on
> the newspaper sheet before he goes to his own." '

Statesmen and other celebrities feature prominently in the paper for the remainder of the century, and here the Hughenden Papers (Benjamin Disraeli) at
the Bodleian give a valuable insight into his political machinations with
Thomas Hamber, The Standard's editor. Hamber, through his support of the
Southern cause in the American Civil War, is also mentioned in correspondence,
now in the Library of Congress; and there seems little doubt that he was in

the pay of the Confederates. Mudford, his successor, though, was made of much sterner stuff:

> 'He was a kind of Chinese Emperor, Japanese Mikado in Shoe-lane - the mysterious and awe-inspiring inhabitant of a Forbidden City, only accessible to a very few principals, attendants and acolytes.'

And here the paper's leader writer, and future Poet Laureate, Alfred Austin, was to walk a tightrope between his editor and his political master, Lord Salisbury.

But the dawn of a fresh century, with its New Journalism, was to bring a change in proprietors to The Standard; firstly C Arthur Pearson, then Dalziel and Hulton before the long stewardship of Beaverbrook from 1923 until his death in 1964. Beaverbrook, of course, has been well documented, Taylor's biography being the classic. But there is still much to be learned from the weekly correspondence between Beaverbrook and his general manager, Robertson.

Apart from the regular searches through The Standard files, much information was gleaned from the diaries of leading personalities of the past 40 years; Nicholson, Duff Cooper, "Chipps" Channon, Muggeridge and Bruce Lockhart. I was fortunate in being custodian of the Lockhart Diaries for some two years, and it was fascinating to read his thoughts on a particular incident and then compare it with the other person's point of view.

To anyone studying the inter-relationship between the press and government during the past 100 years, I would strongly recommend Stephen Koss's master-pieces, "The rise and fall of the political press in Britain", Vols. I and II.

4. THE WRITING

Having gathered the information from such a wide variety of sources, there then came the task of writing it up.

My first thoughts were purely journalistic: to write the history of The Standard as a living entity and not with the benefit of hindsight. If possible, the reader should be left in a certain state of suspense, especially at the end of each chapter: there should be no "jumping forward" out of the present time span.

I was delighted, therefore, after writing the opening chapters, to read Barbara Tuchman's observations in Practising History:

> 'One of the difficulties in writing history is the problem of how to keep up suspense in a narrative whose outcome is known. I worried about this a good deal at the beginning, but after a while the actual process of writing, as so often happens, produced the solution. I found that if one writes as of the time, without using the benefit of hindsight, resisting the temptation to refer to events still ahead, the suspense will build itself up naturally.'

To my mind, many histories suffer from an overzealousness of references, dotted around the page like some plague, and there is a tendency to over-verbosity.

G R Elton has written:

> 'But there are two main technical pitfalls on which it is worth offering advice: the use of jargon in place of real words, and incompetence in the use of real words themselves.

'A strange conviction dictates that a pattern becomes the more intellectually respectable the more it is expressed in abstract language.'

With regard to the history of <u>The Standard</u> from the 1960s to the present day, this threw up the problems of dealing with living people and incidents in which I was participant or a bystander, but, following the advice of Joseph Baylen, the distinguished American newspaper historian, I wrote it as straight journalism, endeavouring to obtain a balanced standpoint.

Certainly, it had been a fascinating experience and had led to much correspondence and gladly-given advice from historians and librarians in Great Britain and the United States.

NEWSPAPERS AS RESOURCES FOR SOCIAL HISTORIANS

Dr Roy PORTER

Fellow, Wellcome Institute for the History of Medicine, London

INTRODUCTION BY Dr Roy PORTER

Ladies and gentlemen, I am one of the users for whom you provide such
excellent services as archivists and librarians so I would like to start with
a thank you. I am a social historian who specialises in the history of
medicine and my particular century of interest is the 18th century, which in
Britain and in many other countries is the first real age of the development
of the mass market newspaper. What I want to do is to say something about the
ways in which I as a user find newspapers particularly helpful to the pursuit
of social history, the particular value of newspapers as distinct from other
kinds of evidence and the way in which the social historian sees newspapers as
actually contributing to the development of an emerging modern society.

The first point I want to make is that it seems to me that historians have not
as yet adequately exploited newspapers as a source of social history. Historians rightly are worried when they confront the evidence of a newspaper
because, they must ask 'is it good evidence?' In other words, when faced with
a jumble of assorted insertions in a newspaper from the 18th or the 19th century, most of them anonymous, it is very hard for the historian to know what
credit to give to these pieces of information. Are they true? Can they be
checked against other sources? Are they pieces of journalism? Are they full
of exagerration? Or are they the best evidence we actually have of many occur-
rences that were taking place? Particularly taking place in parts of the
nation and amongst social groups with which we are generally not very familiar. When we find evidence in a newspaper of a riot, and when we find a newspaper saying that 40,000 people took part in that riot, do we believe it or
not?   There is often no way of checking and that is one good reason why historians have been sceptical about precisely the value of the sort of evidence
often contained in newspapers. That scepticism is doubtless justified but if
newspapers were properly exploited, that is to say if they were combed thor-
oughly and systematically with a sceptical viewpoint and were checked against
other sources of evidence which are indeed available, they might be found more
reliable. Frequently we do have other evidence from bystanders, from police
sources, etc., as to the size of a crowd at a riot, or frequently we have
different estimates in different newspapers of the size of a riot. A radical
newspaper would say that 40,000 people took part, a conservative newspaper
would say that 10,000 people took part and we can roughly judge that the real
number was somewhere in between. Newspaper evidence is not something that we
can merely dismiss as journalism; it often does offer us a real insight into
things which are going on.

Why newspapers are particularly valuable is that they frequently tell us about
happenings which other more reliable, more easily accessible sources say
nothing about, but in my paper, as a medical historian, I try to suggest that
if one studied the history of doctors and medical practice in England in the

18th and 19th centuries using newspaper evidence heavily, one would actually get a different historical picture from the one that we largely get from traditional sources by looking at the medical elite, looking at the medical colleges or indeed from looking at the medical press. And in many ways the picture we would get from studying the general press, London newspapers, provincial newspapers would actually be more accurate than the ones that historians have generally taken as a result of looking at obvious sources of evidence, the lives and letters of the major doctors. We can by using newspapers actually probe more deeply in many ways into the fine texture of social history, than we can if we use merely literary evidence or official records or personal papers and such like.

I believe that this is particularly important for the social historian in that newspapers actually are part of that process of social transformation which we can see happening in England from the 18th century onwards, and accelerating in the 19th century, in other words the development of a society in which information and dissemination of information through the printed media became an increasingly important element of the operation of that society itself. News, the spread of knowledge, the dissemination of literacy, the popularisation of high culture through channels such as newspapers becomes an increasingly important part of our society. We see it all around us nowadays with television above all, but newspapers were the television of the 18th century, and historians, librarians, and archivist should be very well aware of the role played by newspapers in actually spreading new ideas, new fashions, new views, down through strata of society which previously may not have been able to afford expensive books, but which were able to afford buying newspapers which cost a penny or twopence or merely sixpence. And so in many ways newspapers open up a window on to the history of the lower middle classes and the lower classes in society, precisely because newspapers were the agents through which information and ideas and opinions actually got through to such people, and then helped to organise them as important forces in the development of modern society, and that is why newspapers are important, not merely as evidence of the world which has gone, but as agencies in the development of historical change. And it is in that way, with librarians and archivists making newspapers available and with historians seeing the ways in which newspapers are both evidence and agencies, that we can actually work together better to understand the development of our modern society.

* * * * * * * * * * * * * * * * * *

1. INTRODUCTION

This paper will not examine the history of newspapers or the periodical press as such. It will rather point to ways in which newspapers constitute invaluable primary sources of information about aspects of society, economy and culture in times past. To some degree, of course, newspapers have been utilized in this way (though it remains true that those scholars most familiar with newspapers have been concerned with newspaper history as such, rather than with using newspaper evidence to reconstruct the world which they served), and I shall point to studies by general historians which have exploited newspaper resources particularly well. All the same, given the richness of the record of the past contained in the press, it is curious that they have not been more systematically quarried. This is a situation which will surely change with their growing availability on microfilm [1].

In this brief illustrative account I shall not attempt a general survey. I

shall instead confine myself to my own field of research, which focuses around
the social history of England in the eighteenth century. I shall thus say
nothing about the newspaper as a source for political history [2]. I shall
concentrate particularly upon what newspaper evidence can tell us about the
medical history of the Georgian century - the ways in which people were concerned about matters of health, what kinds of doctors and hospitals they made
use of, the medicaments which were on the market, their attitudes towards
health and sickness, life and death. In the body of this paper, I shall explore these issues in two different respects, (a) the newspaper as a simple
mirror of its times - how the newspaper straightforwardly informs us of earlier attitudes and practices; and (b) the newspaper as an agent of change - how
the newspaper as a medium for the exchange and dissemination of information
was instrumental in generating socio-cultural transformation. First I will
say a few words about the quality and reliability of the contents of newspapers as indices of social reality.

Contemporaries were always warning the public - sometimes in the newspapers
themselves - not to believe what the papers said. This applied par excellence
to advertisements ('promise, large promise' was the soul of an advertisement,
remarked Dr Johnson), but to news items as well. We read reports in the press
of men and women aged 130, or indeed of ganders almost as old [3]. We may be
unsure whether their authors (and the newspaper printers) were particularly
credulous, whether instead anything that was sensational and eye-catching was
thought good copy, or whether the printer, desperate above all else to fill
his paper, would simply print indiscriminately anything that was to hand.
Clearly the historian must be on his guard. It is typically impossible to
verify by reference to external sources most of the snippets of information
inserted into the papers. The dilemma cannot be resolved that easily.

For example, we may read (time and time again in fact, for these reports are
extremely common) of a traffic accident, in which passengers were injured, but
that fortunately Dr --- was soon upon the scene. He patched, bandaged, dosed
and advised, and the injured were soon as right as rain, and full of gratitude
to the expert skill and tender care of the practitioner [4]. What is the
underlying truth? The incident may well have happened. The newspaper item
was almost certainly written by the doctor in question. It was inserted as a
puff, a piece of concealed advertising. The doctor may well have paid for its
insertion [5]. Its glowing account of healing and gratitude should probably
be taken with a pinch of salt (occasionally a correspondence follows in subsequent numbers contesting the original version).

Or alternatively we read a paragraph on the advertisement page about another
medical practitioner, praising his patent medicines or his skill as an operator upon the teeth or with appliances for ruptures, and giving testimonials
from satisfied customers who are listed by name. Is this fact or simply
fiction? It is often impossible to corroborate the witnesses listed. But not
always. Not infrequently, in fact, real, traceable people are listed in testimonials - indeed people of quasi-official standing, whose names would carry
weight: clergymen, parish officials, soldiers, sailors, etc. What do we make
of that? Are their names being used without authorization? Or were they
truly grateful patients who genuinely believed in the efficacy of some patent
balsam, balm or bandage? Or were they basically prepared to have their name
used, or anxious to see their name in the paper, in return for a free supply
of the drug in question? Again, we can rarely say.

The veracity of such testimony was frequently contested at the time. In the
1770s, a dispute flared in the London newspapers between the uroscopical
practitioner, Dr Theodor Myersbach and his opponent, the distinguished Quaker

physician, John Coakley Lettsom, who claimed the German was a dangerous fraud [6]. Myersbach had published extensive glowing testimonials of his 'cures'. Lettsom challenged them. Letters then appeared in the papers under the names of some of the people giving the testimonies, defending their accounts and vindicating Myersbach. This may prove the trustworthiness of the original reports. Or it may show that Myersbach's capacity to spin an expanding web of fiction was actually quite imaginative. We cannot say. We do know, however, in this case, that there really were some satisfied customers, since quite independent evidence exists (e.g. letters from David Garrick to his friends) recommending the urine-gazer.

Thus we cannot simply afford to take at face value all we read in the papers. Equally, we shouldn't follow the comparable procedure and assume that all that truly happened left its mark in the press. The pioneer historian of the provincial press, G A Cranfield, once remarked that if one read nothing but eighteenth century provincial newspapers, one could remain totally unaware of the fact that agricultural and industrial revolutions were in progress [7]. (Newspapers do indeed contain economic information, but it is mainly about international trade and prices rather than about developments in local industry or agricultural technology). Illustrating Cranfield's perception, Richard Wilson has demonstrated just how little trace the campaigns launched by agricultural interests in the 1780s to legalize the export of wool have left in the provincial newspapers of the sheep-farming areas. Newspapers did not automatically register all that happened, and if used as if they were photographic 'records' of the past, their evidence would prove deeply distorting[8].

Cranfield's and Wilson's points are important. But they require further discussion. For the 'absences' of the newspapers may not simply be 'wrong', may not simply be failures to record what everybody saw was objectively happening. They may positively and accurately register a truth of their own, that the 'industrial revolution' was, indeed, not something which everybody saw erupting all around them, but rather is essentially a convenient shorthand construct of historians with the benefit (or possibly the handicap) of hindsight. In that sense, the silence of the papers may be rather like Sherlock Holmes' dog that didn't bark. It may do more than point to the shortcomings of the press as a source of historical evidence; it may open up new perspectives on the consciousness of contemporaries.

I have been stressing why we should be sceptical about the evidence of newspapers. Even so, the press remains a nonpareil source for social history. Above all, because it fills us in on the thoughts and actions of certain ranks of society and certain kinds of activities which otherwise are badly underrecorded. We have ample access to the lives of the rich and propertied because these got recorded on paper (in estate records, legal deeds, letters, diaries etc.) and those documents have survived in shoals. We have some fair idea, collectively, of the lives of the poor, because enough of them fell foul of the official established welfare and judicial systems: their names and plights turn up in Poor Law disbursements, in hospital admissions registers, and above all in court records and the annals of crime. Do-gooders also began to undertake surveys of the lives of the poor.

We can write the annals of the rich and of the poor (even if they be short and simple). Oddly, it is often England's expanding petty bourgeoisie who have left least historical trace of themselves, those literate, middling folk who made up the nation of shopkeepers: silent and invisible because few of them kept extensive business records or left diaries, and because, being successful, prudent or law-abiding, few ended up upon poor relief or at the assize courts. For precisely this reason, the Georgian middle classes have suffered historical neglect (E P Thompson has written of patrician culture and plebeian culture amongst the Georgians as if there was little in between) [9)].

Yet the middle ranks formed the newspaper buying classes, and their mark is abundantly left in the pages of the papers. They it is who are being enticed by advertisements to go along to the play or to subscribe to the circulating library, who have attic rooms to let or can make Chippendale chairs, who are donating their annual guinea to the voluntary hopsital, or are writing in to ask for a cure for sciatica; they it is who are asking readers to apprehend their serving maid who has run off with a silver spoon, or who collectively are being described as holding a parade and an illumination in honour of John Wilkes or the Battle of the Nile [10]. When the Georgian bourgeoisie at last finds its historian, the newspapers will come into their own as a kaleidos-copic source of miscellaneous information about their everyday lives. In that sense it is no accident that the rise of the newspaper coincides with the rise of the novel.

2. NEWSPAPERS AS MIRRORS OF THE AGE

Granted the problems posed by newspapers as historical evidence, can they offer a special window onto their times? I believe the information they record can prove of unique value, can significantly and accurately modify the received picture derived from other, more familiar, sources.

Partly this is because of its sheer abundance. Careful scanning of newspapers can demonstrate that phenomena which, from other evidence, we know happened occasionally, were not merely occasional or exceptional, but rather common-place. Take food riots for instance. Historians familiar with government sources and pamphlet literature have long been aware that when grain became scarce or dealers tried to raise its price at the market, buyers would some-times take the law into their own hands, seize the supplies, sell corn or bread at the traditional price, and deliver the proceeds to the owner. It is not until one looks at newspaper reports that one finds that this 'moral econ-omy of the crowd' or 'collective bargaining by riot' was indeed an extremely common occurrence, indeed a normal practice [11].

A parallel would be popular scientific lecturing. It has long been known that a small number of scientific popularizers – men such as William Whiston and James Ferguson – gave occasional lecture courses in the provinces. Biograph-ical sources reveal the odd series of lectures from year to year in Bath, Bristol, Manchester, Newcastle and so forth. Close scrutiny of newspapers for these and other towns, carried out some twenty years ago by A E Musson and Eric Robinson, and by other scholars subsequently, revealed a very different situation. Such courses totalled not a handful but scores; far more lecturers existed than had been previously supposed (they often included local school-masters, physicians or Dissenting clergymen); and their subjects were far more varied [12].

An example such as this suggests a further point. Newspapers reveal not just quantitatively more activity, but a state of affairs qualitatively distinct from the received accounts. Traditional histories of education and learning told us that schooling was in the doldrums in Georgian England, for both grammar schools and the universities were in decay. That is true, but the conclusion is a mirage based upon a myopic focussing upon certain traditional institutions. Get away from those, and we see an abundance of engines of instruction advertised in the newspapers – commercial schools, mathematical academies, lectures in navigation and gunnery, evening classes, itinerant lectures, scientific spectacles etc. Most of these, being ephemeral and one-off, left no record for posterity outside the advertisment or report in the local newspaper. Without the snapshot of local society the newspaper affords, we would have little sense of its rich and teeming culture [13].

The history of medicine offers important confirmation of this fact. Traditional histories of medicine, based on 'official' sources such as the records of the medical Colleges, explained that there existed in earlier centuries an established medical profession, with a hierarchical structure ranging from physicians at the head, through surgeons, to apothecaries at the foot, practising proper medicine; and beyond a small number of itinerants, charlatans and mountebanks, touting their nostrums to the credulous. Medical provision was limited and expensive.

This, however, is nothing but an ideal type which turns out to bear very little resemblance to reality. Numerous different kinds of source materials enable us to get at the reality, but not the least valuable is the testimony provided by newspapers. Eighteenth century papers positively bulge with medical items. Some indeed are the advertisements of itinerant 'quacks' such as James Graham and John ('Chevalier') Taylor. But many give notice of the practices and activities of perfectly regular and reputable doctors, listing their specialities (not infrequently, the cure of venereal infections). Some are resident; others – particularly dentists or oculists – tour on a circuit. Sometimes they recommend their own special cures (self-advertisement did not become unprofessional practice for doctors till at least the mid-nineteenth century). And scores of advertisements are printed for all manner of patent and proprietary medicines, many of them, as with Dr James' Fever Powders, marketed not by fly-by-night mountebanks but by reputable physicians [14].

A wholly different picture of the medical milieu thus begins to appear. Traditionally histories told us that medical skill was in short supply in the eighteenth century. Newspapers show that practitioners were ten a penny, competing against each other for custom. Traditional histories portrayed medical practice as highly 'professional'; the newspapers show it wholly embraced the techniques (such as advertising) of the market economy. Traditional histories said little of the patient; the press reveals just how active and important this figure was. Eighteenth century patients clearly bought up armfuls of proprietary medicines with which to dose themselves, on the strength of newspaper advertisements. Moreover, the correspondence columns of periodicals such as the upmarket and large-circulation Gentleman's Magazine are full of letters written in by the laity, seeking and giving medical advice. Newsaper evidence – trustworthy in this case because corroborated from other sources – thus helps to open our eyes to a very different medical reality: one that was open, one in which lay participation was crucial, one adept in the techniques of the market place, one fully integrated into that surge of 'commercialization', that creation of a 'consumer society', which historians have recently stressed [15].

In a parallel way, newspapers can also afford an important new window onto old outlooks and attitudes. Over the last decades French historians, in particular those associated with the journal Annales, have attempted to go beyond the vagueness of studies of the Zeitgeist, the spirit of the age, on the one hand, or the elitism of the 'history of ideas' on the other, and have instead pioneered l'histoire des mentalités. In general, English historians have not yet followed this lead, partly because of doubts about what would be the proper data bank for such an approach. But newspapers would afford a splendid body of commonplace attitudes, moral platitudes, and national, class and religious prejudice upon which to construct such analyses of the common (though literate) mind [16].

The evidence provided by newspapers of what people did and thought, and what it was thought worth recording, can also prove useful for testing our pre-existing notions about natural beliefs and cultural change in pre-industrial society. For example, we commonly refer to the age of the Enlightenment as a time of sexual permissiveness. Is that assumption a false perspective based upon studies of a small unrepresentative elite from Pepys to Boswell and Byron? [17] The witness of newspapers would suggest that license in erotic act and expression was quite common and may have raised few eyebrows. There is no shortage of bawdy in the Georgian press. The Weekly Courant for 26 November 1717 carries, for instance, the following advertisement:
> 'Any able young Man, strong in the Back, and endow'd with a good carnal Weapon, with all the Appurtenances thereupon belonging in good Repair, may have Half a Crown per Night, a Pair of clean Sheets, and other Necessaries, to perform Nocturnal Services on one Sarah Y-tes, whose Husband having for these 9 Months past lost the Use of his Peace-Maker, the unhappy Woman is thereby driven to the last Extremity.'

One would like to know the story behind that. The interesting fact is that it — with many similar insertions — was actually published.

Similarly, we are told that the age of the Enlightenment repudiated superstition and credulous belief in the supernatural. Does the evidence of newspapers bear that out? Hardly. For there are plenty of reports, through the eighteenth century, of cases of alleged witchcraft. A report in the Northampton Mercury for 2 July 1770 mentions a farmer from Slapton who on the mysterious deaths of a horse and two sheep accused a local widow of witchcraft. The villagers prepared a trial by ordeal for the woman, which was stopped only at the last moment. The newspaper report was scathing in its attitude to this benightedness.

Nearly forty years later, the same newspaper (28 May 1808) was still reporting cases of witchcraft accusations. The newspaper assured its readers that the woman in question, Ann Izzard 'is a very harmless inoffensive woman', but noted that 'the poor in general of the parishes of Great and Little Paxton, and some of the farmers also, really believe she is actually a witch.' In his splendid "Religion and the Decline of Magic", Keith Thomas surveyed the gradual decline of public belief in witchcraft and magic in the seventeenth century, before the availability of newspaper evidence. A follow-up story for the age of the newspaper would be invaluable. It could survey not just the evidence for decline (or longevity) afforded by newspapers, but the role played by newspapers in those processes. For the newspaper was not merely a mirror of its times. It was also an agent in changing them.

3.   THE NEWSPAPER AND SOCIAL CHANGE

Victorian newspaper editors in particular celebrated the press as one of the great engines of improvment. The eighteenth century had fought and won the battle for the freedom of the press. Now the Fourth Estate, by its fearless championship of justice, liberty and truth, would guarantee the course of progress. It would be a mistake to take this often self-serving ideology at face value. Most eighteenth century London papers were under the control of political paymasters of one or other party hue; their provincial equivalents were typically owned by small capitalist printers for whom cash, circulation and copy rather than crusading were what counted [18]. Of course, there was a radical press; but the press was far from radical as a whole, and it is noteworthy that England, with its relatively free press, never had a revolution, whereas so many nations where the press was censored or shackled, did. We should not expect that the press directly wrought socio-political transformation.

But to say this is not to deny that the emergence of the newspaper was instrumental in social change. In many respects, it worked for greater integration of attitudes and activities throughout the land. Information of all kinds — from news of war overseas to official proclamations to the latest West End fashions — now sped down more quickly, more certainly, to the dark corners of the land. The newspaper bridged the communications gap — and therefore the culture gap — between metropolis and province.

Moreover, the newspaper also helped bridge a class gap. It was a relatively democratic instrument of information, freely available to all those who could read and who had a few coppers to spare (or who were fit to be seen in a coffee house or a tavern or any other public place where the papers were for the asking). The coming of the newspaper helped to bring a certain political awareness to the whole nation, argued the radical journalist, William Cobbett. Describing the rural Surrey of his infancy in the 1760s, Cobbett wrote, [19]

> 'As to politics, we were like the rest of the country people in England, that is to say, we neither knew nor thought anything about the matter. The shouts of victory and the murmur of defeat would now and then break in upon our tranquility for a moment, but I do not remember ever having seen a newspaper in the house.'

Things rapidly changed. Foreigners were soon calling the English a nation of newsmongers. All the same, if cheap printed material integrated all those who could read, and could afford a paper, it may also have helped to reinforce the divide between literate and oral culture themselves (although we must remember that bridging devices, such as reading newspapers out loud to the illiterate, were common).

The rise of the newspaper was the triumph of the new. People who in earlier generations might have spent their evenings poring over family Bibles and treasured copies of Pilgrim's Progress now developed a taste for novelty, for the ephemeral, and not least an absorption in the here-and-now, that taste for chit-chat, gossip and trivia which newspapers fostered. This is not to argue that the rise of the newspaper, harbinger of 'mass culture', diluted 'standards'. It is, however, to stress that the newspaper was integral to two cardinal eighteenth century developments [20].

Firstly, the emergence of innovation as a dynamo of capitalism. News fanned a taste for the new. Fashionability increasingly became a desideratum in itself (and to some degree shed its pejorative overtones). And newspaper advertising, overt and concealed, became the medium through which the market for fashionable commodities broadened out from the local to the national.

This development is particularly conspicuous in the field of medicine. Before newspapers became common, the quack or nostrum-monger was dependent almost wholly on his personal presence as he toiled his way with his zany, monkey and portable stage from town to town. With the advent of mass-advertising in provincial newspapers, the nostrum-proprietor could instead establish one central manufacturing warehouse, advertise his wares the length and breadth of the country in the newspapers, and arrange for their delivery through the newsagents. Indeed, printers themselves commonly became the major outlets for fashionably advertised and gaudily packaged commercial medicines. John Newbury, newspaper proprietor and leading promoter of children's books, possessed the largest stake in the best-selling nostrum, Dr James' Fever Powders (notoriously slipping a puff for them in his best-selling "Little Goody Two

Shoes"). Analyses of the process of industrialization nowadays stress the importance of the quickening of consumer demand as a factor in commercial acceleration. Advertising was crucial in articulating that demand, and newspapers formed a key advertising medium [21].

Secondly, the newspaper played a major role in the triumph of 'culture'. Before the eighteenth century there were of course numerous 'cultures' – oral culture amongst the people at large, a powerful Protestant religious culture, a literary and artistic culture amongst the polite and propertied elite, and so forth. The eighteenth century witnessed an additional development, the mushrooming of a widespread commercial, urban culture, cashing in upon the fact that more people had more money and time to spare. The circulating library, the book shop, the print shop, the theatre, the concert hall, the assembly room, the coffee house, the shopping parade, the club – all these became fashionable resorts and foci of leisure activities, just as hospitals, schools and comparable charities became centres of conspicuous philanthropy [22].

All such activities were buoyed up by the advent of the newspaper. Papers could be read in places of resort such as the clubs and coffee houses. Newspapers advertised the services of culture-instructors such as dancing-masters and musicians, and listed the attractions of theatres and concert halls, reporting upon performers and performances and listing who graced the audience. The sayings of wits, the clothes of the fasionable, forthcoming attractions – all found their mention. The magic circle of the newspaper – being noted in it by name, or at least being one of its readers – came to be definitive of membership of the monde, whether it was the greater metropolitan and polite world, or merely in in-circle in Exeter or Newcastle. In so far as the secularized civil society depends upon cultural emulation for its cement, in so far as commercial capitalism depends for economic growth at least as much upon service industries as upon manufactures, the newspaper proved an indispensable midwife for English's buoyant market society [23].

4. CONCLUSION AND SUGGESTIONS

The newspaper is thus both a window onto the history of the birth of the modern world, and one important agent in that history. Scholars have given us a body of excellent histories, both of individual newspapers and of the press in general, in particular focussing upon their political content. Curiously, we lack any major study of the wider socio-cultural impact of the advent of the press (comparable, for example, to Elizabeth Eisenstein's pioneering analysis of the cultural impact of the printing press as such) [24]. Such would of course be no simple task, since it would be in danger of merging into the much broader history of print culture as such, or of the rise of literacy, or of that growing separation of elite from popular culture which Peter Burke and others have analysed [25].

In one respect, the task of assessing the impact of the newspaper is relatively easy. For although some copies of some newspapers are irretrievably lost, we do possess a clear record of which towns hosted which newspapers from which date. In this sense, the congruence between milieu, medium and message is uniquely concrete in the case of newspapers: we can be sure (for example) of what a few hundred, or a few thousand, people in Worcester or Halifax were reading on a particular day – The Worcester Post-Man or the Halifax Advertiser. We can never have that kind of assurance with any other kind of printed matter.

There is alas of course a severe obstacle: the peculiarly ephemeral nature of the newspaper itself. Library catalogues, subscription lists and the like often tell us who owned which works of theology, novels or history books; no-one saw fit to record their purchases of newspapers that way. The private journals of eminences from the past frequently give us their considered opinions on the latest novel or book of poetry. What readers actually made of the newspapers they purchased cannot so easily be read off from direct comments in their correspondence. But letters and diaries do contain a good spattering of casual mentions of reading the papers, sending them on to friends and family, even occasionally of writing to the editor in protest. And personal archival sources such as family recipe books or commonplace books often contain passages cut out or copied out of the newspapers. Assessing the meaning of newspapers to their readers is a perfectly feasible research project. It has not been attempted. It would be pleasant if the joint efforts of librarians, archivists and scholars alike would make it a reality.

REFERENCES

1   One welcome project is the microfilming of Eighteenth Century English Provincial Newspapers by Harvester. Already published or shortly to be published are the holdings of Bath, Derby, Ipswich, Newcastle and Gloucester newspapers.

2   See for up-to-date discussions containing excellent bibliographies:
    Black, Jeremy, 'The English Press in the Eighteenth Century'. London, Croom Helm, 1987, esp. ch.5, and
    Harris, Michael, and Lee, Alan, (eds.), 'The Press in English Society from the Seventeenth to Nineteenth Centuries'. London and Toronto, Associated University Presses, 1986, esp. William Speck 'Politics and the Press', pp. 47-63.

3   There is a good sampling of this sort of stuff in: Morsley, Clifford, 'News from the English Countryside'. London, Harrap, 1979.

4   There are scores of instances of this kind of insertion, for example, in the early numbers of the Bath Journal, which I have used heavily for the generalizations about the medical content of newspapers which follow.

5   For puffery see Nevett, Terry, 'Advertising and Editorial Integrity in the Nineteenth Century', in: Harris and Lee (eds), op. cit. (ref. 2), pp. 149-67.

6   For what follows see Porter, Roy, '"I Think Ye Both Quacks": The Controversy Between Dr Theodor Myersbach and Dr John Coakley Lettsom', in: Bynum, W F and Porter, Roy, (eds), 'Medical Fringe and Medical Orthodoxy 1750-1850'. London, Croom Helm, 1986, pp. 56-78.

7   Cranfield, G A, 'The Development of the Provincial Newspaper, 1700-1760'. Oxford, Clarendon Press, 1962, 26f, 90f, 211f.

8   Wilson, Richard, 'Newspapers and Industry: The Export of Wool Controversy in the 1780s', in: Harris and Lee (eds) op. cit. (ref. 2), pp. 80-106.

9   Thompson, E P, 'Patrician Society, Plebeian Culture', in: Journal of Social History, Summer 1974, pp. 382-405.

10 Admirable on these social opportunities and pressures is Wiles, R M,
    'Freshest Advices. Early Provincial Newspapers in England'. Ohio State
    University Press, 1963.

11 Thompson, E P, 'The Moral Economy of the English Crowd in the Eighteenth
    Century', in: Past and Present, Vol.50 1971, and Stevenson, J, 'Popular
    Disturbances in England 1700-1870'. London, 1979.

12 Musson, A E, and Robinson, Eric, 'Science and Technology in the Indust-
    rial Revolution'. Manchester, Manchester University Press, 1969.

13 See Hans, N, 'New Trends in Education in the Eighteenth Century'. London,
    1951.

14 See for example:
    Brown, P S, 'Medicines Advertised in Eighteenth Century Bath Newspapers',
    in: Medical History, Vol.20, 1976, pp. 152-68.
    Barry, J, 'Publicity and the Public Good: Presenting Medicine in
    Eighteenth Century Bristol', in: Bynum and Porter (eds), op. cit. (ref.
    6), pp. 29-39.
    For dentists see Hillam, F C, 'The Development of Dental Practice in the
    Provinces from the Late 18th Century to 1855' Ph.D. thesis, University of
    Liverpool, 1986.

15 For the Gentleman's Magazine see Porter, Roy, 'Laymen, Doctors and Med-
    ical Knowledge. The Evidence of the Gentleman's Magazine', in Porter,
    Roy, (ed.), 'Patients and Practitioners. Lay Perceptions of Medicine in
    Pre-Industrial Society'. Cambridge, Cambridge University Press, 1985, pp.
    283-314; the other essays in this volume offer important perspectives on
    patients' choices. For consumerism see Mackendrick, N, Brewer, J, and
    Plumb, J H, 'The Birth of a Consumer Society'. London, Europa, 1982. For
    the medical market place see Holmes, G, 'Augustan England. Professions,
    State and Society 1680-1730'. London, 1982.

16 See the discussion in Burke, Peter, 'Revolution in Popular Culture', in
    Porter, Roy, and Teich, Mikulas , (eds), 'Revolution in History'.
    Cambridge, Cambridge University Press, 1986, pp. 206-225.

17 For up-to-date assessment see Rousseau, G S, and Porter, Roy, (eds),
    'Sexual Underworlds of the Enlightenment'. Manchester, Manchester
    University Press, 1987.

18 See the discussion in Black, op. cit. (ref. 2).

19 Quoted in Porter, Roy, 'English Society in the Eighteenth Century'.
    Harmondsworth, Penguin, 1982, p. 241.

20 See the general discussion in Porter op. cit. (ref. 19), ch.6, and the
    literature cited on pp. 400-01.

21 See the discussion in:
    Porter, Roy, 'The Language of Quackery, 1660-1800', Burke, Peter, and
    Porter, Roy, (eds), 'The Social History of Language'. Cambridge,
    Cambridge University Press, 1987, pp. 74-103.
    See also Looney, J J, 'Advertising and Society in England 1720-1820. A
    Statistical Analysis of Yorkshire Newspaper Advertisements'. Princeton
    Univesity Ph.D. thesis, 1983.

22   Plumb, J H, 'The Commercialization of Leisure in Eighteenth Century
      England'. Reading, University Press, 1973.
      Cunningham, H, 'Leisure in the Industrial Revolution'. London, 1980.
      For a specially good regional study see Money, J, 'Experience and
      Identity. Birmingham and the West Midlands, 1760-1800'. Manchester,
      Manchester University Press, 1976.

23   See the excellent discussions in Cranfield, op. cit. (ref. 7), and Wiles,
      op. cit. (ref. 10).

24   Eisenstein, E, 'The Printing Press as an Agent of Change'. Cambridge,
      Cambridge University Press, 1979.

25   Burke, Peter, 'Popular Culture in Early Modern Europe'. London, Temple
      Smith, 1978.

DISCUSSION

Q.   Andrew Phillips, British Library

I think that it is very interesting that you pose that question at the end.
In a sense what I would like to ask you is; what particular difficulties and
lacunae you find when approaching newspaper collections in libraries in which
you worked because I think that there are some things which the librarians and
archivists, if I can put it this way, could do something about. There are
other things which maybe extremely difficult to do anything about, and I
wonder if we could begin to look at where that divide might be from your
experience as a user and historian.

A.   Dr Roy Porter

Yes, can I very briefly answer that question. I think that there are lacunae
which are irrepairable, there are just simply gaps in runs of newspapers,
which we can do nothing about at all. Quite often I have found that detailed
probing of librarians or the grapevine will actually reveal information which
is valuable, but which is not readily available, for example; when looking in
local record offices at runs of early provincial newspapers it is often very
revealing to discover where that particular collection actually comes from.
Because to discover that it was found in the attic of a farmhouse somewhere
deep in the countryside and it had been there, been collected indeed by a
tradesman or a farmer in the 18th or early 19th century, tells us a lot about
something else, which is what people did with newspapers. Did people automatically throw them away, read them, discard them, or did they actually file
them, bind them, treasure them, go back and reread them etc.. Now the more we
know about how particular collections have actually come to be preserved the
better, and I have sometimes found that there is somebody around who half
remembers where a collection came from or something like that. But if that
sort of information could be more systematically made available it would certainly be a real help to historians such as myself.

Q.   Unidentified

Question about the readership in the 18th Century. Was the lower class really
reading as much as has been suggested?

A.   Dr Roy Porter

I think that the brief answer to that is by and large most probably no. But
the second answer to that is we really do not know too much about that as yet
because a great deal of work still remains to be done on the whole question of
lower class literacy and not least the availability of newspapers and periodicals like The Spectator to ordinary people.

A lot of foreign visitors to Britain were very impressed in the 18th century
by claiming that lower class workers, porters, cab drivers etc., in their
spare moments were reading newspapers. Or that you paid a halfpenny to get
into a coffee house and you sat and read the newspapers, and they all kept on
saying, the English are great newspaper addicts. It looks as though maybe the
habit of reading newspapers actually spread further down the social strata
than we often believe. Certainly the newspapers were not primarily aimed at
the lower class reader, that does not mean to say that they were actually
reading them, probably not The Spectator but certainly one imagines that quire
a few of the provincial newspapers that came out once or twice a week were
read by lower class people, because quite frequently one sees jobs advertised
in them etc., which lower class people would be actually applying for. So it
sounds as though the provincial newspaper were often geared to quite a wide
social strata.

Q.   Unidentifed

It is important to distinguish between newspapers as a primary source and as a
secondary source which is often mixed up - really in some aspects it is always
a primary source if it reflects what people thought regardless of whether the
facts are accurate or not. The impression that one gets from a newspaper, the
so-called facts that are given and given over to people is as important perhaps as the accuracy or the validity of the facts themselves. So if you look
at a newspaper critically as a historian and I look at it both as an historian
and as an archivist, you have to realise that important distinction and you
can know a great deal if you can keep that distinction in mind.

A.   Dr Roy Porter

I think that is a very valid point in the sense that the newspaper is both a
way of trying to get at reality but it is also creating a reality, a mythology
of its own. If one wants to study the development of popular attitudes the
function of the newspaper in actually creating opinion, fostering prejudice,
mobilising particular political views is extremely important and sometimes one
can actually see the tensions and the discrepancies between these two
functions.

Obviously we need to know a great deal more about the newspaper and it is a
problem because frequently we know who read which books because people made a
note of it or kept the books in their library and we have library catalogues.
We know far less about people's newspaper reading because they actually recorded that reading so much less it being that bit more ephemeral.

I do not believe that the task is hopeless and if we all reassembled in ten or
fifteen years time then some of these questions would be much more nearly
resolved.

THE USE OF RETROSPECTIVE NEWSPAPER RESOURCES IN THE LIBRARIES OF THE
FEDERAL REPUBLIC OF GERMANY: 8 THESES [1]

Dr Willi HÖFIG
Newspaper Librarian, Staatsbibliothek Preussischer Kulturbesitz,
Berlin (West)

1. INTRODUCTION

We Germans are convinced in our heart of hearts, even though we sometimes deny
it, that there is a suitable Goethe quotation for every problem which concerns
us. I have been supported in this view by my success in locating a comment by
Goethe on the problem of the use of retrospective newspaper stock. Please,
therefore, lend an ear to the following extract from the Tag-und Jahreshefte
1808 which I ask you not to take as only a ludicrous notion:
>'Convinced all along, and even more so in recent years that newspapers
>are only there to keep the crowd at bay and to delude momentarily,
>unless an external power prevents the editor from telling the truth or
>an internal partisan forbid him the very same, I read no more... The
>'Allgemeine Zeitung', however, kindly sent to me on a regular basis by
>Mr von Cotta, accumulated at home and so, by way of the orderliness of
>a Chancellery colleague, I found the years 1806 and 1807 neatly bound
>just as I was about to set out for Carlsbad. As I usually took a few
>books with me at such opportunities, I found it comfortable and pleas-
>ing to take this political library with me, and it gave me not only
>unexpected education and entertainment, but also friends, who, on
>becoming aware of the volumes, requested them periodically, so that in
>the end I could hardly get my hands on them again.' [2]

It is not so easy nowadays for the librarian to make reliable predictions
about the use of his newspaper collection. Only local usage is perceptible
from day to day, perhaps also inter-library lending from his own library. A
better picture is obtained from the editorial offices of union catalogues,
such as exist in the Federal Republic - especially for newspapers - at Bremen
and Berlin. Here negative requests can be examined so that a survey of supply
and demand is possible [3].

The systematic analysis of inter-library loans can determine this demand more
exactly. In the first half of 1983 the incoming loan forms for newspapers at
research libraries in Aachen, Berlin, Hamburg and Stuttgart were copied. The
same thing happened at the Berlin Union Catalogue and at both the central
newspaper catalogues. Analysis of this material has up till now been delayed
for financial and staffing reasons, however, the results I should like to
submit are not so perishable because they concern the principles of newspaper
usage.

152 libraries altogether in the Federal Republic of Germany were included in
the survey. Selection could not be planned because of the nature of the
study; it arose from the actual accumulation of loan forms at the key points
where they were copied. In keeping with the diverse nature of the German
Library system, the libraries whose users request newspapers on inter-library
loan belong to very different categories. 53 of the returning libraries are
university, polytechnic, college and advanced vocational college libraries, 36

public libraries, 28 academic public libraries, 17 subject and special libraries, 13 state and regional libraries and finally 5 district libraries and
related institutions. Almost three quarters of those libraries included in
the survey are geared to satisfying the research needs of universities, colleges and advanced vocational colleges or the institutions collecting and offering relevant material as supra-regional institutions for specialist areas of
research. A quarter of the participating libraries belong to the public library system which - at least in theory - should provide universally for a
general public. The two library domains cannot be compared with each other
quite so simply from the point of view of their functions and scope. Supra-
regional lending in the Federal Republic is predominantly lending between
research libraries which, - commensurate with the special structure of the
German library system - is also available to public libraries but not used by
them to an extent which would correspond with their share in the library
system. So far the preponderance of research-oriented libraries in the lending of newspapers is not characteristic of newspapers as a material but rather
a peculiarity of the German lending service. If the number of newspapers
requested per library is seen in relation to the proportion of different library categories, then characteristic outlines emerge which can be related to
newspapers as library stock.

University libraries make up 34.9% of our sample; they account for 75.2% of
all inter-library loans - i.e. 29.4 loan forms per university library. Public
libraries on the other hand, which as a category with 23.6% are only slightly
less strongly represented than university libraries, generate only 5.3% of
newspaper loan forms. On average each public library accounts for 3 loan
forms.

2. SUMMARY OF THE THESES

2.1. Thesis 1
Newspapers from retrospective collections are required by users of all types
of library, primarily, however, by users of research libraries in the Federal
Republic of Germany.

University libraries require ten times as many newspapers as municipal libraries in the public library sector: on average 30 loans per university
library as opposed to 3 in public libraries during the same period.

Thus our data have been subdivided for the first time; we would however like
to know more about the libraries whose users have the wish to read or examine
actual newspaper stock. The result of our survey is an average of 14.7 loans
per library. Given that data collection lasted in all 3 months, this number
of loan forms per library is ridiculously small, when one remembers that
interlibrary lending in the Federal Republic at the moment reaches a volume of
2.5 million loans annually. It is a curious feeling to tackle a subject which
- looked at purely statistically - would hardly be worth mentioning because of
its insignificance in relation to the problems of inter-library lending as a
whole; and that is exactly the crux of the matter when it comes to resolving
the problems which are piling up and are not made any easier by being linked
to phenomena of another order of magnitude. The absolute number of loans is
very small; between 10 and 24 loans forms per library. Yet the figures are
not distributed evenly among despatching libraries. Data is made up of 2
components. Numerous users request a newspaper now and again along with other
material; few users request newspapers exclusively on inter-library loan, but
in large numbers. So, alongside a large number of libraries with occasional

newspaper requests, we have others whose demand for newspapers is continuous
and greater than that of the others, even if the absolute figure still remains
small. For simplicity's sake I will call the latter from now on 'newspaper
libraries'. During the data collection operation they were responsible over a
period of 3 months for pushing between 51 and 110 loan forms for newspapers
into the German lending system; they are - in descending order - the university libraries of

Münster (110)	Marburg (69)
Dortmund (102)	Bochum (64)
Mainz (99)	Cologne (54)
Hamburg (71)	Tübingen (51)
Frankfurt a.M. (70)	

as well as the library of the Technical College in Aachen (62). Those are the
libraries whose users work with the newspapers to a great extent and order
them via inter-library loan. This enumeration is disposed to support my first
thesis that loan traffic in newspapers is primarily loan traffic among research libraries, more precisely university libraries. It also makes it clear
that it is a question for the most part of our 'old' university libraries.
Here is not the appropriate place to elaborate on the structure of German
higher education. Face to face with the 'old' universities are the new institutions of the 60s to 80s, the literature needs of which have been determined
by thoughts on library planning over many years. The idea, that new institutions would have to rely on loans to a greater extent to provide for their
users, because of their own poor book stock, is not borne out by our data as
far as newspapers are concerned.

It is an interesting question as to how our data is divided among the individual regions of the Federal Republic. Unfortunately, the answers lead us
away from our concrete theme of usage to more formal questions of lending
which can only be of peripheral interest in this context. Suffice to say that
the lion's share of requests emanate from the libraries of North-Rhine Westphalia, as half the 'newspaper libraries' are located there, while the second
half is distributed between Hesse, Baden-Württemberg, Rhineland-Pfalz and the
city state of Hamburg. North-Rhine Westphalia and its libraries thus lie at
the top; there follow in descending order Hesse, Baden-Württemberg, the north
German lending region in which Schleswig-Holstein, Bremen and Hamburg are
included, finally Bavaria and Lower Saxony; Berlin brings up the rear. Conversion to the number of users interested in the material under investigation
results in the same sequence, so that, in spite of considerable variations in
detail over all regions, an equivalent figure of an average of 2.2 newspaper
requests per user was arrived at. This figure is surprisingly low when we
compare it with the general impression given when examining newspaper loan
forms. We have already indicated that we are dealing with two quite different
aspects of newspaper usage.

To return to the question of the weighting of the libraries concerned! If only
three 'new' university libraries appear among the ten most important libraries
in our discussion, and therefore newspaper lending is seen as essentially
lending among 'old' university libraries, nevertheless two of the 'new' libraries Mainz and Dortmund, lie in second and third place amongst 'newspaper
libraries'. Why this should be so is evidenced by a look at the role mass
communication research is playing at these universities. We can accept that
the special emphasis on journalism or mass media research within the general
framework of university research at Dortmund, Bochum, and Mainz, the new university libraries appearing in the sample of 'newspaper libraries', is not
without influence on the existance of a special need at these centres for
journalistic source literature. The names Koszyk, Noelle-Neumann and Heinz D
Fischer are known in communication research even outside the Federal Republic.

However, in the case of the 'old' university libraries, the relatively high proportion of newspaper requests in the lending system cannot be explained just like that. With the exception of Münster, which has the largest share in newspaper lending, the remaining 'old' university libraries among the 'newspaper libraries' have no institute or seminar for mass media research at their university. Simply considering the teaching structure of the respective university does not offer a satisfactory explanation of the larger coverage of newspapers deemed necessary.

However, the data allow us to formulate the second thesis,or, at least its first half; it reads:

2.2. Thesis 2
The participation of newly founded West German university libraries in newspaper lending is directly proportionate to the importance of their teaching facilities in mass media research.

We have established more closely at which institutions our users are to be found and within what framework research requiring newspapers takes place. Our data allow us to answer the question as to which titles are requested and for which years, at what locations these titles appear and the arbitrary combination of the criteria of place, period and title, as well as, finally, their association with the themes of the requested newspaper articles.

Let us look first at places of publication. They are always given on the forms under investigation or filled in later because information about place of publication represents a _sine qua non_ for the identification of the relevant paper. I can think of titles such as _Reporter_ or _Tempo_ which appear in many places and are not even limited to one language group, while a title such as TIMES is scattered in innumerable variants over the whole Anglo-American world as well as large parts of Asia and Africa. Subdivision of newspapers requested according to place of publication offers a highly characteristic, one would be tempted to say _deceptive_, picture. Over half of all newspapers requested (52.3%) originate from the area occupied today by the two German states. 30% of places of publication lie in the Federal Republic, scarcely 7% in the German Democratic Republic and 16% in Berlin. If we follow the sequence of states and geographic regions downwards, according to the number of newspaper places of publication sought, with one exception to be discussed later, Austria and Switzerland, completely or predominantly German-speaking countries, appear with figures of 6%, somewhat later the places formerly belonging to Germany which became Polish, Russian or French during the wars of the twentieth century (3.1%). If we include those places of publication which used to belong to Austro-Hungary and lie today in different states of Central and Eastern Europe and the Balkans, we arrive at a figure of 71.6% for newspapers requested on loan with present or former German-speaking places of publication. We are, therefore, faced with the fact that 71% of the material which German libraries obtain for use by their newspapers users was published in a geographic area which was German-speaking at the beginning of this century.

We have already established that newspapers requested are used predominantly for work at universities. We now learn, in addition, that this work takes place largely from an ethnocentric point of view. My third thesis runs thus:

2.3. Thesis 3
Newspapers used in German libraries come primarily from the German-speaking world.

These findings are depressing whatever one may think of the cosmopolitan nature of German research. There is a small chink of light in the fact that in third place behind places of publication in the Federal Republic and Berlin, but still ahead of the German Democratic Republic, we find France with 9.1% of places of publication sought. Newspapers which appear in France represent the second largest region – after those appearing in the German language area, a fact which has been taken into account by the Staatsbibliothek in Berlin which is responsible for supra-regional provision of foreign newspapers to libraries in the Federal Republic. As a result it has acquired microfilms of the most important French newspapers from the beginning and in continuation and holds them ready for lending.

To summarise, the ranking list runs as follows:

Position	Country	%	Position	Country	%
1.	Germany (FRG)	29.9	10.	Germany (former regions)	3.1
2.	Berlin	15.6	11.	Italy	2.2
3.	France	9.1	12.	Central & South America	1.8
4.	GDR	6.7	13.	Soviet Union	1.5
5.	Switzerland	6.3	14.	Netherlands, Belgium	1.0
6.	USA and Canada	6.0	15.	Scandinavia	0.5
7.	Austria	5.3	16.	Spain	0.5
8.	Czechoslovakia	3.6	17.	Poland	0.5
9.	Great Britain	3.5			
					97.1%

For the rest of the world there remains scarcely 3%.

TABLE 1
Ranking list of countries where newspapers are published

But this picture is deceptive: expert intervention is necessary. We know that the Neue Zürcher Zeitung is held at 82 German libraries, the Moscow Pravda at 49, the London Times at 47, the International Herald Tribune at 40, the Moscow Izvestija at 38, the New York Times at 32, the Guardian at 30, the Observer at 23 [4]. The presence of about 20 prestige papers at practically every library which would like to be taken seriously, tells us nothing about the actual availability of the material. What is the position with earlier volumes, for example? Are the requested editions available, for example, the domestic edition of the New York Times which is only to be found at a few locations ?

The following survey shows how things actually stand:

Title	Current number of libraries	Requested number of volumes	Requested which years
Neue Zürcher Zeitung	82	25	1908–1981
Pravda, Moscow	49	1	1961
Times, London	47	7	1879–1974
Internat. Herald Trib.	40	14	1949–1965
Izvestija, Moscow	38	1	1918
N.Y. Times	32	24	1936–1982
Guardian	30	1	1982
Observer	23	7	1946–1964

TABLE 2
Availability of prestige papers

The survey shows clearly that, on the one hand, early volumes are requested which are not available in the libraries which can offer the relevant title today: for example, the early volumes of the Neue Zürcher Zeitung (NZZ) from 1908 on, although every larger library can produce a copy of the NZZ. It is somewhat surprising that the volumes of the NZZ requested on loan go as far as 1981, those of the London Times to 1974 and those of the New York Times to 1982. Although our data do not clarify this matter with any certainty, the answer may be sought in the newspaper library truism which goes thus: there is no complete newspaper volume in one library; or in other words: there are no two identical volumes in different libraries. The notorious gaps in coverage of prestige newspapers make supra-regional lending a subsidiary device to relieve local defects.

The picture given here, where we have grouped places of publication of requested newspapers together according to countries or geographic regions, is modified by determining the ranking sequence of individual places of publication. Of a total of 302 places of publication which occur in our data only 16 reach a volume of over 1% of the titles sought: and within this first 16 the sequence covers a wide range.

60.3% of all loan form relate to places of publication which occur more than 30 times in the data as a whole; 11% to those which are requested between 11 and 30 times; 13.1% of the data relates to newspapers from places of publication which occur 4 to 10 times; and finally, 15.6% to those requested from once to 3 times. Thus to thesis 4:

2.4. Thesis 4
The user requests primarily newspapers from a few important places of publication.

The librarian can therefore, by the skilful selection of the places of publication of his retrospective stock, (inasfar as microfilms are available to build up a relevant collection) cover most of the expected demand.

Number of loan requests per place of publication	Total requests per group of places of publication	Loan requests %
1-3	326	15.6
4-10	273	13.1
11-20	181	8.7
21-30	49	2.3
more than 30	1260	60.3

TABLE 3
Requests by place of publication

Which towns then assume this key role as important places of publication?

The figures are;

Position	Town	Number of loan requests	Requests%
1.	Berlin	323	15.6
2.	Paris	179	8.6
3.	Hamburg	103	5.0
4.	Vienna	89	4.3
5.	Frankfurt/Main	80	3.9
6.	New York	74	3.6
7.	London	68	3.3
8.	Prague	64	3.1
9.	Zurich	60	2.9
10.	Stuttgart	56	2.7
11.	Munich	55	2.7
12.	Leipzig	40	1.9
13.	Cologne	35	1.7
14.	Bremen	35	1.7
15.	Dresden	25	1.2
16.	Basle	24	1.2

TABLE 4
Ranking list of important places of publication

The most important towns for the West German library user when he wants to consult newspapers are Berlin, Paris, Vienna and Hamburg; in one out of 6 instances he is looking for a Berlin Paper, a title from New York or London in only one out of 30 cases. Basle, with only just over 1% among places of publication sought leads the group of those towns which only account for a few titles: that third of the data which is distributed over non-German Europe and the Americas, with less than 20 requests for newspapers from a particular place from all libraries of the Federal Republic which took part in lending during this three month period. No librarian will be able to keep newspapers from all these places in stock, given that most of them have not been filmed and cannot be filmed as a priority because they are only of local importance. And so to the next thesis:

2.5. Thesis 5

While two thirds of newspaper lending is concentrated on the capitals of the German-speaking region, and newspapers from Paris, London and New York, the remaining third cannot be determined more exactly because of its diversity; yet user interest is all the more probable the nearer the place of publication lies to Central Europe.

The question of whether users at particular libraries prefer newspapers with particular places of publication, be it on the basis of the research and teaching emphasis of the respective college or of traditional links, should be of interest. To answer this question we have to go back to the list of ten libraries with the most extensive newspaper lending activity. As you will remember, this concerns the university libraries of Münster, Dortmund, Mainz, Hamburg, Frankfurt, Marburg, Bochum, Aachen, Cologne and Tübingen.

The ranking list of places of publication sought in lending deviates for each of these libraries from the average which we have established for the data as a whole. Most users look in general for newspapers with Berlin as place of publication - except for readers in Dortmund and Aachen who request Parisian newspapers most of all. Paris, at second place on the ranking list, also holds this place for individual 'newspaper libraries' - with the exception of the university library of Tübingen whose users - after the Berlin papers - prefer papers from Zurich and Frankfurt, the first doubtless because of the geographic location of Tübingen. The university library of Tübingen also deviates from the standard list of the most important places of publication inasfar as Brussels and Lausanne reach fourth and fifth place here and Stuttgart and Munich are placed above the average: geographic proximity to the places of publication is crucial here. The first 4 positions in the ranking list of the university library of Dortmund include the French-speaking places of publication: Paris, Geneva, Lausanne and Brussels; except for Paris they do not appear in the overall list. The university library of Munster is the exact opposite: except for 2 volumes of New York newspapers most titles requested in Münster are for German places of publication: Hamburg, Vienna, Stuttgart, Munich and Leipzig correspond to the average of the total data, while Dortmund, Mainz, Halle/Saale, Innsbruck and Konstanz appear as places of publication of additional titles, and finally the Baden-Württemberg town of Aalen (63,000 inhabitants). Interest in local information is apparently particularly great in Dortmund.

Each library participating in lending has its own list of newspaper places of publication which are sought in lending. That is only to be expected; what is rather surprising is that there is so much agreement. On one hand, there is the Technische Hochschule Aachen which lies in the westernmost part of the Federal Republic and as the last of the great colleges bears the name of 'College of Advanced Technology' and is involved in teaching and research in this area, while participating in humanities and economic and social sciences. Among the newspaper loan requests are newspapers from Paris, Berlin, Cologne, Munich, Frankfurt/Main, also from Hamburg, Vienna and Zurich. Contrast this with the city and university library of Frankfurt/Main - a centrally located large university, the library characterised by the incorporation of a special library for the natural sciences, while the social sciences play a leading part in teaching activities. The majority of newspapers requested are from the towns of Berlin, Basle, Paris, Hamburg, Vienna, London, Zurich, Munich; also Dresden and Budapest. Differences between Aachen and Frankfurt are obvious but they are so indistinct that they cannot contribute much to a closer identification of users in Aachen or Frankfurt. This leads to our next thesis:

2.6. Thesis 6

Differences in user preference for the geographic provenance of newspapers are slight according to the originating library. In individual cases they can be explained by the historic relationships of libraries and institutions in a geographic context.

In the newspaper warehouse, which is what all the lending libraries together form, the whole press since the beginning of daily journalism is available – at least in theory; to what extent practice deviates from this is determined in accordance with the holding library's idea of stock maintenance. But the question of whether newspapers are lent or kept for reference, of whether microforms facilitate accessibility in individual cases, or of whether the loan request returns to the readers as a failure after a long journey through libraries which indeed possess the volumes sought but do not wish to lend them, is irrelevant in the investigation of newspaper needs – and that is what concerns us here. Germany has no central newspaper library, such as Great Britain is fortunate to have, and the availability of our newspaper stock is a problem which is not neglected but rather of burning importance even if it does not belong in the present context. And even without this problem newspaper volumes requested on inter-library loan are an indication of the information needs of our library users. More meaningful for the user than the place of publication is the year of publication. To what period does our user turn? We have already identified this user as a student, with primary interests in German events or better still, the German-speaking area in its widest sense. He/she prefers Berlin papers to all others, prefers to work in a university at which mass media research plays a role but needs the impetus of his/her accademic teacher towards the use of journalism as a source. After a review of the previously presented data, this is the image we have of the end user of our endeavours.

Let me dwell on this picture for a moment. It enables us to correct our estimate of the types of newspaper users which have been derived from the library's daily clientèle. Do not misunderstand me: these other types do really exist. They are however not that embodiment of the library user which has emerged from the data under investigation. We can think of the mass of requests for copies of front pages of newspapers on particular days which are produced as gifts for persons born on that day: we call them jubilee copies, and orders for them have increased to such an extent that some libraries no longer produce them themselves but refer the user to microfilm firms which have developed a source of additional income by producing these copies. There is no doubt that the user who orders a jubilee copy forms part of the daily work of the librarian; but apparently he is not as typical as we thought. And what about – a real German phenomenon – that refugee from the former German, present day Polish, regions or from the GDR who would like to advance his claims to social services by means of newspaper advertisements and reports, because his papers have been lost in the flight? He is also a type who belongs to everyday library work and is also not the normal type of library user despite our prejudices. Let me finally point to one sort of user who is not excluded from our survey but about whom nothing can be said because he does not appear in it: that is the user who is looking for up to date information from - sometimes exotic - press accounts. Display copies in libraries satisfy him, not lending from which the publications of the current year are excluded. But our concern here is retrospective stock and so we must now try to answer the question: how retrospective should our collections be?

The dates of publication for 2069 newspaper volumes can be deduced from our

data. They reach from 1729 to 1983. 19 loan requests fall within the 18th
century and are fairly evenly distributed. The distribution becomes more
interesting from 1800 on. Clear variations are evident from decade to decade
which can be seen as the fluctuating interest of users in interpreting the
events of the time, in so far as the daily press, as source literature, pres-
umes – be it for historic research or literary or communication studies – that
the user has an interest in the period to which the relevant newspaper
belongs. In the light of the knowledge that newspaper users in the Federal
Republic are interested primarily in the German-speaking area, we may limit
the more or less strong interest of users in the decades since 1800 to German
history as reflected in the extent of newspaper lending.

Newspapers from the decade 1800-1815 are requested twice as frequently as
material from the 18th century as a whole; the newspapers requested from
Breslau via Gotha, Hildesheim and Leipzig to Sagan, Schwerin and Zittau have
exclusively German places of publication and the articles requested deal with
subjects of local history and history. Yet the number of these titles which
are needed for perusal, and for which therefore the whole newspaper volumes
are requested, is higher for this decade than requests for individual articles. This general historical interest does not include the Napoleonic period
and that of the wars of liberation; if they feature in teaching and research
at German universities this is not evident from the use of the press documents. All the more suddenly comes the upsurge for 1848/49; newspapers from
Barmen, Berlin, Cologne, Paderborn, Elberfeld, Frankfurt a.M., Mannheim, Mainz
and Frankfurt (again) to Pirmasens and Überlingen are evidence of the interest
in the revolution of 1848. Readers prefer to peruse the volumes as a whole
and the articles when specified are recognizable as documents of contemporary
history.

As quickly as interest grows, so does it fade: the years between 1851 and 1870
only encourage a few interested persons to order newspapers. A mixed bag of
titles from Nice, London, Berlin, Augsburg and Paris are requested, with
theatre, music and local history as their chief components. With the foundation of the Empire in 1871 user interest increases and rises continuously to
the end of World War 2. The only decade for which there are noticeably fewer
loan requests is that of 1911 – 1920: World War 1 does not appear to be particularly popular as a research topic. On the other hand in the following
decades there is a growing number of libraries which possess newspapers from
this period and can refer their users to their own stock, a factor the importance of which can only be reckoned generally as it can not be estimated precisely. The decade 1921 – 1930 and the following one is the most intensively
researched at the moment, if we can trust the mass of loan requests. The time
of National Socialism and World War 2 is apparently gone through in detail.
Although there is a series of newspaper-microfilms from both these decades,
with the help of which some of the requests have already been absorbed, the
years from 1921 – 40 are the most strongly represented in loan requests and
the titles come from places of publication which cover the whole range of the
relevant geographic regions already named. The immediate post-war period
comes in for considerably less attention; the number of enquiries rises for
the period to about 1970 then falls away; there may be one coincidence here
between on the one hand the better provision by libraries of current newspaper
material and on the other hand less interest from the readership in the documentation of the immediate present by newspaper articles.

2.7. Thesis 7 (This may serve as a summary of this view.)
The interest of the user encompasses material without a time limit which is
determined by respective research emphases. User preferences for particular
periods are irregular and fluid. Frequent variations are probable.

Our time is limited. Let me therefore turn to the thematic structure of the
data. The subject groups from which the figures come could not be other than
relatively approximate, as only the titles of articles requested were available for examination. The following grouping was the result, somewhat unexp-
ected in my opinion:

Ranking team	No. of loan requests	%(100% = 1658 loan requests)
1. Features	841	50.7
2. Arts	285	17.2
3. Contemporary history	277	16.7
4. Local History	116	7.0
5. History	92	5.5
6. Church, religion	19	1.1
7. Technology, science	19	1.1
8. Sport	9	0.5
No article specified	351	
formal	4	

TABLE 5
Subject groups of the total material

In more than four fifths of all loan requests a particular article is indicated (82.4%) so that a subject arrangement can be drawn up with some certainty. Half of the libraries surveyed (77 of 152) have also been sent loan
requests in which complete volumes or series of volumes were demanded for
examination. Such inspection can be due to many reasons, so that a subject
arrangement is not possible with these requests. It so happens that this kind
of loan request is chiefly related to pre-1900 material for which subject
indexing has been sporadic up till now. The bibliographic listing of German
newspaper articles in the International Bibliography of periodical literature
by Dietrich, which was undertaken during the decades 1908-44 has certainly
encouraged information about individual article titles. [5]

Almost 70% of all subject-related requests for newspaper articles concern
articles which are to be found in the sections 'Features' and 'Arts'; somewhat
less than 30% among comtemporary historical, local and general historical
material. Again one wonders. It is generally believed that newspapers assist
in historical research; however, only one of the four instances of use concerns the special subject of history, while the other three relate to literature, theatre, visual arts, music, fashion and film or documents on cultural
matters. The breakdown of the surprising 70% into subject areas provides
further evidence:

Subject area	No. of loan requests	% (100%=1095)
Literature incl. texts	577	52.7
Culture incl. texts	285	26.0
Theatre, music	140	12.8
Essays, philosophy	31	2.8
Visual Arts, film, fashion	24	2.2
Undifferentiated	38	3.5
Features and cultural matters in total	1095	100.0

TABLE 6

Feature articles requested according to subject matter

Most of the articles requested are concerned with literary phenomena; whether articles and reviews of literary publications are sought or the literary texts themselves, the first mention of which in a newspaper attracts the user's attention. We already expect to find a Berlin paper in first place: The Vossische Zeitung it is, with articles from the years 1844, 1851, 1890, 1906, 1910, etc. finally 1930, 1931, 1932. Here we are talking about catching up with literary history, second place then will be taken by current literature: the literary section from the Frankfurter Allgemeine Zeitung for the years from 1956 is in demand. The old Frankfurter Zeitung (1866 - 1943) is taken for the same subject from 1878 to 1936, the Frankfurter Rundschau between 1947 and 1963. Use is made of the Hamburg Welt just as frequently as the titles named above: the literary pages from 1953 to 1978 are made full use of; a popular post-war source also is the Hamburg Zeit with contributions from 1949 to 1969. In southern Germany users are interested in the Stuttgarter Zeitung (contributions between 1953 and 1976) and the Süddeutsche Zeitung of Munich (articles from 1919 to 1978). In this the most important subject area it is clear that German language newspapers take priority: over 300 newspaper titles from all countries and in all languages are sought for literary articles but only the named papers are requested frequently; we can add the Prager Tagblatt from Prague between 1919 and 1928, from Vienna Die Presse from 1952 to 1978; and finally the Neue Zürcher Zeitung with articles from 1942 to 1981, Le Figaro litteraire from 1947 to 1972 and the Daily Telegraph from 1962 to 1966.

The subject area culture covers contributions on cultural politics and general cultural matters. The picture is monotonously similar to that already described: under the key word 'cultural' the Vossische Zeitung still comes top (volumes 1889 to 1930 requested), followed by the Berliner Tageblatt between 1906 and 1928; and then follow 200 additional titles with one to two volumes each. The topic music, theatre breaks the familiar grouping: the lead is taken by Le combat (1947-60) and Paris-Presse/L'Intransigeant (1948-59), followed by the Frankfurter Rundschau, and, in this subject area only in fourth place, the Vossische Zeitung; interest in the theatre is often also interest in current productions, which 'Auntie Voss', which was only published until 1934, cannot offer.

2.8. Thesis 8
Articles and documents from the cultural sector, particularly literature, are
primarily sought from newspapers. The press as an historical document takes
a back seat. The ethnocentric view of the German user is especially evident.

I would overstretch your patience if I insisted on presenting the same picture
for each topical group. Allow me in conclusion to outline briefly the special
group history.

Subject area	Number of loan requests	% (100% = 485)
Contemporary history	265	54.6
Texts of contemporary history	12	2.5
Local History	116	23.9
Historical persons	58	12.0
History in general	34	7.0
History altogether	485	100.0%

TABLE 7
Article requests for history by subject area

If we delete 'local history' in the first instance, requests in other subject
areas live up to the conventional picture of newspaper use: no title particularly to the fore, geographically and linguistically dispersed. Articles
from the Daily News, Daily Worker, Daily Telegraph are requested in historical subject areas, also from Il Giornale D'Italia and Le Figaro. Geographic
diversification is great in this area; however, that also means that no handy
picture, no overview has emerged from the multiplicity of requested titles.
It is a different matter with 'local history', for which the broad spread of
newspaper titles is no less applicable but here is directed not at geographic
and linguistic horizons but at small newspapers, the provincial press. Requested items are, for example, the Forster Tageblatt of 1932-35, the Höxtersche
Zeitung of 1883, the local supplement to the Magdeburgische Zeitung of 1902.
Work on the emigrant problem within the framework of local history and the
German refugee problem are explained by the appearance of the Lycker Zeitung
of 1933 and the Washington Post of 1969.

At this point I should like to conclude or rather break off my survey. To
exhaust the available data one would have to debate detailed matters the relevance of which to libraries would probably have to be clarified. But of what
subject could one not say that? Sufficient that Goethe who spoke of the
entertainment value of the bound volumes of Cotta's Allgemeine, and called
their use 'comfortable' and 'pleasing', has been endorsed in so singular a
fashion.

REFERENCES

1   Part of the results, without those presented here, were published in:
    'Zeitungen in Bibliotheken' (Newspapers in libraries) ed. Willi Hofig and
    Wilbert Ubbens on behalf of the Newspaper Committee of the Deutsches
    Bibliotheksinstitut. Berlin, DBI, p. 284-306.

2   'Goethe's Works.' Complete edition, the last under the author's super-
    vision. Vol. 32. Stuttgart & Tubingen, Cotta, 1830, p. 33-34.

3   'Negative loan requests for foreign newspapers', in: Zeitschrift für
    Bibliothekswesen und Bibliographie vol.22, 1975. p. 215-220.

4   'Foreign newspapers in German libraries', in: 'Das Angebot von Zeitungen
    auf Mikroformen' (The provision of newspapers in microform). Dortmund,
    Mikrofilmarchiv der Deutschsprachigen Presse 1976, p. 24-30.

5   'Internationale Bibliographie der Zeitschriftenliteratur'. (International
    bibliography of periodical literature) ed. Felix Dietrich (and others),
    1897-1964.
    Supplement A: Verzeichnis von Aufsätzen aus deutschen Zeitungen (Index of
    articles from German newspapers). Vol. 1-31. 1909-44.

DISCUSSION

Q.   (Questioner unidentified)

Is there any censorship in German libraries of the papers one could take as
there has been in some English libraries? I am talking of restriction of
newspapers by socialist councils.

A.   Dr Höfig

There may be some problems in some small public libraries depending on local
authorities, but what I spoke about was the use made of the inter-library loan
mainly by research libraries - there is no such censorship there.

Comment. Susan Swartzburg, Rutgers University

I would really like to comment that a continued study of the use of inter-
library loans and newspapers over a period of years might give us a very interesting notion as to what researchers are looking at, and we would be able to
see, perhaps, changes in the way scholars use newspapers. I would also like to
thank you in Germany for your very open access to German archives and to using
old newspapers.

Q.   Dr Belfrage, Sweden

I am interested as to what extent microfilms have been used for inter-library
lending. In Sweden, we have been very reluctant to send the real newspapers
and I think we are restrictive in sending some of the microfilms too. I
think, although I am a librarian, that it is necessary for us to be more
generous.

A.   Dr Höfig

As for the situation in the Federal Republic the inter-library loan research I
reported on as to the foreign titles is almost exclusively for microfilm.
Microfilm is sent on inter-library loan and they come back and usually you
can use them again. As to the German titles this is very different. We have
not been able to film every German title of course and as the time span for
which the research is needed goes back to the 18th century, this is what our
task is. But every library of course has its own policy of lending and these
are the 'negative' forms which I reported on, so would have not been fulfilled. So there may be, somewhere, stock in a public library or elsewhere
which says it will not send it on inter-library loan.

Q.   Ian Gibb, British Library, retired.

As the great majority of requests seem to be for articles from newspapers
rather then whole issues or runs, it would seem that photocopies from microfilm could satisfy most of them. Is that so?

A.   Dr Höfig.

Yes , that would seem to be true.

THE USERS OF NEWSPAPERS OUTSIDE OF LIBRARIES

Helmuth BERGMANN

Periodicals Department, Universitätsbibliothek, Wien

1. THE DESCENT OF INFORMATION

To get news and to spread it meets the human demand for information starting
with his existence. A short glimpse at the history of news shows us the following: newspapers did not necessarily depend on printing in their early
times. With small editions and a modest size usually a small number of tran-
scribers was enough. The circulation of papers resulted from street-sales and
from passing on after reading. The intentions in buying newspapers were in
the early times as they are today - mainly curiosity and satisfaction of the
advantage of information compared with the non-reader. Thereby two phenomena
are remarkable:

    1.1. The descent of information between social classes.
    1.2. the descent of information between the urban and the rural areas.

1.1 Up to the eighteenth century reading newspapers - like reading in general
- was impossible for a broad class of the population. This was not only due
to illiteracy, but also to the high price of a paper (around 1800 one copy was
in Vienna 8 to 10 times as expensive as today). Lower social classes were not
able to afford a newspaper - even when they were able to read. Today the
price is of no importance, still a descent of information exists in the society. As example the situation in Vienna: four top newspapers share the
Viennese readers (Neue Kronenzeitung, Kurier, Neue AZ, Die Presse - in order
of the size of their circulation). The two first mentioned, the so-called
boulevard press, are available everywhere and have an enormous street sale.
The Neue AZ (the newspaper of the Austrian Socialist Party) is carried almost
hidden in particular quarters of Vienna so as not to be seen with it in the
streets. A banker or a medical doctor shows himself only with Die Presse in
the streets. (Die Presse includes an important economic feature and is of the
highest social standard). A further argument for the social descent of information is the tendency of the higher social classes to read various newspapers
(sometimes they have to read them for professional purposes), while the middle
and lower middle classes prefer the lower level of intelligence as presented
in the boulevard press and even there they often read just the head-lines of
the one paper they prefer. Another reason to read only one newspaper is the
readers' expectation of finding his own opinion supported by it. Still we all
know that in the end the paper forms the opinion of this reader. (Here an
expression of the Austrian writer Hans Weigel may be mentioned: 'The black is
the letters, but most people read anyhow just the white.')

1.2 The descent between the urban and the rural areas has additional reasons
which are mainly due to geographical and economic factors. The spread of the
population in the rural areas forces the dealer not to increase the number of
newspapers he is prepared to offer as the additional handling costs would not
allow any profit in the business of selling newspapers. He can only offer

papers which are required. It would be presumptuous to provide in an Austrian holiday resort in the Alps 20 copies of the <u>Daily Telegraph</u> or the <u>Figaro</u>, while 50 copies of the German <u>Bildzeitung</u> are an absolute necessity. Besides this all said under point 1 is also valid for the rural area.

When it was mentioned before that the newspaper forms the reader's opinion this is true in many cases. One of the main reasons for publishing a paper besides this is still to negotiate a profitable transaction with it (I especially think of Mr Rupert Murdoch). This is even easier as in the Western world the economy is actually forced to advertise. This fact even leads so far that free copies with additional parts which are financed only by advertising are delivered by mail to the residences. Other reasons for publishing a paper are due to the wish to spread special ideas of religious or political nature (though the terms have fluid boundaries). I do not want to take up the matter of papers in one-party-states; their base of existence is the state or the party, the edition is secured. More problematical is the position of party-newspapers (or those which are close to parties) in countries with a pluralist system. In almost all of these countries the circulation of party papers is decreasing constantly. In Austria for example a party-newspaper was discontinued in March 1987 as the party's and official subventions were not sufficient. Two other papers were saved only with great efforts. The continuance of the <u>Neue AZ</u> is discussed once a year. Obviously you cannot make any profit with party-papers as the economy prefers to advertise in newspapers with wider circulation.

2.   CIRCULATION

The circulation of a paper is not only carried out by the seller. Each number has various readers. In the international comparison (according to national media-analysis) the number of readers of one issue fluctuates between 1.2 and 3.5. This bandwidth is due to the population of one country, the number of newspapers and their circulation as well as the preference of reading of the inhabitants. The number of readers also varies within national borders: In Vienna with 1.5 million inhabitants there are 1.7 readers per number, in Graz with 250,000 inhabitants there are 2.4 readers. In Vienna five important daily newspapers are published, the same in Graz.

Now one question is imposed on us: How much time is used for reading - especially for reading papers? Research by the Austrian Statistical Directorate in 1981 shows, that in Austria there is daily an average of 1 hour 24 min. spent on reading, thereof about one hour for reading papers. Similar results were reached in a study from Hungary which was performed with students in Szeged in 1974.

Who are the readers following the buyer? We have to differentiate three areas of use in order to answer this question:

    a) in the family
    b) at work
    c) in public places

(a) In the family: according to the research by the Austrian Statistical Directorate of 1981 we can conclude that the first reader of the residence is usually the buyer of the paper - mostly the head of the family. The second readers are the children aged between 14 and 19 years. Only at last the wife or husband gets the paper. These are generalized facts, there are sometimes sporadically very severe variances.

(b) At work the newspaper is used only very seldom by further readers than
the buyer. Normally the breaks at work are just long enough for the buyer to
read his paper. Unfortunately it is hard to say how much time is spent reading newspapers on the way to work as most of the researchers on reading do not
cover this aspect.

(c) In public places the number of readers is not countable. These are
places from the so-called Wandzeitung at the publisher's buildings to the
entrance-halls of hotels up to the legendary Viennese coffee-houses.   In the
Viennese coffee-house, a type spread all over Europe, you find the popular
papers with 50 or more readers; even the exotic titles (such as The Sun,
Pravda, or Washington Post) are used by more than 5 readers.

3.   NEWSPAPER USERS

We always talk about newspaper-readers, but we should always speak more accurately of the newspaper-users. A paper is not read like a book from the beginning to the end, but instead only parts are used for personal information.
Which parts are used depends on the user's interests. This does not mean that
people interested in culture only read the cultural pages and people interested in sport only read the sport pages. It is even mentionable that the
readers of sport magazines only notice their favourite sport and just take a
glance at the others. It would be a misjudgement to expect that politicians
only open the paper at political comments and the economic features - some of
them even find the cultural pages.

The editorial layout of a newspaper allows conclusions about the target group
of readers. As example again newspapers of Austria: Die Presse is published
with a daily enclosure called Economist, but with only one page of local news
and sport; the Neue Kronenzeitung places the TV-Programme on its back page,
its cultural page is daily in a different place, if it can find a space at all
between sex, crime and sport.

A study at the University of Graz in 1980 inquired of more than 700 students
which parts of the newspaper they prefer. There were significant correlations
between the branch of studies and the newspaper parts which were read - with
some enormous variances which were due to personal interests and social
origin.

It is therefore proved by all sociological observations and researches that no
newspaper user reads all parts of a paper; this happens also outside of the
libraries and not only in libraries where research on special topics is undertaken.

4.   SURVIVAL OF NEWSPAPERS

The immediacy of the newspaper is the reason that its contents are not up to
date after just a few days. The mortal shell remains. The time of the pure
waste of paper is gone - in the long history of newspaper it only lasted for a
short period. Before the time of abundance the old papers were at least used
for lighting a fire, as wrapping material or for book-binding (is there a
nicer recycling for a librarian than book-binding?). The short life of newspapers and their recycling leads also to the fact that up to now they have
found their way only very incomplete into libraries. Incomplete in the number
of titles, incomplete in the totality of their holdings. The current way of

newspaper-recycling and the lack of space and money in libraries does not support the desire for totality.

5. CONCLUSION

Should you need for your research on historical relations or events older issues of newspapers, two ways present themselves:

    a) to use a library (I wish you good luck!)
    b) the establishment of an archive of your own when you are young (I wish you a lot of space!)

REFERENCES

Gehmacher, Ernst, 'Buch und Leser in Österreich'. Wien, 1974.

Bergmann, Helmuth, 'Die Bibliothek und ihre Benützer'. Wien, Österreichisches Institut für Bibliotheksforschung, Dokumentations- und Informationswesen, 1985. (Biblos-Schriften, 33).

Baltl, Hermann et al., 'Lesegewohnheiten und politisches Interesse von Grazer Studenten'. Graz, Institut für Österreichische Rechtsgeschichte an der Universität Graz, 1981.

'Reading research in the socialist countries'. Budapest, National Széchényi Library, 1975.

'Tagesablauf: Ergebnisse des Mikrozensus September 1981'. Bearbeitet im Österreichischen Statistischen Zentralamt. Wien, 1984.

THE GENERAL MANAGEMENT
OF A NEWSPAPER COLLECTION

Else DELAUNAY

Conservateur au Département des Périodiques, Chef de Service du
Catalogue Générale des Périodiques, Bibliothèque Nationale, Paris

1. INTRODUCTION

By way of introduction I would like to give you a short presentation of the
Department of Periodicals at the Bibliothèque Nationale to which I belong.
Set up in 1942 but not opened to the public till 1945, the Department of
Periodicals, according to the law on legal deposit, receives, registers, cat-
alogues, preserves and gives access to all periodicals published in France.
Of course, legal deposit of periodicals was made to the Bibliothèque Nationale
before 1945 but until then the Department of Printed Matter, together with the
General Office of Legal Deposit, did the processing.

Today the Department of Periodicals has a staff of 135 permanent agents and 13
temporary agents; Miss Le Nan, chief librarian, is head of the Department.
About 6000 issues of periodicals arrive _daily_ at the library (the law stip-
ulates the deposit of 4 copies from the publisher and one or two copies from
the printer). The holdings are kept in either Paris or Versailles.

In Paris, the Department is located in the Richelieu building as well as in
the Vivienne building (opened in December 1985). The Office of legal deposit
of periodicals and the different offices of computerized cataloguing (Bibliographie de la France, Supplément I: Serials; CNEPS (National Center of Registration of Serials)) are situated at the Vivienne site; reading room, stacks,
offices of retrospective cataloguing and of foreign periodicals as well as the
administration are situated at the Richelieu site. In Paris, the staff
includes 113 permanent agents and 10 temporary agents. The stacks cover about
14,000 linear meters with a yearly increase of about 380 meters. The Parisian
stacks contain all the holdings of national newspapers and of important reference periodicals, French or foreign.

Our Annex in Versailles keeps and gives access to almost 80% of all periodicals received by the library, registration having been made previously in the
Paris offices. The Annex comprises three ten-storeyed buildings of which the
first was opened in 1934, the second in 1962 and the last one in 1970. Mrs
Olivier is head of the Annex that has a staff of 21 permanent agents and 3
temporary agents. The yearly increase of the holdings covers about 450 linear
meters and includes technical publications, trade-union journals, professional
publications, bulletins from different associations, children's magazines, as
well as French local daily newspapers, foreign daily newspapers, foreign periodicals, yearbooks, overseas publications, parish bulletins and local administrative publications. The stacks in the Annex cover approximately 46,000
linear meters. The reading room in Versailles is opened every day except
Monday, and comprises 40 seats. So the Annex in Versailles is indeed important to the Department of Periodicals.

Stacks in Paris and in Versailles have almost reached their saturation point.
Therefore it has become necessary to think of other "annexes". Since 1980,
within the "Salvation Programme", considerable subsidies have been given to
the Bibliotheque Nationale by the Government every year which have made it
possible to set up two new centers. One is in Sablé, 300 km West of Paris.
It was particularly designed for restoration and microfilming of books. The
other one, in Provins, 100 km East of Paris, was set up for preservation of
newspaper holdings and preparation for microfilming of local editions of
running local newspapers, as well as for restoration of old newspapers by
thermosizing and for microfilming. The Center in Provins has a staff of 19
agents at the moment and the stacks cover 1,800 linear meters, especially set
up for newspaper holdings. The Center works for the Department of
Periodicals.

This brief introduction to our Department seemed useful to me before getting
to the heart of the purpose of my paper: The General Management of a Newspaper
Collection with the many problems such a subject comprises : acquisitions,
users' needs, preservation, accessing, financial resources ... I myself have
spent quite a long time in the Department of Periodicals, especially within
the area of retrospective cataloguing (here I have had alas often the opportunity to note the merciless decay of the holdings that I had to check for the
cataloguing) but also in the Preservation section where Mrs Petitou, who is
also present here, succeeded me. Therefore, of course, I have worked out my
paper by light of my experience in that department.

2.   FRAMING OF A NEWSPAPER COLLECTION

Before dealing with all the acute problems relating to preservation and accessibility of newspapers I want to consider several points in the setting up
of a newspaper collection. If this is not a difficult question for national
libraries getting most of their holdings through legal deposit, it is a difficult one for other libraries. When one has to build a collection of current
and/or retrospective newspapers, several points should be considered. In the
first place, the selection of newspaper titles to be acquired must be settled
on. To this end one will generally take up the usual criterion for selection
of the library concerned: if the library is specialised in such and such a
field (e.g. economics, politics, finances, literature, humanities, etc.), a
selection of daily and weekly national and foreign newspapers dealing with
such subjects should be chosen. Of course, users' needs and suggestions
should be taken into account. Indeed, choices should depend very much on the
different kinds of research work for which users attend the library. For
instance. at least in France, since World War II, a very large part of historical research work on daily life, political developments, etc., is elabor-
ated by means of newspapers.

As soon as the selection has been settled upon, it should be decided if the
library ought to get newspapers in paper form or on microfilm (when the latter
is available which is frequently the case). In the case of retrospective
newspapers, microfilm will be the only possibility. As far as current
newspapers are concerned, microfilm is more expensive than copies in paper
form. But in return, as time goes on, the latter will need heavy preservation
care. Furthermore, the microfilm format helps to save precious space in the
stacks and facilitates enormously accessibility and photocopying.

The reading room for newspapers should have special equipment: vertical desks
for reading of large size bound volumes, big tables for cardboard boxes ... A
special dark room for microfilm reading should be available with a number of

reader-printers depending on the number of users.

Furthermore, bibliographic access provided to the users should include different kinds of catalogues, computerized or not, retrospective bibliography, union lists, on-line search to locate newspapers in other libraries inside or outside the country, with the possibility of providing photocopies to the users. Terminals should be set up for on-line search of newspaper indexes, press cuttings, etc.. But I only mention these points as they will be discussed in the workshops.

On the whole, the building of a newspaper collection depends above all on the library budget which varies, of course, depending on the importance of the library: number of users, quantity and quality of the research work done by the users or the library staff, etc.. The origin of funds may be public and/or private. Anyway experience shows that, generally, the budget for acquisition and preservation is hardly large enough to cover the needs of the library in this field. Thus, before the setting up of any newspaper collection it is primordial to consider all parameters which may limit the extent of such a collection, taking into account the special nature of such a library material (the newspaper), users' needs as well as financial means. Some libraries do not want to keep newspaper holdings over a long period. In such case it is more reasonable to get copies in paper form as they are predestined to be destroyed after a certain period.

As to the national library in a developing country where legal deposit may not exist, the principal object should be to acquire and to keep all national newspapers in order to preserve the total production as well as a certain range of foreign newspapers allowing users to have access to all round information. According to the financial resources of the library, systematic microfilming of newspapers should be undertaken in order to keep safe the original copies and to give access only to the microfilm (including photocopy and other photographic reproduction). This would prevent the need for expensive preservation conditioning of the original copies, which could then be kept, unbound, in clean and safe stacks set up with shelves of a "Compactus" type.

3. PRESERVATION AND RESTORATION

In the Preservation section of our Department I was particularly confronted with deterioration of our holdings of old, large size, daily or weekly newspapers. Our collection in the Department of Periodicals dates back to 1800. If the wear due to frequent reading throughout years is important, in spite of well bound holdings handled in a proper way, the poor quality paper used for newspapers, since 1860 approximately, has made their preservation even more precarious. We all know that mechanical wood pulp paper has an inherent acidity which increases with time. That means that after fifty years margins turn yellow and become brittle, and after a hundred years pages will crumble and even break so that all restoration will be extremely difficult and, of course, expensive. Moreover, damage caused by atmospheric industrial pollution from which most big towns suffer today is also to be considered.

It seems as if we have reached the break-down point in the field for some years already. Deacidification has become the great business of all libraries keeping old book or newspaper holdings.

Consequently, the principal object of the management of a newspaper collection is undeniable: preservation of the copies, for without proper preservation,

access to holdings is not possible and so the reader cannot get the information he needs and to which he has a right for his research work.

At the Bibliothèque Nationale, which is responsible for preserving the
national printed heritage, we do our utmost – but it is still not enough – to
strengthen preservation of our collection of newspapers published in France
and received by legal deposit. Holdings kept in Paris (at the Richelieu site)
are bound; in Versailles, newspapers are kept, unfolded, in large cardboard
boxes.

Preservation, such as we conceive it today and to the degree of our financial
means, includes several more or less important elements. Here I shall only
touch the different points briefly, for requirements and difficulties of preservation are well known to all librarians responsible for preservation of
newspapers. But I shall try to give an enumeration as complete as possible.

3.1. Elements of preservation

Proper checking of the holdings:

- Proper checking of the state of the newspapers (margins, pages,
  binding, etc.), estimation of wear due to handling, and of increase
  in deterioration caused by the inherent acidity of wood pulp paper
  and by atmospheric pollution.

- Permanent checking of atmospheric conditions in the stacks where
  the holdings are kept: moisture, temperature, dryness, light ...

- Dust removal

- Location of parasites and mould and other risks.

As soon as any damage is noticed, repairing of the materials should take
place, in other words restoration.

It may be of minor nature. On that account a small restoration shop housed
next to the stack is very useful. Small damage can be repaired quickly here,
for instance tears, light lacerations, light damage of bindings, awkward fold-
ings, etc.. I think particularly of damage due to frequent handling of the
copies whether old or recent.

But decay of the paper due to its acidity does concern all newspapers published after 1860 and leads to heavy restoration. Newspapers are printed on
particularly poor paper and their large size make them still more fragile.
Even if the bound copies have not been handled frequently throughout years,
the paper will turn yellow and brittle; finally it will crumble up. In the
hope of preserving it, it must then be restored. Deacidification and sometimes also disinfection become absolutely necessary.

Having arrived at this point I must refer to the "Salvation Programme" elabor-
ated by the Bibliothèque Nationale from 1978 to 1980. Since 1980, the French
Government has given the Bibliothèque Nationale a yearly grant of 10 million
francs in extra subsidies for the saving of the holdings. Within this Programme a certain number of estimates were made so as to be aware of the financial requirements of such a saving operation: deacidification, restoration,
microfilming, microfiche, binding, etc.. In newspaper holdings alone, it was
estimated that about 40 million sheets should be treated (laminating and
microfilming). So we have to face a tremendous task.

access to holdings is not possible and so the reader cannot get the information he needs and to which he has a right for his research work.

At the Bibliothèque Nationale, which is responsible for preserving the
national printed heritage, we do our utmost - but it is still not enough - to
strengthen preservation of our collection of newspapers published in France
and received by legal deposit. Holdings kept in Paris (at the Richelieu site)
are bound; in Versailles, newspapers are kept, unfolded, in large cardboard
boxes.

Preservation, such as we conceive it today and to the degree of our financial
means, includes several more or less important elements. Here I shall only
touch the different points briefly, for requirements and difficulties of preservation are well known to all librarians responsible for preservation of
newspapers. But I shall try to give an enumeration as complete as possible.

3.1 Elements of preservation

Proper checking of the holdings:

- Proper checking of the state of the newspapers (margins, pages,
  binding, etc.), estimation of wear due to handling, and of increase
  in deterioration caused by the inherent acidity of wood pulp paper
  and by atmospheric pollution.

- Permanent checking of atmospheric conditions in the stacks where
  the holdings are kept: moisture, temperature, dryness, light ...

- Dust removal

- Location of parasites and mould and other risks.

As soon as any damage is noticed, repairing of the materials should take
place, in other words restoration.

It may be of minor nature. On that account a small restoration shop housed
next to the stack is very useful. Small damage can be repaired quickly here,
for instance tears, light lacerations, light damage of bindings, awkward fold-
ings, etc.. I think particularly of damage due to frequent handling of the
copies whether old or recent.

But decay of the paper due to its acidity does concern all newspapers published after 1860 and leads to heavy restoration. Newspapers are printed on
particularly poor paper and their large size make them still more fragile.
Even if the bound copies have not been handled frequently throughout years,
the paper will turn yellow and brittle; finally it will crumble up. In the
hope of preserving it, it must then be restored. Deacidification and sometimes also disinfection become absolutely necessary.

Having arrived at this point I must refer to the "Salvation Programme" elabor-
ated by the Bibliotheque Nationale from 1978 to 1980. Since 1980, the French
Government has given the Bibliotheque Nationale a yearly grant of 10 million
francs in extra subsidies for the saving of the holdings. Within this Programme a certain number of estimates were made so as to be aware of the financial requirements of such a saving operation: deacidification, restoration,
microfilming, microfiche, binding, etc.. In newspaper holdings alone, it was
estimated that about 40 million sheets should be treated (laminating and
microfilming). So we have to face a tremendous task.

To this end I want to quote some very enlightening figures worked out by Miss de Lépiney, head of the Center in Provins.

The laminating undertaken by the Central workshop for restoration in Paris and especially by our Center in Provins consists in covering each sheet recto-verso (after a mutual aqueous deacidification) with a transparent material (a polyamid sheet called "Cerex") by means of a thermosizing machine named "Reliant". Each machine requires a staff of 6 or 9 full time working staff. In Provins, it was estimated that 160,000 sheets could be "doubled" in this way every year. As the average cost of doubling a sheet is about 30 francs, it turns out that doubling of 40 million sheets would cost about 1200 million francs; the whole operation would represent abount 250 years of machine time with a full time work form. At present, the Bibliothèque Nationale has only three "Reliant" machines at its disposal. If they were used only for news-papers, the doubling would require 83 years of the machines running full time, which is not the case at this time. Actually, a single "Reliant" machine (the one in Provins) is 100% allocated to newspapers. Thus it has been possible to double 300,000 sheets since 1981.

If it would be possible to accelerate doubling and fix a five years programme with the object of doubling 40 million sheets, it would be necessary to have:

a) 50 "Reliant" machines
b) a staff of 300 to 400 agents
c) about 240 million francs a year for doubling only, besides
   working supplies, salaries, etc..

I think I need not tell you that the Bibliothèque Nationale would never be able to carry out such a programme, and particularly now as we have passed into a period of budgetary retrictions (staff, working supplies, etc.).

And what is perhaps still more upsetting is the fact that in ten or twenty years, the state of these 40 million unrestored sheets will be so bad that neither restoration nor microfilming will be possible.

It is a fact that though our first concern is older newspaper holdings, the current newspapers arriving every day will soon also raise problems. There-fore it is so important to have in hand a mass deacidification system for large size library materials. In Canada, thanks to the Wei T'o system, mass deacidification of books is already carried out. In France, together with the United States (Library of Congress), a system quite similar to the Canadian system has been developed in order to allow simultaneous deacidification or 600 in-octavo volumes (of about 400 pages each). A process tank (80 x 80 x 130 cm) has been set up in our Center in Sablé and the system should be run-ning as of next September. Later, it will be possible to fit it out for deac-idification of large size volumes (large in-folio) after having modified the baskets holding the volumes. It is still too early to estimate the exact capacity of such a system for mass deacidification of newspapers. If all retrospective newspaper holdings should undergo such a treatment before rest-oration, recent newspapers should also be treated before entering the stacks in order to be protected from acid attack.

Mass deacidification and restoration are therefore the major elements of pres-ervation. But they are as much more efficient if they are followed up by another key element of preservation: systematic microfilming of restored library materials. When possible it is better to microfilm before restor-ation but in many cases, newspapers are in such a poor state that they must

first be restored. Once more I cannot go into details; I only want to under-
line how much any management of a newspaper collection requires a real microfilming policy, and especially for holdings needing restoration. The microfilm protects the original copy as it replaces it, even if access to the original copy may be necessary for some special research work. Moreover, the
microfilm allows the keeping of original copies in stacks set up especially
for newspaper holdings and located far from the reading room and even from the
library itself. At the Bibliothèque Nationale, we send all our completely
microfilmed holdings out to Provins where the stacks are especially equipped
for newspaper holdings.

Another preservation element is <u>binding</u>. It protects against wear due to
frequent, and sometimes careless, handling of the copies. Thus, at the Bibliothèque Nationale, all national newspapers published in Paris and some important local newspapers are systematically bound. From traditional binding we
have passed on to a kind of industrial binding: the <u>Aclé binding</u> that allows
us to save money and time (in two hours time, two binders can fit a binding
containing two months of a daily European newspaper). The Aclé binding consists of stitched "books" each one made of several issues held together by
means of steel clips which are fastened to the binding itself with thin steel
wires. The sides of the binding are made of acid free cardboard covered with
acid free paper; the back is covered with unbleached linen. Such a system
offers evident advantages: quick fitting, low costs (about 140 francs per
binding), possibility of binding without having available all numbers of the
period considered (it is easy to insert lacking issues when they arrive),
possibility of complete opening of the volume in case of microfilming (the
guard with which each issue of the newspaper is equipped during the binding
widens the inner margin). (A sample of an Aclé binding was available at the
Symposium.)

Nevertheless, this type of binding is still too expensive to be used for all
newspapers kept by the Bibliothèque Nationale. Therefore other methods giving
an adequate protection had to be chosen: unfolded, well pressed, newspaper
issues are kept in <u>acid free cardboard boxes of the exact size of the newspaper concerned.</u> The boxes are made of reinforced grain of leather (weight:
1,750 gr) according to technical clauses, pH 7. They are manufactured by
Cauchard Ltd. Most newspaper holdings in our Annex in Versailles are, or will
be, kept in such boxes. They should preferably be placed flat on the shelves.
For practical reasons we have to keep them vertically just as bound volumes.
When communicated to the reading room the boxes need some more handling as it
is necessary to count the issues in the box before and after communication.
But when the holdings are microfilmed, the original copies may perfectly well
be permanently stored in such boxes giving protection enough against dust,
light, moisture, etc..

However, one must not forget that the <u>stacks</u> that house newspaper holdings are
just as important to their preservation. Atmospheric conditions, light and
environment must be checked carefully. But these are problems well known to
us all, I think. Here I shall rapidly recall them.

   <u>Temperature, moisture or dryness</u>: an adequate number of
   thermohygrometers (according to the air space) should be available to
   ensure permanent control of these vital elements for preservation of
   library materials.

   <u>Light</u>: it is also important to provide a lightmeter in order to
   measure light radiations and protect library materials in a proper way.
   Light should not exceed 50 lux.

Environment: it has been noticed that industrial pollution in the towns accelerates the acidic deterioration of wood pulp paper. But there may be other risks such as mould, insects etc.. In that case it is necessary to disinfect the stacks as well as the holdings, even new holdings arriving in the stacks.

Finally, the staff commissioned to the stacks and to the reading room should have special training as this staff is in daily contact with the holdings and thus plays an essential part checking for wear and damage, reading of thermo-hygrometers and lightmeters, location of parasites, mould, leaks, proper dust removal, pointing out of damaged bindings and torn pages, etc., supervision of the handling of the volumes or boxes in the reading room (e.g. bound volumes should be placed on special desks for reading of newspapers).

Photocopy. As far as newspapers are concerned, photocopying from originals is prohibited at the Bibliothèque Nationale because of their size and their general brittleness. But thanks to the microfilm reader-printer, it is possible to get photocopies directly from the microfilm.

3.2. Questions

What I have said here concerning preservation and restoration of retrospective newspaper holdings, particularly as to the astronomical figures representing the needs of the Bibliothèque Nationale in this field, leads me quite naturally to the thought which imposes more and more on all librarians from the great national libraries in the world: is it really possible to meet deacidification and restoration of such masses of library materials? Will it be possible to provide space enough to keep the holdings after being treated (laminating by thermosizing increases by 100% the space needed for the holdings)?

While we are waiting for an answer, deterioration of the newspapers accelerates. Microfilmed, but not deacidified, holdings are often kept in a poor state. It is only holdings restored before microfilming that may be considered safe. Facing a steadily more invading production, will it be possible to keep all newspapers in paper form? Henceforth and after long and careful reflection, as librarians can we imagine, and even plan, total or partial disposal of original copies in paper form when they have been completely microfilmed according to international standards on microfilming and preservation of microfilms?

Would it not then be useful to keep samples of the originals or, perhaps, a complete holding of some titles as reference copies? Or better, would it not be possible to share tasks in a different way, a certain number of district libraries becoming responsible for preservation, restoration and microfilming of newspapers published in the district considered? Should each country only preserve and restore its own newspapers and, eventually, newspapers published in its ancient or present overseas possessions? Would it not be possible to return foreign newspapers to the countries where they were published if the country had no holdings, or only incomplete holdings, of the originals. So many questions which prove that a new preservation policy of newspapers should indeed be developed.

It is urgent to open a debate in order to know about difficulties and, perhaps, learn of solutions found or chosen here and there. In short, to give rise to common reflection that may allow us to draw some guidelines which might help each of us to a better development of a national policy in this field.

It is evident that national libraries getting national publications by legal deposit must be careful for different reasons. I should like to quote a few paragraphs from an article written by Albert Labarre, head of the Office for preservation and restoration at the Bibliothèque Nationale; the title of the article is: 'Causes and Finality of Preservation' (published in Liber in 1985):

'...Several reasons tell in favor of the preservation of original copies, among others:

- legal reasons: the copy of legal deposit should be the one remaining to bear witness when all other copies will have disappeared;

- technical reasons: it is not sure that the support of microforms and reproductions will last longer than paper; moreover, it is possible that handling of reproductions might be more careless than of originals. Therefore the original copy must be available when it will be necessary to make a new reproduction;

- intellectual reasons: some particularly interesting research work needs material contact with the original ...'

Here I have only had the possibility to give a brief survey of the acute problems posed to those who are in charge of managing, preserving and giving access to newspaper collections. I think that our Symposium should be an ideal opportunity to start the debate on this primordial question. A workshop is programmed on this matter. It should bring us to a better understanding of the problems, and allow us to exchange viewpoints, difficulties and also solutions so that we shall be able to compare the situation in the different countries we represent here. International co-operation seems necessary. Choices have to be made. Our meeting should facilitate such choices.

BIBLIOGRAPHY

Banks, Joyce M, 'Note sur la désacidification de masses à la Bibliothèque Nationale du Canada', 1985. (Note on the mass deacidification at the National Library of Canada).

Bony, Françoise, 'Conservation: l'Exemple de la Bibliothèque du Congrès', (Preservation: example of the Library of Congress), in: Livres Hebdo, no.4, January 20th 1986, pp. 62-64.

'Désacidification à la Bibliothèque', (Mass deacidification at the National Library), in Nouvelles de la Bibliothèque nationale [du Canada], Vol.14, no.3/4, March/April 1982.

Diverses notes etabliés par le Centre de Sablé (J.M. Arnoult et coll.) pour les besoins du Stage de conservation prodigué par ce Centre depuis 1984. (Different notes made by the Centre in Sablé for the training course on preservation which takes place in the Centre every year since 1984).

Gibb, I P and Green, S P, 'Considerations relating to the Retention or Disposal by the British Library of Newspapers after microfilming', in: 'Minutes of the Second Meeting' [of the British Library Consultative Group on Newspapers]. British Library, November 1983.

Green, S P, 'The British Library's Newspaper Library in a New Era', in: Journal of Newspaper and Periodical History, Vol.I, no.1, Winter 1984.

Johansson, E, 'The British Library Newspaper Library: Looking Ahead', in: Journal of Newspaper and Periodical History, Vol.II, no.3, Summer 1986.

Labarre, Albert, 'Causes et Finalité de la Conservation', (Causes and Finality of Preservation), in: Liber, no.24, 1985.

Labarre, Albert, 'Le Plan de Sauvegarde des Collections de la Bibliothèque Nationale 1980 -1985. Note établie en juin 1986'. (The "Salvation Programme" of the Bibliothèque Nationale, note made in June 1986).

Lépiney, Lionelle de, 'Rapport annuel des activités du Centre de Provins en 1985' et 'Eléments de note établis en août 1986'. (Annual report of the Center in Provins, 1985, and parts of a note made in August 1986).

Smith, Richard D, 'Progress in mass deacidification at the Public Archives', in: Canadian Library Journal, Vol.36, no.6, December 1979.

DISCUSSION

Q. David Kranzler, New York, US National Microfilm Archives

In view of the fact that microfilming will be carried out wherever feasible, except for those that need deacidification and in view of the fact of the upcoming technology of discs and lasers, would you not say that the astronomical figures that you gave at the beginning are perhaps anachronistic because if you eventually will microfilm (and it takes a lot less time and effort to microfilm that it does to deacidify those pages), I can foresee within 10 years for example with modern technology, the task requiring far less time and money.

A. Mme Delaunay

I do not know exactly what to answer because I think that the figures are so astronomical, so enormous, so we will never be able to do this and the microfilming of course will go on. But we still need money and my colleague, Miss Perraud, knows a lot about the lack of money for the microfilm programme. But anyway I think we have to decide perhaps in a more proper way, and in a more precise way what we want to do. For the moment the problem in the National Library is that we do microfilm, we do preserve, or I should say we do keep the holdings which have been microfilmed. We do everything at the same time, and that is to say that we cannot do very much and I do not think that that is the right way to try to do it. We have to get a new policy and say we will microfilm and not restore all, we will share the task as I said at the end. I do not think that we can microfilm and restore and preserve everything, it is not possible. I do not know if I have answered your question very well, but it is an enormous question for us today.

A.   Bob Harriman, Library of Congress (Chairman)

I also believe that in most instances that the decision cannot be put off
while you wait in the hope that technology will provide some new opportunity.

A.   Mme Delaunay

Of course we do wait, we hope also that new technologies might provide a solution.

A.   Mr Mannerheim, Royal Library, Stockholm.

I think that the arguments you quoted at the end of your paper for preserving
the original were very valid arguments, but I would like to add one more to
those. That is that microfilming is a very complicated business and we who
are doing it know that there are bound to be some mistakes in microfilming; if
you after microfilming dispose of the original you have lost the information.
So my opinion is that you should have such a complete microfilming programme
as is possible and in addition you should preserve the originals. But this
question of restoring the originals is of course a problem. From my viewpoint
in Sweden, where our collections are smaller the problem is not so big
actually, if you have a complete microfilming programme you can stop the use
of the originals and if they are not used they are, though brittle, in a fairly good condition in our collections.

A.   Mme Delaunay

I quite agree with you, but I think that our holdings are very often in a
poorer state than in Sweden.   They have been used very much since the last
World War, as I have said; for historical research we have a lot of users of
newspapers and for perhaps too long a time the originals have been used,
because our microfilm policy did not start early enough and was not complete
enough and still is not. We should do much more, but we still lack money,
staff and so on; you all know about this. But of course if you have a very
complete microfilm policy you might keep the holdings somewhere else and in
very good conditions. Anyway, if you do not deacidify it is finished in 20 or
40 years; there will not be any paper any more and you cannot restore them any
more.   So as far as we have no mass deacidification for newspapers, there is a
problem even when you have the complete microfilm. For the moment we keep
them of course and I quite agree with you we should keep them because there
are gaps in microfilm, mistakes and so on, but for the moment it is not very
satisfactory because we have the microfilm, it may not be very good, and we
have also the holdings, but they are just crumbling, so there we are. And we
have no mass deacidification; maybe we will have it in a year or two, as there
are new developments of course.

Q.   Mr Mannerheim

Why do you waste money on binding newspapers, those newspapers you are microfilming? Why do you not use that to microfilm some more? One other question
I would like to take up about the preserving of the original. Most of you
have visited or will visit the British Library, there the bound volumes are
preserved vertically, and you have said that you are doing the same. Do not
follow these examples if you have the possibility because it is a tremendous
stress to the originals to be preserved in that way. Try to keep them in a
horizontal position.

A.   Mme Delauney

I quite agree with you too. But we cannot change all our stacks and the shelves. We can do it in new stacks when we make new equipment, but in the old
stacks we cannot because again it is just a question of money, and as to the
Acle binding of course we do bind all the newspapers, some foreign newspapers
and all the most important national newspapers in France. Of course we should
microfilm them and I think when they are available on microfilm (some of them
are), we purchase them too. Anyway, the Aclé binding is very cheap compared
with microfilming, and it can be done very quickly. We cannot show it to you
now but it is a very easy system, quick fitting as I have said and 140 francs
– that is not very much for a binding and two hours for two not very well
trained binders, but two binders for that kind of work, it is not very expensive. If we could bind them in that way and could keep them, and not give
them to the users, have them microfilmed them instead and then keep them flat
on the shelves, that should be the right way, and finally deacidification
also. Then that would be the optimum conditions but I am not sure that we can
manage all this for a long time.

The new stacks in our centre in Provins are equipped especially for newspapers
and there they are kept flat on the shelves.

Q.   Ms Penny Griffith, National Library, New Zealand.

I actually believe keeping newspapers just in case you made a mistake in
microfilming is a very bad reason. I think that it is important that your
quality control at the time of filming is good and that you make an intermediate positive to make your user copies from, so that your master negative is
safe and keep it in good conditions. I really believe that the strongest
argument for retaining the newspapers is, and I speak here as a representative
of a national institution, the responsibility for keeping the national
imprint. We would not think of throwing away the national imprint of periodicals and books after we have microfilmed them, why should we throw away newspapers? We do retain the filmed copies now in our library and we shrinkwrap
them unbound. The shrinkwrapping itself reduces the amount of air around the
copies and that slows down the process of self-destruction and we will keep
them in remote storage for use only in exceptional circumstances, probably by
people interested in ink, or paper, or type. But I do recommend keeping newspapers as bibliographical items.

A.   Mme Delaunay

Yes we agree. The problem is still a huge one because we have so many of them
in such a poor state, but of course I think that the original copy should be
kept. The National Library should keep a complete holding, or as complete as
possible, but maybe that we still should reach another policy and perhaps
share tasks in the country because it is really such an enormous task for a
single library even if it is the National Library.

MICROFILMING: WHAT YOU NEED TO KNOW

PRESERVATION BY MICROFILMING: some considerations on the planning of newspaper microfilming and its consequences for libraries and users

Johan MANNERHEIM

Head of Newspaper Section, Kungliga Biblioteket, Stockholm
and responsible for
the National Newspaper Microfilming Programme of Sweden

CONTENTS

1.   INTRODUCTION: Taking a national approach

As a librarian you are always confronted with the contradiction between use and preservation of the material you are managing. For those who are occupied in a national library, as I am, this contradiction is specially sharp. Among the written or unwritten rules guiding a national library's work, the preservation of the national literature for future generations, especially in its printed form, is one of the library's main tasks. This task has no end, the preservation should if possible go on till eternity. The crux is only that preserving has no meaning if nobody uses the preserved material.

The national library has even a responsibility of its own, beyond for instance university libraries, to serve people from all walks of life with books, pamphlets, periodicals and newspapers which are not accessible elsewhere. And among these categories the contradiction between use and preservation is most acute for the material with the worst paper – the newspapers.

The reason for me to take this national approach is that microfilming newspapers always becomes a national endeavour, whether it is done by a national library, a university library, some joint committee or a private company. Microfilming should never be a single library's project to protect its newspaper collections and make them more available. The complexity and substantial costs of a newspaper microfilming programme and the need for standardization speak strongly for that.

The number of newspaper copies, which are still complete and in acceptable condition, are also very few in comparison with books. In Sweden, for instance, copies of many newspapers only exist in the three old legal deposit libraries, and these copies are partly destroyed by heavy use. Many countries which have gone through war are in a much worse situation. Therefore, any library's newspaper holdings are of national importance.

Today newspaper microfilms already constitute a considerable part of the newspaper collections of many libraries. In a world wide Survey on national newspaper collections made by the IFLA Working Group on Newspapers 1981-83 66% of
92 answering institutions had microfilms in their collections. 65% of them
knew of retrospective newspaper microfilming projects and 50% of microfilming
of current newspapers going on in their countries. In most of the countries
at least some newspaper editions were filmed, while supplements and newsbills
usually were not.

2. ROUSING AN INTEREST

If you want to rouse an interest for extensive microfilming of newspapers, you
should not bother much to embroider a text about better access to newspapers
or about microfilms being convenient to handle or to send, and other things
like that.

These things are true, but in my experience it is much more rewarding to speak
and write about the important part of the national heritage which will be lost
if the responsible persons are not doing anything. At this very minute information is destroyed and can never be regained. That is also true.

It is certainly a national obligation for every country to preserve its newspapers. Therefore the costs for a newspaper microfilming programme should
burden the state budget.

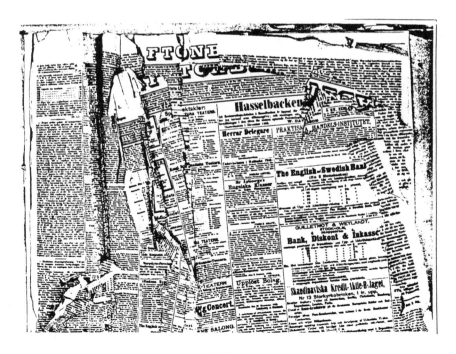

FIGURE 1
A collage from the collections of Kungliga Biblioteket in Stockholm
Aftonbladet January 1866

In many countries with a federal structure this is unrealistic. There you might have a programme on a co-operative basis. In other countries you must rely, at least partly, on private funds.

One thing is common in all these cases. A comprehensive and good microfilming programme is expensive. You will get the required funds only if you manage to rouse an interest for your programme. To do that, you must first state the facts.

It might be self-evident to you that the newspapers will not last long, if nothing is done to protect them, but it is not self-evident to the public, the officials and the politicians.

2.1. The ageing of newspapers

You have to make it clear, that all newspaper paper from about 1865 and there-after is ageing swiftly. A good picture of this process is the yellowing of a forgotten newspaper in a window. Most people have experienced that. In our collections the same happens, only a little slower. You can serve small pieces of brown-yellow, brittle paper gathered from the shelves and floors of your newspaper stacks, and ask people to fold them. You can show volumes with torn and loose and missing pages. (See Figure 1).

It is impossible to say anything scientifically exact about how fast the age-ing goes, as ageing tests are relative, not absolute. Storage conditions vary and so does the stress through use. Therefore you must rely on your exper-ience. This is the way I put it in 1982 when The Royal Library of Stockholm was campaigning for a retrospective programme:

'A rough summary of the results can be expressed thus:

Newspapers 10 years old have fairly good durability.
Newspapers 30 years old have distinctly reduced durability.
Newspapers 50 years old have poor durability.

This is true for newspapers printed on mechanical wood pulp paper, a paper which became dominant in Sweden around 1865 and still is used.

Newspapers which are thirty years old and have not been used are most commonly whole and fine, but fragile. If they have been used many times they have tears and other damage.

Newspapers which are older than fifty years are damaged by each use. If they have been used many times part of the text is lost.

So it is not the case, that newspapers destroy themselves turning to dust. The real process is just as serious. The newspapers are be-coming so brittle, that they cannot endure any handling. Even with the utmost caution the newspapers will break into pieces by use or reproduction.
...

This very day about half of the newspapers in danger are fifty years of age or older. Within twenty years about three quarters of the newspapers will reach this age.

With the present tempo of microfilming the average age at the time of filming would be well over one hundred years. That means that the

average newspaper, when it is put under the camera, already has been
of poor durability for fifty, sixty, seventy years. Each time it has
been used during this period it has got some damage, usually resulting
in loss of text!

It is evident that if you carry out retrospective microfilming at the
present utterly low level of ambition, an important part of our cultural heritage will get lost beyond rescue. But there is still time to
prevent the catastrophe in the main, if the programme of the (Swedish)
Newspaper Microfilming Committee is quickly realized in the time suggested by the committee, fifteen years.

Time is thus expensive. Texts are getting lost. The filming is furthermore becoming more and more expensive, as the material is getting
damaged and the puzzle of bringing different copies together for an
original for a film of quality is getting more difficult for each year
that passes by.'

2.2. The value of newspapers

When the librarian is pointing out the catastrophic situation for the newspapers, the authorities still might say: "So what!" From their point of view
it is a correct position to take. Newspapers are traditionally regarded as a
third class material filled with trash, misunderstandings, biased selections
of uncontrolled facts and plain lies.

We know of course that this is exactly one of the main reasons why newspapers
are so valuable: they reflect the opinions and quarrels of their time and
place, well founded or not. They are part of the process creating history.
But this is not for the librarian to say.

You have to ally yourself with the users, mainly historians in the broadest
sense of the word. They will point out that with the newspapers an important
part of our cultural heritage will be lost. And they can say it with the
necessary authority.

In Sweden the Royal Library arranged a half day symposium under the title:
'The newspaper as a mirror of time - a cultural treasure facing destruction'.

The interesting thing was the broad spectrum of scholars attending. History,
economic history, history of literature, history of art, sociology, ethnology,
law, journalism and science of government were all represented. One of the
participants stated: "You cannot find a scholar of humanities or a social
scientist, who does not benefit from older newspapers". Others emphasized the
importance of old local newspapers for laymen and organizations looking for
their own history in short necrologies and paragraphs. In newspapers you will
find material which is unattainable elsewhere. The importance of keeping
originals after microfilming was stressed by art historians.

When you eventually have convinced your officials, government and other parties concerned, their interest must be focused on a practical newspaper microfilming programme.

3. MICROFILMS VERSUS ORIGINALS

There are two main arguments for saving at least one newspaper original after
microfilming. The first is that a newspaper microfilm is not the same as the

original, the other that the original is needed for safety.

3.1. A newspaper microfilm is not a full substitute for a newspaper

The obvious difference between the newspaper and the black and white microfilm is the colour. You do not fulfil your national obligation of preserving the newspapers if you do not preserve the colour pictures and the coloured head-lines, rules and surfaces of the newspaper.

Some black and white pictures also cause problems. Xylographs (wood engrav-ings) from the nineteenth century, for instance, often have thin black lines in the white surface and simultaneously thin white lines in the black surface. This will not be reproduced in a microfilm picture.

The evidence of the technique is also destroyed. For a specialized newspaper researcher, studying the past production techniques of newspapers, the micro-film is worthless.

3.2. The original is needed for safety

Nobody is perfect. That is another reason for keeping the original after microfilming. In such a big venture as microfilming mistakes are bound to happen.

A photographer misses pages or even whole issues. A blurred picture makes the text unreadable. A film is scratched or insufficiently rinsed. All these things occur and sometimes they are missed by the controllers. But sooner or later somebody else finds the fault and then you will need the original badly.

Another safety aspect is the risk of destruction of whole files by war or disaster. If you dispose of the originals you will have only one archival copy (usually the camera negative) on which the preservation for the future relies. It is much safer to have one or two paper copies left as well, housed in other locations than the archival film, preferably in the country-side, where stores are cheaper and the air less polluted.

These archival paper copies should be protected from wear by strict user res-trictions. Users should use microfilm, with exception only for those few cases when the film fails to be a substitute.

4.   ALTERNATIVE TECHNIQUES

It is not my task to provide an elaborate discussion on other techniques than microfilming, as they will be dealt with in other forms during this Symposium, in the workshops on conserving the original and on new developments. There-fore I confine myself to discuss the impact they might have on the national newspaper microfilming programme.

Mass conservation of all newspaper originals of a country is unrealistic. It would be a task much more expensive and time consuming than microfilming. Besides, conservation does not protect the originals from further use and wear. The best protective measures to preserve originals are to minimize their use by microfilming. If this is done, conservation might be a comple-mentary measure in some cases.

Microfilm has a long term problem: the film is ageing and a new copy of the old film if always one little step coarser than the original film. This means that in the long run, that is several hundred years, when you have made seven, eight generations of microfilms, some texts will be unreadable and there will not be much left of the pictures.

Digital storage, for instance by optical disc, does not have this inherent limitation. In principle, but not always in practice, a copy is exactly of the same quality as the original.

Today's CD/ROM and other optical disks are not ready for newspaper preservation. The guaranteed lifetime of the disks is less than twenty years. Newspapers cannot be stored in ASCII code, as pictures, layout and headlines are important parts of them. Picture storage in newspaper format is possible, but still very space consuming in digital form. The costs are therefore far beyond library budgets.

However, in the future, newspapers will most probably be stored and used in digital form instead of microfilm.

A possible conclusion would be that it is better to wait for technical development, which certainly has been fast in this field. This is not wise for two reasons.

The first is that microfilming is not wasted work. It is possible to scan the microfilms and convert them into digital form. It is not unlikely that this will be normal procedure in the future, as microfilming reduces the scanning area and standardizes its size.

The second reason is that the longer you wait the more newspaper copies are torn or destroyed. This will make the preserved file incomplete and increase the preservation work.

My view on the relations between microfilming and the alternative techniques can be summarized in a few sentences: you should microfilm now to rescue the newspapers. It is fine if you can change to a still safer medium in the future. Then it will be possible to convert microfilms to that medium instead of making new microfilm generations. The different preservation techniques complement rather than contradict each other.

This conclusion calls for setting up a microfilming programme. It is not advisable to do so, however, before you are aware of the problems of editions and the differences between current and retrospective microfilming.

5.   IS A NEWSPAPER A NEWSPAPER? THE PROBLEM OF NEWSPAPER EDITIONS

Since 1979 I have been responsible for the continuous microfilming of Swedish newspapers. The task given to the Royal Library was to make a complete newspaper film, covering all current Swedish newspapers including their supplements, editions and newsbills (placards with the main headlines). While my colleagues and I were investigating the publishing pattern of all Swedish newspapers, an existential question grew in my mind: is a newspaper really a newspaper? Or to be exact: is this copy of Sweden's most circulated evening paper Expressen of June 8, 1987 an Expressen of June 8, 1987? The answer is: No! Expressen is not Expressen. A newspaper is not a newspaper.

When somebody in Haparanda, which is a small town north of the Polar Circle, 1000 km from Stockholm, buys Expressen in the afternoon, he will get the first edition printed in the morning in Stockholm, which the Expressen people call

FIGURE 2

Expressen, 8 June 1987. Last and first pages of the first Stockholm edition (above) and the last Stockholm edition (below)

"first national". A person who simultaneously buys <u>Expressen</u> in Kalmar, a
somewhat larger town at the east coast of southern Sweden, 300 km. from Stockholm, will get "number one", which is the first edition printed in
Joenkoeping. This copy was printed a little later than the first Stockholm
edition. The first Stockholm edition was transferred to Joenkoeping page by
page by Telefax, then it was changed a bit by editors in Joenkoeping and eventually printed. Someone who buys <u>Expressen</u> in Stockholm at about the same
time as the others, will get "first city" which usually is the fourth, sometimes the third edition printed in Stockholm. But if he waits till about 6
p.m. he will have the fifth and last Stockholm edition. That is provided
nothing extraordinary happens in the world forcing <u>Expressen</u> to produce a
sixth Stockholm edition. If you assemble and study the copies, you will find
that there are not many identical pages in the first and last editions of
<u>Expressen</u>. (See Figure 2).

A newspaper is not a newspaper. That means that many notes and bibliographies
in dissertations are incorrect. "<u>Expressen</u>, June 8, 1987, page 1". That
means nothing. These bibliographic, existential problems are therefore the
scholar's and researcher's problems, but the librarians must help to solve
them. For example, the librarians should be able to inform researchers about
<u>Expressen</u>'s usually nine editions, five printed in Stockholm and four in Joen-
koeping, and also be able to inform about the marks which make the editions
recognizable. <u>Expressen</u>'s first Stockholm edition has five dots under the
title, and for each regular edition one dot is taken away. (See Figure 3).
The first Joenkoeping edition is marked with a versal R and four dots, which
are successively taken away.

FIGURE 3
The Stockholm editions of <u>Expressen</u> 8 June 1987. The publishing pattern calls
for five editions printed in Stockholm, but this day there was one extra edition

5.1. Geographical and chronological editions

Editions can be divided into two kinds, geographical and chronological. The case of <u>Expressen</u> is a typical example of a chronological edition. It has a large circulation and is printed on many presses during a long time. Then it is easy to make many editions in order to bring the latest and hottest news and win the race against other newspapers.

The geographical editions are more regular. A newspaper has perhaps bought another paper in a neighbouring town. The buyers keep the title, but make the contents identical with their main newspaper, apart from the first page and some local pages. But even in these geographical editions, now and then changes are made also in those pages which principally are common. There are also mixed forms, which stand somewhere between geographical and chronological editions. So the distinction is not exact, only useful.

Irrespective of the kind of edition, a new edition always gives the editors of the newspaper an opportunity to correct faults and to change articles for other reasons. Therefore the order in which editions are printed is of interest.

Sweden had in 1984 around 170 main newspapers. There were also 40 geographical editions with a title of their own. Finally there were about 70 other editions without a separate title, making the total number of different newspapers in Sweden about 280. Around 50 of the "unnamed" editions were chronological. The other 20 were geographical, but could only be identified by stars or dots and in a few cases by words like "east" and "west". The Swedish press is not much different from the press in other countries with many newspapers. In the survey of national newspaper collections 35 countries (of about 55) admit having editions and in 25 of these countries at least some of the editions are collected. The conscious collection of chronological editions is most rare. It seems not be be realised that the differences can be just as extensive between two chronological editions as between geographical editions.

5.2. Defining newspaper editions

What is a newspaper edition? How does it relate to editions of books?

Newspaper people as well as libraries are using the word "edition" not only for the phenomena just described.

For instance it is used for the concepts of language edition and weekly edition. Those editions have normally not a single page identical with the main newspaper. Therefore language editions and weekly editions should be treated as separate titles by microfilming.

Sunday editions are not true editions either. They could be treated either as weekly newspapers in their own right or as part of the main newspaper carrying a variant title.

Now, let us rephrase the question. What is a true newspaper edition? How does it relate to editions of books?

Book publishers might print a new edition some months after the first; more often it will take a year or more. In the newspaper world everything goes much quicker. With a few exceptions, all editions are printed within a few hours. The next day of issue the newspapers start all over again.

Within the microcosm of one day in one newspaper's life, you could use the bibliographical tools of the 'books' world, edition, issue, printing etc. I do not think that would be very rewarding to do. To do it for a long period would simply be impossible, at least for librarians.

Another special feature is the complexity and vividness of many newspapers. When describing a newspaper it is convenient to use expressions like the publishing pattern and the pattern of editions, as those editions, supplements and newsbills which actually are printed vary a little from day to day.

Because of this complexity it is definitely wise to confine oneself to use one term for the different appearances of a newspaper; edition. For books, edition means edition of the same work. The second edition contains basically the same work as the first edition, maybe in revised or enlarged form. For a true newspaper edition, the same must be the case. If not, the term has lost its bibliographical meaning and usefulness.

For newspapers, I suggest the following definition:

A true newspaper edition is created

- when a newspaper is reprinted with any change in the appearance, however small (apart from pressmarks)

- if the number of pages changed from the previous printing does not exceed half the total.

An edition could be occasional, but usually it is part of the publishing pattern of the newspaper.

If the differences concern more than half the pages, we have a case of two different newspapers with some pages in common.

A good thing with this definition is that it is useful for the scholars. When studying a newspaper with true editions, the reader will know that the basic material is the same, but that several pages might have been changed between the editions. The definition will also help to distinguish between geographical editions and separate newspapers from the same publishers. And it can, as will be shown later, be helpful for current microfilming of editions.

5.3. Preservation policy for editions

If newspaper editions are not preserved, part of our cultural heritage is getting lost. It is clear from the survey that very few countries collect all their editions, but many countries are collecting some. In some countries at least, those answering our survey were not aware of newspaper editions.

Microfilming editions might generally have a lower priority than the microfilming of at least one copy a day of each newspaper. The demand for editions by users is probably not high as the awareness of their existence is low. Therefore their destruction will proceed comparatively slowly. But in the long run, they will be used both by researchers and the public, and then they also have to be microfilmed.

However, if you put current microfilming on your programme, I strongly recommend filming the editions directly, when precise knowledge of them is obtainable.

6. CURRENT VERSUS RETROSPECTIVE MICROFILMING

Going into the newspaper rescuing business it seems natural to start with some old, important newspapers, microfilming them in retrospect before they totally disintegrate. But if you want to set up a smart national microfilming programme, you have to consider current microfilming as well.

Current microfilming means microfilming newspapers weekly, monthly or yearly just after they were published. Current microfilming is in many ways much easier. The newspapers are in better condition. The paper is still white (or pink in some cases). If the copy is badly printed you can have another from the printer or publisher. If you ponder about editions or supplements, you simply ask the publisher. The newspapers are unbound. The rules for legal deposit can be changed to facilitate the filming. You can secure a steady income from subscribers of your newspaper microfilms.

Summing up, this means that you get more for your money by current microfilming than by retrospective.

If you have a complete current programme, covering all living newspapers in your country, including supplements, editions and newsbills (newspaper placards) – then at least you can be confident that your preservation problem is not growing any more. You can be sure that all retrospective microfilming done in the future will reduce the number of unfilmed newspapers in danger of being lost.

7. BIBLIOGRAPHICAL WORK IN CONNECTION WITH MICROFILMING

Microfilming newspapers is a golden opportunity to make contributions to your national bibliography.

Because of the low status newspapers have held historically in academic and library circles, existent bibliographic descriptions of newspapers are often on the level of a simple catalogue entry. It has not been considered worth the effort to do something worthy of the name bibliography. Newspapers are not very easy to describe as they often are complex, with editions, periodical supplements and, in some countries, newsbills. They also are like human beings, they change all the time. Titles, especially subtitles, publishers, printing offices, editors, political tendency, size and of course editions and periodical supplements will vary during the lifetime of a newspaper. In our experience not many current newspapers are constant in all these respects as long as a year.

If you set up an ambitious newspaper microfilming programme, you are obliged to gather much of this information for the filming's sake. It would be bad economy not to save this information for the future in bibliographical form. The reader of a newspaper microfilm needs a picture with a text that gives him access to the contents, a text describing both the newspaper itself and how it is filmed. This picture is called the bibliographical target.

When we were designing our bibliographical target, we both listened to scholars using newspapers and looked at the Swedish tradition formed by Bernhard Lundstedt in his Sveriges periodiska litteratur (Sweden's periodical literature), which goes to 1899. (See Annexes 1 and 2).

You have to be very careful, when you choose the piece of information to be registered, as every added part in the long run will multiply to weeks or months of work. Avoid giving information which is not easily obtainable for you.

We soon found that there is an essential difference between the description of current and old newspapers, not owing to the newspapers themselves, but our situation.

7.1. Bibliographical targets for current microfilming

With current microfilming the bibliographical target is a snapshot of the newspaper just as it is now. The target is valid till further notice, that is until some change appears which affects it.

When writing the description you have the advantage of being able to solve most problems by simply asking. The master printer and the editor are available and know what they are doing.

It is possible to get safe information about the editions and the order they are printed in, about supplements and newsbills, and about the publisher, all the kind of information which is difficult to obtain for old newspapers.

We have even influenced some of the Swedish newspapers to mark their editions better.

It is certainly good economy to gather the information while it is easy to get. Later it might even be unobtainable.

7.2. Bibliographical targets for retrospective microfilming

With retrospective microfilming the bibliographical target gives a picture of the newspaper for a long period, preferably the whole publication period. In our case we mostly confine ourselves to the years we film. The headings will in this case be followed by long lists of items with dates reflecting all the changes the newspaper has undergone. (See Annex 3).

Sources for the descriptions are in this case the newspapers themselves, official records and available printed information. We use, for instance, "annonstaxor", which are union newspapers advertising price lists. They started in 1880 and contain useful information about the different newspapers. We are also helped by some biographical works on newspaper men and women.

The main source, however, is the newspaper collections themselves. In order to make a complete film you have to go through the copy chosen for micro-filming anyway, looking for defects. That is a golden opportunity to gather bibliographical information. It will also make the work more interesting for your staff.

8. SETTING UP A NEWSPAPER MICROFILMING PROGRAMME

As situations in different countries vary, the national microfilming prog-rammes will also differ. Therefore it is both impossible and meaningless to try to prescribe one programme or another. But it might be useful to supply some arguments and experiences from other countries.

It is easy to underestimate the need of personnel, accommodation and funds by basing the calculations on some obvious parts of the programme and forgetting other inevitable or desirable parts. There are points which should be considered before deciding, otherwise they might pop up as an unpleasant and maybe expensive surprise later.

The following is intended to give a fairly complete picture of the elements of a programme.

8.1. Scope

There are several policy decisions to make which will determine the scope of the microfilming programme and have tremendous implications for costs and manpower.

8.1.1. Defining newspapers to microfilm

It is necessary to draw a line between those newspapers which should be part of the project and those newspapers and other objects which should not. One possibility is to microfilm the newspaper collections just as they are with inconsistencies and oddities caused by librarians' willpower and negligence through centuries. This non-method seems natural for retrospective microfilming and it has one good point: users are already used to the collections.

A more intellectual attitude is to define a newspaper. For current microfilming you have to stick to some definition, like the one made up by the IFLA Working Group on Newspapers: a serial publication which contains news on current events of special or general interest, the individual parts of which are listed chronologically or numerically and appear usually at least once a week. Perhaps you do not like the idea of including the special newspapers. Perhaps the authorities prefer some definition already existing in your legislation for other purposes.

However, if we focus on preservation, all items on bad paper, in large format and of interest for the users should be microfilmed. Therefore not only general newspapers, but also special newspapers, advertisement newspapers and other newspaperlike periodicals should be considered.

Old newspapers printed on rag paper in small format are usually in excellent condition, at least in my country. In spite of that, it is my opinion that they should be included in the programme to promote their accessibility. There is not much to save here, as they only constitute a small part of the programme – in Sweden, less than five percent.

8.1.2. Current or retrospective microfilming or both

The question of current or retrospective microfilming or both has already been discussed. In Sweden, we started a complete current programme for general newspapers in 1979, and when that was in hand, it was followed in 1983 by a retrospective programme comprising all unfilmed newspapers and planned to be finished in fifteen to twenty years.

A retrospective programme should have a limited time schedule, as time is eating the newspapers. If you are in the lucky position that you can stop all use of the copy, which in the future will be microfilmed, then a somewhat longer time schedule can be accepted.

8.1.3. Priorities

If you cannot convince the authorities of the necessity of a complete microfilming programme, the question of priorities gets more important. You could
also search for partners to share the costs, so you get the most out of your
money. In our experience, it is easiest to find partners for newspapers which
are heavily used. The same newspapers are also more exposed to wear and damage than others. On this level there is therefore usually no sharp contradiction between the 'economy first, preservation first and access first' attitudes.

You could also let geographical and political criteria influence the selection. It is important to cover both the whole country and the whole political
spectrum during the newspaper period.

To plan newspaper microfilming from a purely chronological point of view is
not advisable. It is unscientific, as it is not age itself, but use that
destroys the newspapers. It is also bad economy. Let us imagine that you
start by filming all newspapers of the 1860's, then continue with newspapers
from the 1870's, etc. It would mean chopping all newspapers in ten year
pieces and lead to increased administrative work through the whole chain of
production: selecting originals, bibliographical work, preparation, photographing with correct targets, controlling, marketing and distribution. It is
much better to microfilm a newspaper from start to end or to the point where
current microfilming of the newspaper has started.

8.1.4. Editions, supplements and newsbills

Another policy matter is the question if each newspaper should be completely
microfilmed, including editions, supplements and newsbills.

I gave my opinion on the importance of editions in section 5.3. Different
ways of microfilming them will be discussed in section 8.6.

Supplements are parts of the newspapers and should not be separated from them.
Therefore the normal procedure should be to microfilm them as issued. If that
is not done for some reason, it is mandatory to make a note about it in the
film itself.

Printed newsbills, that is placards advertising the most important news of the
day, are used in many countries to promote the selling of single copies. (See
Figure 4). You should consider collecting and microfilming newsbills. They
are certainly part of the newspaper's publishing pattern. They reflect the
newspaper's evaluation of news and are highly rated as documents imbued with a
scent of time by media people, picture editors and others.

8.1.5. Number of distribution copies

Another important aspect of the programme, which directly affects the costs,
is the number of distribution copies (user copies). There are mainly two
considerations to take into account.

The first is to evaluate the need for access to the films for research and
other purposes in different places in your country. Microfilms are certainly
most suitable for inter-library lending. But you have to weigh the cost of
inter-library loans against the cost of microfilm duplicates.

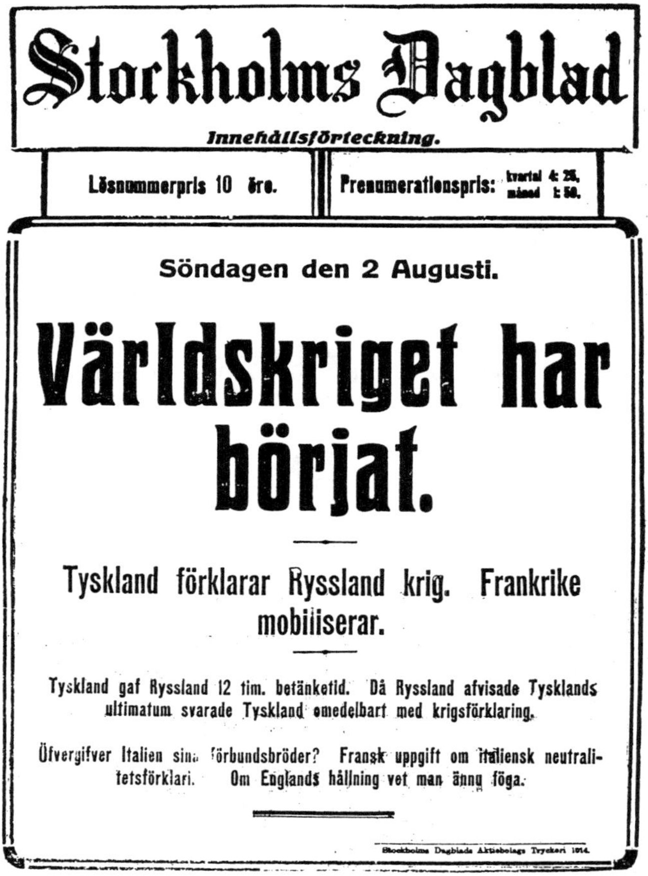

Stockholms Dagblad

Innehållsförteckning.

Lösnummerpris 10 öre. | Prenumerationspris: kvartal 4: 25, månad 1: 50.

Söndagen den 2 Augusti.

Världskriget har börjat.

Tyskland förklarar Ryssland krig. Frankrike mobiliserar.

Tyskland gaf Ryssland 12 tim. betänketid. Då Ryssland afvisade Tysklands ultimatum svarade Tyskland omedelbart med krigsförklaring.

Öfvergifver Italien sina förbundsbröder? Fransk uppgift om italiensk neutralitetsförklari. Om Englands hållning vet man ännu föga.

Stockholms Dagblads Aktiebolags Tryckeri 1914.

FIGURE 4
Newsbill of Stockholms dagblad 2 August 1914. 'The World War has started'

The other consideration is to estimate how much storage space there is to gain by replacing originals by film copies.

In Sweden for instance, there are seven deposit libraries since 1979. Only two libraries - those which have national library tasks - get newspaper originals. These two, and three of the other libraries, get complete duplicates of all newspaper films from the Royal Library budget. The remaining two deposit libraries have to borrow or buy newspaper microfilms just like all other libraries. The result of this policy is that the growth of newspaper collections totals about 600 meters of shelves a year in the deposit libraries instead of 1800 meters a year.

8.2. Format

According to the world wide survey 1981-83, all answering libraries with newspaper microfilms have 35 mm unperforated roll film. Only six libraries had films in other formats also.

Why is that? Let us look at the alternatives.

16 mm unperforated roll film has several advantages over 35 mm. It is cheaper. It occupies less space. There is a wider range of equipment to choose from. There are cameras which make two camera negatives at one exposure. Manufacturers have developed several computer controlled search systems for automatic or half-automatic access.

The problem with 16 mm is that its small format will mean reduction ratios like 1:40 and 1:50 for large originals in newspaper format. It is just about possible to make a readable camera film with these reduction rates. This is not enough, as the quality of user films, being copies of copies of the camera film, will be insufficient. This problem - the effects of film generations - will be further discussed later.

16 mm roll film could be used for microfilming of press-cuttings with a reduction rate between 1:12,75 and 1:25,5.

For newspapers the microfiche format is a more serious alternative. Actually newspaper microfilming is done on microfiche in some cases, but usually with a reduction ratio which makes the fiche unusable as part of a preservation programme.

It is, however, possible to make non-standard microfiche with, for instance, six exposures on each. This would give an acceptable reduction rate. The disadvantage with this solution is the higher cost and the problem of keeping the microfiche in order. A large newspaper like Dagens Nyheter, a month of which will fill three 35 mm rolls, will need no less than 300 fiches a month, around ten for each day.

A possibility worth investigating might be to make the archival microfilm on 35 mm, but then convert it to user copies on fiche or even 16 mm roll film with a larger reduction.

Anyhow, standard for newspaper filming, is today 35 mm unperforated microfilm. There is even an international standard made for that format.

8.3. Colour

I do not know of any colour microfilm of newspapers produced today. But there are some developments which make colour microfilm worth considering for part of the programme.

The first is that multicolour pictures are getting more and more frequent in newspapers. In England, Today is even boasting of having colour throughout. Newspapers of the same type will certainly appear in other countries.

The second development is the occurrence of new colour microfilms, like Cibachrome from Ilford, with much better preservation qualities than before.

If you do not go so far as to use colour microfilm, there is another thing you should do. The microfilms should contain information for the user about colour in the originals. In the few cases that multicolour is used throughout it should be stated in the bibliographical target. When colour occurs now and then, there is a new micrographical symbol, decided by the International Standard Organization, ISO, for the purpose. (See Figure 5). It is placed in the margin. In Sweden, we use the symbol whenever colour occurs only for older newspapers. For most modern newspapers, where colour is normal in mast-heads, headlines, rules, frames and backgrounds, the symbol is used only for multicolour pictures.

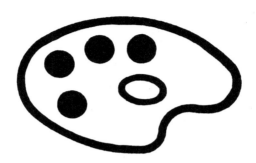

FIGURE 5
Micrographic symbol for colour in the original

8.4. Standards

There are several international standards which are helpful, when forming the newspaper microfilming programme. The most important is ISO 4087, "Micro-filming of newspapers on 35 mm unperforated microfilm for archival purposes".

The newspaper microfilming standard gives prescriptions and recommendations concerning among other things:
- image placement and reduction ratios
- arrangement of the file
- film targets
- micrographic symbols
- processing the exposed film
- quality specifications for legibility, optical density and contrast
- correcting the processed camera negative,
- intermediate and distribution (or user) copies
- container inscription.

The present version, which dates from 1979, has in my opinion, some short-comings especially in the sections on film targets and the arrangement of the file. Editions are not even mentioned. The standard is under revision, so there are good opportunities to improve it.

Other ISO standards of interest are:

ISO 417, "Photography – Determination of thiosulphate and other residual chemicals in processed photographic films, plates and papers – Methylene blue photometric method and silver sulphide densitometric method"

ISO 446, "Microcopying - ISO No. 1 Mire - Description and use in photographic documentary reproduction"

ISO 2014, "Writing of calendar dates in all-numeric form"

ISO 3166, "Codes for the representation of names of countries"

ISO 3334, "Microcopying - ISO test chart No. 2 - Description and use in photographic documentary reproduction"

ISO 4331, "Photography - Processed photographic film for archival records - Silver-gelatin type on cellulose ester base - Specifications"

ISO 4332, "Photography - Processed photographic film for archival records - Silver-gelatin type on poly(ethylene terephtalate) base - Specifications"

ISO 5466, "Photography - Practice for the storage of processed safety photographic film"

ISO 6196, "Micrographics - Vocabulary"

ISO 6200, "Density of silver-gelatin type films"

In many countries there are national counterparts to some of these international standards.

8.5. Laws helping and laws causing problems

Planning current microfilming of newspapers, you should consider rewriting the deposit law.

It is possible to prescribe that the deposit copy should be delivered in a form which suits the microfilming. This has been done in Sweden from 1979, when the current newspaper microfilming programme started. According to Swedish law most editions should be delivered in the form of changed pages.

This is fair, because it is most time-consuming and unreliable, in practice impossible, to search out the changed pages in retrospect by looking for differences in the text, while the newspaper printers possess the information during the printing and just have to save it for their deposit delivery.

Another legal aspect is the relevance of copyright law. Before starting a newspaper microfilming programme it is important to check how the copyright laws of your country might affect the microfilming, the making and selling of film copies, and then making and selling of paper copies from the films.

It is advisable to take up negotiations with representatives of the newspaper publishers.

8.6. Microfilming editions

In section 5 editions have been discussed in some detail. The importance of preserving them was stressed and microfilming recommended. If you want to incorporate editions in the newspaper microfilming programme, you must find suitable methods to deal with them.

Language editions and weekly editions should be treated as separate titles in microfilming. The same is possible with Sunday editions. Another possibility is to microfilm the Sunday edition chronologically with its main newspaper.

More difficult to decide is the treatment of true editions, editions with more than 50% of the pages identical with the preceding edition. Microfilming these identical pages over and over again does not give value for money. Moreover it makes it difficult for readers to find what they are looking for among all the duplicates.

In an investigation of all Swedish newspapers printed in four days in October 1971 it was found that about two thirds of the pages were unique, the rest duplicate pages.

There are obviously many exposures to save. There is also a problem connected with saving them. You have to know which the duplicate pages are.

It is impossible to find that out by comparing pages. I have tried. Different pages are fairly easy to find. But to become convinced that two pages really are identical is difficult. It takes more than a minute for each page – and the result is still unreliable.

So for current microfilming it is necessary to convince the newspaper producers that they should pick out the pages, by agreement or by law. Even so it is inevitable that some mistakes will be made in this process. There will be some duplicate pages and also, which is more serious, a few gaps in the microfilm.

Therefore it is recommended that the editions are kept complete and intact in the national collections of originals, even if that will cost some stack space.

In the Swedish current newspaper microfilming programme editions are to a large extent represented by their changed pages. We estimate that 25-30 per cent of the exposures are saved that way. The method is used both for geographical and chronological editions.

The main edition is always completely microfilmed, including all supplements, in a series by itself. The underlying idea is that most users will need the main edition only and would just be distracted by edition pages.

With geographical editions one possibility is to keep each edition together for the whole period on the roll. Thereby all the local pages for one area are kept together, which is practical for most users. The consequences are that if somebody wants to read the whole newspaper issue, including pages in common, he has to read the main edition also, which is on another roll or in another part of the same roll.

With chronological editions the number of editions usually varies from day to day. It is not always fair to identify the third edition of one day with the third edition of another day. Those users who are not content with reading only the main edition will normally wish to check all edition pages of the days they are interested in. In this case it is therefore natural to keep the edition pages together day by day, constituting one edition series.

A method I have seen used is to microfilm all variants of a certain page immediately after the same page of the main edition. This is not recommended, as it makes it difficult for the reader to identify the editions. It is better to keep all the pages of one edition together and let them represent the edition of that day.

With retrospective microfilming you are lucky if you can find a pattern governing the change of pages between editions. If not, the choice stands between microfilming complete editions, including many identical pages, and not microfilming editions at all.

8.7. Film generation and film preservation

If the camera film is used it will soon be scratched, smeared and destroyed. If it is stored in polluted air, sometimes hot, sometimes cold, sometimes dry, sometimes moist, it will age swiftly.

The preservation of newspapers by microfilming will be a failure if the microfilms are not preserved properly. It is therefore important to consider the storage climate of the films as well as the set of duplicates needed.

Duplicates are copies of microfilms usually made by contact printing in a 1/1 ratio.

8.7.1. Film generation

The camera film is also called a microfilm of the first generation. A duplicate of the camera film becomes the second generation, a duplicate of that film a microfilm of the third generation, etc.

For each generation the pictures get slightly coarser. The legibility of small details is impaired. It is also difficult to avoid changes in contrast by duplication. Thereby a few middle and light tones are lost for each generation. Finally the duplicate gets unreadable and uninterpretable.

When planning a microfilming project, you should at an early stage consider the chain of duplicates which may be made and set the quality norms such that even the "youngest" generation will be good enough. This could, for instance, be a hard-copy on paper made from a fourth generation duplicate.

If the contents of the newspapers will be preserved for a long time, you must have an archival film which is never used. For reading, copying and inter library lending distribution copies are used. If there is need for many distribution copies at once or in the future, you should make a master film, from which the distribution copies are made, to protect the archival film from damage.

In this way you get sets of microfilms of different generations. In Figure 6 are some diagrams showing examples of such microfilm chains.

The polarity of the exposed camera film is negative. The originals appear negative on the picture. If you use ordinary silver print film (or vesicular film) to make duplicates, the polarity is reversed for each generation. If you use diazo film the polarity stays the same.

As you can see in the diagrams, the need for a positive or negative appearing picture in the distribution copies affects the chain and can lead to an extra intermediate.

The orientation of the emulsion is reversed for each duplication. Generations 2, 4, 6 etc. are preferable as distribution copies since the emulsion of the

roll is protected by the back of the film and most microfilm readers are built
to protect the side turned inwards on the roll.

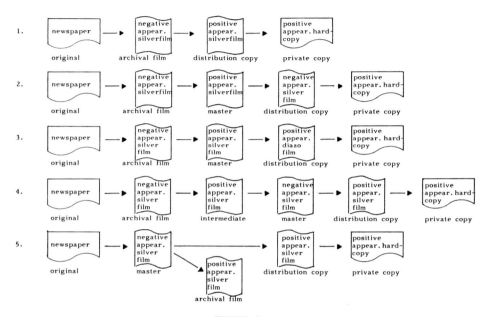

FIGURE 6
Examples of microfilm chains. The film is 35mm unperforated rollfilm throughout

The first chain is not recommended. It does not contain a master to protect
the archival film.

The third chain is not recommended either as the distribution duplicate is a
diazo film. Diazo and vesicular films are used as they are cheaper than silver film. They are not suitable for archival purposes. Diazo film, for instance, is light sensitive after development. For newspaper microfilming they
are seldom used, as the distribution copy certainly has an archival character
for the library which owns it.

I am not going to recommend any of the remaining chains as the best. They all
have advantages and drawbacks. Other chains are also possible. The choice
depends on other aspects of the microfilming programme, polarity preferences
etc. In Sweden we use the fourth chain for the time being. The intermediate
is used as a distribution copy after the master film has been made.

However, I think two points must be stressed.

The microfilm chain should contain both an archival film and a master besides the distribution copies.

Test sets of microfilms must be made before decision. They should be based on originals of different qualities and comprise the whole chain from camera film to hard-copy so you can see that the quality is good enough also in the last thinkable generation.

8.7.2. Film preservation

The best protection of the archival film is to protect it from use. The archival film should only be used by generation duplication, that is making a master or making a new archival film, when the old one shows ageing symptoms. The archival film must always be a silver film. It should normally be of the first generation to preserve the best quality.

The film must be kept in containers which do not affect silver film, for instance aluminium or a polyester of the same kind as in the film itself.

A correct storage climate has an extremely pure air, a temperature in the range 10-15 degrees centigrade and a relative humidity in between 25 and 35 percent. The changes within 24 hours at any point in the room must not exceed 1 degree centigrade and 5 percent relative humidity.

There are mainly two methods to accomplish this. The first is to build a climate chamber which meets the demands above. It is not easy and not very cheap to obtain such a stable climate in a store of considerable size. A suspicious attitude to the contractor is recommended. Double aggregates might be necessary - if one fails, the other goes on.

The other method is to create a microclimate of pure air of the right humidity in the container. The container is then put into a store with the right temperature. For safety you keep the relative humidity under 50% in the store. The problem with this method is that the containers must be absolutely tight after they have been sealed.

In both cases you must run a spot test programme to check the condition of the archival films. The films must be conditioned and then reconditioned when inspected or used to avoid condensation of water.

For master films a climate under 20 degrees centigrade and 40 percent relative humidity is to be recommended.

Distribution duplicates should be used and not protected. Of course they should not be mistreated or damaged by scratching equipment. Beside the waste this will indirectly affect the preservation of master and archival films as the use of them will increase.

8.8. Originals

In section 3 it was emphasized that not all information of the newspapers is preserved in microfilming. Therefore a microfilming programme does not entitle us to dispose of all originals.

The number of copies might however be reduced. In my opinion every country should preserve at least one, preferably two, complete original copies of the newspapers published or printed in that country. If two or more copies are preserved, they should be located at different places for safety and accessibility reasons.

With current microfilming it is best to dispose of the microfilmed original and save others. There is no need to bind newspapers, if their use is restricted to the absolutely necessary. Instead it is recommended to put them in boxes in plano. Not only is it cheaper, it also facilitates reprographic work in the future. Through current microfilming it is possible to reduce your country's need for storage growth both now and in the future.

With retrospective microfilming you might be able to reduce your country's storage area at once after the microfilming of a newspaper is completed. It is possible for most libraries which acquire the film to dispose of their originals. The few libraries which should harbour a 'national' copy of the original can on the other hand replace worn volumes with better copies. Volumes which have been taken apart for filming must not be rebound. They can be stored in boxes just as current newspapers. Loose leaves from periods when they did not carry running title, date or pagination, cause problems. They should be marked if there are no intact bound copies left which maintain the order.

8.9. Selling and marketing

Microfilming newspapers means becoming a micro-publisher. You will have subscribers to your current titles. You sell retrospective microfilms as a kind of encyclopaedia. Soon you will have a backlist too. Special features of this sort of publishing are small editions and printing on demand. The market will mainly be libraries and the newspapers themselves.

If your funds are insufficient to have a complete programme, it is of importance to find partners to share the costs. The search for partners for a certain newspaper must begin long before the microfilming can start. The most probable partners are the newspaper itself, if it is alive, and local and regional libraries. In this case it is natural to share the costs equally between the partners. You certainly will get more from your money if you find several partners as microfilming and intermediates together, in my experience, cost five to six times as much as printing a distribution copy, the work of library personnel not counted.

Also where you have sufficient funds it is helpful to circulate pre-publication lists of the retrospective microfilming about a year before filming. If you get the orders in time you can print all the copies at once, which is cheaper and reduces the handling of the master film. Library journals in your country might accept articles including such lists free of charge. In Sweden we have with some success turned directly to such libraries and newspapers, which in our judgement need film.

You should also prepare complete sales lists or sales catalogues of your master film stock. (See Figure 7). In our case the Swedish government bought all negatives of a former newspaper microfilm publisher, providing us with an extensive backlist just a few years after the newspaper microfilm programme started.

For the international market and the information of libraries in other countries we list our titles in Microforms in print, which is recommended by the IFLA Working Group on Newspapers.

FIGURE 7
Newspaper microfilm sales catalogues from British Library, London, and
Kungliga Biblioteket, Stockholm

9. PREPARATION BEFORE CURRENT MICROFILMING

When you are planning newspaper microfilming it is important not to underestimate the preparation work that has to be done before microfilming, both by library and micrographic personnel. As the preparations for current and retrospective microfilming differ considerably I will treat them one by one.

9.1. Planning microfilming of a certain newspaper

Before current microfilming of a certain newspaper can start there is some initial work to be done. First, the library staff should investigate the publishing pattern of the newspaper, if they are not already aware of it.

How many editions are there? Are they true editions? Which are the signs used to distinguish them from each other? In what order are they printed? Are there regular supplements? Does the newspaper print newsbills (i.e. placards with the most important headlines)?

When this is mapped down it is possible to decide upon the disposition of the film, that is in which order editions, supplements and newsbills should be filmed.

To reduce the number of exposures by edition filming one of the editions has to be appointed main edition. The main edition is the edition that will be completely microfilmed, including all supplements. In principle any edition could be used as the main edition. In practice we often pick out the last printed edition, which usually is in accordance with the publisher's view and vocabulary. The majority of microfilm users, which only read the main edition, will then get the most corrected version of the newspaper.

The microfilm of the other editions will not contain supplements included in the main edition. It is also possible to save more exposures by letting true editions be represented by their changed pages. The changes are then ultimately related to the main edition to ensure that all pages not in the main edition are filmed with the other editions.

The arrangement of the editions must also be made clear. If the editions are geographical you might wish to have them separate for the whole period. If they are mainly chronological it is better to film all editions of one day directly after one another.

In Sweden we microfilm the newsbills in a series separate from the newspapers, as they are not always tied to a certain edition.

Finally it has to be decided if the different series of a newspaper should be on separate rolls or after each other on the same roll. You should also give the periods on the rolls some thought. The disposition of the films is further discussed in section 11.

FIGURE 8
The identification target

9.2. Writing of targets and instructions

When the disposition is ready, the targets of the film have to be written.

The _identification target_ (see Figure 8) is the target which library personnel should be able to read without putting the film into a microfilm reader. A manuscript for the microfilming personnel is formulated containing the identification title, place of publication and symbols for series on the roll (for instance M for the main series, E for the edition series and M+B for a film roll with the main series first and the newsbills at the end of the roll).

Then you write the _bibliographical target_, which gives readers of a newspaper film the necessary information about the publishing pattern and the disposition you have chosen of the films of that particular newspaper. You also write down all other information, which according to your decision should be included in the bibliographical description.

The bibliographical target can also serve as basic instruction for the microfilming personnel on how to film the newspaper in question. In some cases it is necessary to write an extra _filming instruction_, for instance with the text of a dividing target.

Finally you have to make _delivery instructions_ to the newspaper publisher or printer to streamline the delivery of his microfilm copy with the microfilming.

9.3. Running preparation

Up till now, everything described under this heading is initial work, which is done once and for all for each newspaper. In our experience it is not necessary to bother library staff with a thorough preparation of the recurrent deliveries. The newspapers can, after a test period, go directly to the microfilming unit - that is if there is another copy.

Library staff must however also have access to a newspaper original. (In our case it is the 'national copy' which will be preserved for the future.) It is mandatory to check the delivery against the bibliographical target **before** filming. The target is then rewritten if there are changes which affect the description of the newspaper. Actually, many newspapers change several times a year. Word processing technique is recommended to keep the bibliographical targets updated.

The microfilming staff must on the other hand do a thorough preparation of the originals. It is recommended to do this in a special routine before the newspapers are put under the cameras. The preparing person checks that the newspapers are complete for the period and in good condition for photographing. The order of the newspapers is checked against the valid bibliographical target and other instructions. Missing and unusable copies are claimed from the printer or publisher.

Glued and metal-stitched papers are taken apart. Small tears are laid together. Only if the copy will be disposed of after filming can you permit self-adhesive tape. A careful spray of water could be given to the papers before they are put under a light press.

The number of exposures is counted, so you can decide on the period per roll. The targets are prepared and put on their right places together with possible symbols according to the standard. Special instructions to the photographer might be included, like urging him or her to make two exposures to cover uneven text print or a dark picture.

10. PREPARATION BEFORE RETROSPECTIVE MICROFILMING

For retrospective microfilming the first step is the choice of main copy for filming.

When unbound newspapers are available in reasonable condition, they are to be preferred. If there are only bound volumes, many of them must be disbound. If not, text in the inner margins will be lost, even if it is readable in the original and on the exposed camera film. The varying angle of the paper towards the light will cause an uneven exposure and partly unreadable distribution copies. In this case the binding technique used might influence your choice of copy. The less glue and knife used by the binder, the better.

Library personnel then have to prepare for the filming by going through the newspaper from its first to its last issue. The aim is both to find out if something is missing (or in a terrible condition) and to find out how the newspaper was constructed to be able to write the bibliographical target.

Annex 4 shows the form used for this work in Sweden.

When something is missing, the hunt after another copy starts. It will obviously simplify the work if there is a union catalogue of newspaper holdings in your country.

In our experience it is important to be able to look beyond the circle of deposit libraries. If an issue is missing or misprinted (e.g. heavily smeared, exceptionally thinly printed or having unprinted pages), usually the same is the case in all deposit copies. This is understandable as it is practical to take all deposit copies out of the production at the same time and from the same press. If you turn to a library which has got their copy by subscription the chance is much better of finding a readable original.

But when other kinds of faults or damage, created after printing, appear, it is obvious that other deposit libraries might have a better or more complete copy.

While going through the file the personnel should also gather information from other sources necessary to write the bibliographical target. In our case we regularly use about twenty sources, for instance registers of periodicals and joint stock companies in the National Archives of Sweden.

It is not unusual that during these studies you find editions and other closely related newspapers with partly the same text in the same setting.

When the bibliographical target is finished, preparation by microfilming personnel can begin. Their work is mainly the same as for current microfilming, but there are some obvious differences, which make the work more delicate and time consuming.

The brittle condition of newspapers older than thirty years forces the staff to handle the material with utmost care, like avoiding rash movements and even using supporting leaves when necessary.

Bound volumes are taken apart.

Defects with loss of text are much more frequent than with current filming. Claims can of course not be directed to printers and publishers, but to the library staff. It is their task to have knowledge about other copies and contacts with their owners.

If the missing part is found in another copy, we use three different methods. The first is to send the gapfilling volume to the microfilming unit. The second is to microfilm the missing part plus two exposures before and after. The film strip is sent to the microfilming unit, which will develop the strip and splice it into its right place. The third method, used to fill holes, lost corners and other similar small defects, is to send an electrostatic papercopy of the missing area to the microfilming staff, which will put it under the original, making the page complete on the microfilm.

11. DISPOSITION OF THE FILM

The aim of newspaper microfilming is not only to preserve newspapers, but also to give scholars and public better access to them.

The conversion from originals to microfilm in itself gives libraries new possibilities in this respect. But the way newspapers are presented on the film is also important to consider if you want to achieve easy access for users to the often complicated material which is newspapers.

11.1. Disposition of series on rolls

It has already been mentioned that in preparation you have to decide on series and periods on the rolls.

If the microfilm of a newspaper contains other series than the main series, for instance editions or newsbills, it is practical to have them on separate rolls as most users are satisfied with only the main series.

A series consisting of few exposures leads, however, to an extremely long period on the roll (if you are not accepting the bad economy of extremely short rolls). This is not advisable with current microfilming, where time of delivery is of importance. It might then be better to have several series on the roll separated by a division target.

There is also a marketing aspect to this question. If you microfilm the editions and newsbills on separate rolls you will find that there is a larger market for the main series. On a price sensitive market you will sell more of the main edition if it is separate and thereby cheaper. On the other hand you will certainly sell less of the editions. Of course this is also a matter of principle. The one extreme attitude would be that you should adapt yourself totally to the demands of the market (in this case the libraries) and the other that any user should have the right to see the complete newspaper microfilm.

11.2. Periods on rolls

It is not advisable to let the roll space decide the roll division completely. The periods on the rolls must be acceptable from a systematic and bibliographical point of view. That means that you, just as in binding periodicals, normally choose one, two, three, four or six months, one or several entire

years before other periods. Extensive newspapers are microfilmed with half a
month or one third of a month etc. per roll.

For small current newspapers with few exposures you might consider a maximum
period of for instance one year, even if they do not fill half the roll.
Otherwise the users have to wait several years for the film.

11.3. Disposition of the roll

A newspaper microfilm should in my opinion have the following parts. (See
Figure 9). (The following description is in accordance with the Swedish
standard SS 622351. This is not the place to discuss the differences from ISO
4087 which is under revision).

1. The film begins with a leader, minimum 450mm in length.

2. Then comes a picture with the micrographic symbol "Beginning of roll".

3. After that there is an identification target containing title, place of
publication, country, indication of series on the roll and period on the roll,
legible to the naked eye (e.g. to library personnel without a microfilm
reader). It contains also the names of institutions responsible for the
microfilming and the year of filming, which can be given in smaller lettering.

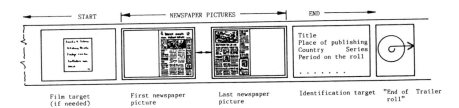

FIGURE 9
Disposition of the roll

4.   Then there is a <u>bibliographical target</u>. It was discussed in the section
on bibliographical work. I strongly recommend that the description of the
newspaper and the description of the newspaper microfilm are kept apart.

5.   Then follows the <u>technical target</u>, which makes it possible to control the
technical quality. It contains the reduction rate used, a metric reference
graduation, an ISO test chart for legibility control, grey surfaces for density and contrast control and registration number of the raw film.

6.   Every film should contain an <u>explanation of</u> the micrographic <u>symbols</u> used
in your newspaper film. The symbols in the standard ISO 4087 are shown in
Figure 10. To this you could add other symbols you find practicable. You
should certainly add the colour symbol mentioned in section 8.3.

Beginning of reel
(ISO 7000, sheet 76)

First symbol of microfilm to
be given as a separate image

Incorrect numbering – incorrect
data (ISO 7000, sheet 79)

To be placed in the margin when
the incorrect figure is given

End of reel
(ISO 7000, sheet 75)

Last symbol of microfilm to
be given as a separate image

Original difficult to read
(ISO 7000, sheet 77)

Due to print through, print
smeared, print faded, etc.
To be placed in the margin
opposite the part difficult
to read

Missing pages and/or issues
(ISO 7000, sheet 81)

Damaged text – wrong binding
(ISO 7000, sheet 78)

Loss of text because of torn
pages or wrong binding. To be
placed in the margin or where
the text is missing.

Repetition of image
(ISO 7000, sheet 80)

In cases where a second
image is taken because
of varying density on
the original this symbol
should be placed at the
bottom of the first page
and at the top of the
second.

FIGURE 10
Symbols applicable to microphotography

7. After that follows in most cases the newspaper pictures.

8. There might be other targets, for instance a film target with information about the specific roll, dividing targets to separate different series on the roll or to separate years or months and annotation targets to remark on something within the film. The symbol "Missing original" could for instance be used as an annotation target to tell that pages or issues are missing.

9. At the end of the film the identification target is repeated. This is good if the roll is wound backwards.

10. Finally there is the symbol "End of roll" and a trailer, minimum 450mm in length.

12. CONTROL

As a newspaper microfilm publisher you are responsible for the quality even if you are buying the actual microfilming from outside. Nobody else can assume the ultimate responsibility.

The level of perfection should be set with preservation in mind. A partly unreadable or incomplete microfilm is certainly a waste of money. (Here I mean incomplete in relation to existing originals.) And so is a scratched camera film or a film where the pictures are fading away. The disposition of the film must also be correct with right targets in right places. Otherwise the users will be misled.

But there are many other faults which might be considered as minor defects or lack of beauty. A film with such faults must not be corrected. The fault should be considered in future production.

Some kind of control system must be included in the microfilming programme. In our experience the internal control made by the microfilming staff or firm is not sufficient. Just as in preparation some of the work has to be done by library personnel.

12.1. Control by microfilming personnel

Microfilming personnel are trained to check that the camera negative meets the standard demands for density and contrast. They also find many other obvious faults and correct them. Beside the negative control they make a rough control of all duplicates.

12.2. Control by library personnel

The "library control" should be done on a duplicate to protect the camera film.

First a legibility control is done by microscope on the test patterns which are part of the technical target. The demands should not only ensure the legibility of the copy itself, but the legibility of several further microfilm generations.

Further control is made in a microfilm reader:

Bibliographical control ascertains that the disposition and the targets of the roll are correct.

Completeness control is done to see that no issues or pages are missing.

Picture control is made to check the quality of the single picture. The original might be damaged or have a fold concealing the text. Thinly printed text might be unreadable on the copy. The leaf might have moved during exposure causing blur. A slight blur is enough to make the text unreadable on a hard-copy on paper although the text is readable on the microfilm. Uneven light on corners or on the curved inner margins of bound volumes causes loss of text. Standard symbols are used wrongly. Deep scratches might occur here and there. Innumerable are the faults which have passed your eyes after having checked some million exposures.

The legibility and bibliographical controls must be done on every microfilm roll. Completeness and picture control can be done frame by frame or by sample while doing the bibliographical control.

In the beginning of a project the control must be very thorough. It is wise to be prepared for a long period of learning and adjustment. I regard two years for a current and a little more for a retrospective newspaper micro-filming project as normal.

12.3.   Control by other institutions

Finally there is the important rinse control, vital to the life length of the archival film. The residual thiosulphate content of the processed camera film must not exceed the limit prescribed in the standard. In Sweden this is checked by a government body specialised in testing, Statens provningsanstalt.

13. CATALOGUING THE FILM

An inevitable consequence of microfilming newspapers is that you have to cat-alogue the films. However, I am going to deal with the cataloguing of news-paper microfilms only briefly since the IFLA Working Group on Newspapers is preparing guidelines for newspaper cataloguing.

The cataloguing has to reflect the publishing pattern, including editions and newsbills, so far that the users are able to order the correct series of rolls. For current microfilming we are preparing an annual catalogue of Swedish newspapers and their microfilms. (See Annex 5).

You should consider using a numerus currens system for the shelving of the film rolls. Thereby the rolls can get their permanent place at once and you must never move them to other shelves just because your collection grows. If you have many newspaper titles and maybe several series within the titles there is much work to save now and in the future by such a system. For a user, ordering becomes somewhat more complicated. On the other hand he will know exactly how many rolls a period comprises and is protected from unrealis-tic ordering and surprising restrictions.

In Sweden every roll carries its individual number on leader and trailer as well as on its container. Four of the five libraries which get all Swedish newspaper films use the system for their storage.

14. CONSEQUENCES FOR LIBRARIES AND USERS

The aim of newspaper microfilming is to preserve the newspapers.

The cessation of the current destruction of newspapers and their contents can therefore be regarded as the main result. It is certainly the main defensive achievement.

But microfilming newspapers is also offensive. It opens new roads for research and librarianship.

14.1. Better access creates demands

Newspaper microfilms are easy to handle, easy to use, easy to get paper copies from and easy to send - in comparison with originals. Another good feature is that they are not originals. So if a microfilm copy vanishes or gets destroyed it is no catastrophe. You just print another one. Even a national library can consider giving the users open access to the microfilm collections.

These advantages of microfilm can only be exploited if you have enough room and usable microfilm readers and reader-printers. Inter-library loans can be fully utilized only if the libraries know the locations. This could for instance be accomplished by preparing a joint catalogue of user copies of newspaper microfilms.

The better access to the material will lead to an increase of users. University teachers will find it more realistic to give students subjects involving newspaper research.

So if the easier handling will reduce the need for staff involved in user service, the swelling number of visitors will increase the need.

There is, however, still a another factor just as important as access and that is knowledge.

14.2. Better knowledge

The preparation and bibliographic work done in connection with microfilming will increase the knowledge of your newspapers, their editions and their connections drastically. This knowledge will not only be found in bibliographical targets and catalogues, but also in the minds of the staff. Together they will constitute a centre of information and their ambitions will rise. Newspaper librarianship is much more than moving newspapers and newspaper microfilms back and forth.

It is important to make use of these resources in the service of scholars and other users. Newspaper users and librarians should be linked together and learn from each other for mutual benefit. The newspaper microfilming project should not be isolated but form the base of a newspaper information centre. It should be supplemented by a reference library, including newspaper indexes, news yearbooks and other date-oriented works, and by access to national and international data bases of newspapers and news agencies to form a true hemerotheque.

Thus the level of information service will be heightened and newspaper research supported and inspired.

DISCUSSION

Q.   John Baker, New York Public Library

Can you tell us where the master negative is stored? Is it stored in Stockholm or is it stored elsewhere? And can you also tell us under whose supervision the control of the master negative rests?

A.   Mr Mannerheim

I think what you are really asking about is our archival film, because we have
both an archival film and a master film; the master film is the one we make
new distribution copies from and there is no hard restriction on that copy.
The archival copy is preserved 60 kilometres from Stockholm. We are preparing
it, though it is not quite ready; there they will be in a climate chamber and
there are two ways to do that. One is to have a climate chamber with a
correct humidity and pure air and low temperature. It should be 10 or 12
degrees centigrade something like that. But we have found in Sweden that it
is very difficult to build such stable climate archives, we have had bad experiences, so we will try another solution which means that we will put the
microfilms in bags from a laminate of different plastics and aluminium. They
should be airtight, and in these bags we will create a micro-climate which
then has the correct humidity and pure air. This enables us to have different
humidity for different kind of film bases which is a good point. Then these
bags will be stored in a climate chamber which has the right stable temperature and where the demands of humidity are lower, so that you will not have
mould; it should be under the mould level so to say, that means it should be
under 50% humidity. There has been developed in Sweden, I do not know if it
is international, a way to control films preserved in this way, by simply
weighing the bags, because if a bag is not airtight, the humidity in the bag
will change and thereby the weight of the bag. So when you are preparing it
you weigh the bags and to check you can weigh them again.

The Royal Library has the responsibility, it is not the National Archives in
this case.

ANNEX 1

EXAMPLE FROM: Lundstedt, B, 'Sveriges periodiska litteratur'. 1-3. Stockholm 1895-1902.

205. **Adressen.** 1775 $^2/_1$—76 $^{31}/_{12}$. Stockholm, J. G. Lange 1775 och A. J. Nordström 1776. Fr. o. Ant.

Utgafs »efter Gjörligheten en eller flere Nummer i Weckan»; 4 s. 4:o, 2-spalt. (16,5×12,7); 18 dlr for 100 nr. Haraf utkommo 1775 nr 1—42 och 1776 nr 43—82.

Litterär tidning utg. af *C. C. Gjörwell*, »som här införde hwad han ej kunde nyttja i sina andra skrifter, såsom sammandrag af tryckta rättegångshandlingar, samt det märkvärdigaste ur wåra provins-tidningar, o. s. v. af oeconomice-politico-historiska ämnen».

206. **Lunds Weckoblad.** 1775 $^5/_1$—82 $^{13}/_{12}$, kallades **Nytt och Gammalt*** 1783 $^9/_1$—1812 $^{29}/_{12}$ och **Lunds Weckoblad Nytt och Gammalt** fr. 1813 $^9/_1$—(fortgår). U. o. o. tr. 1775—89 [= Lund, C. G. Berling]; Berlingska Boktryckeriet 1790—1874 $^{30}/_4$; Fr. Berlings Boktryckeri och Stilgjuteri 1874 $^5/_5$—89 $^{29}/_2$ samt Berlingska Boktryckeri- och Stilgjuteri-aktiebolaget fr. 1889 $^1/_3$. Fr. 1775—1876 $^5/_1$; Fr. o. Ant. 1876 $^8/_1$—$^{30}/_{12}$ samt Ant. fr. 1877.

1 v., O.; T. o. F. 1775 $^5/_1$—77 $^6/_3$, 1786 $^1/_1$—1812 $^{23}/_{12}$, 1813 $^1/_1$—14 $^{29}/_{12}$ och 1846 $^8/_1$—1863 $^{26}/_{12}$; O. 1777 $^{12}/_3$—85 $^{15}/_6$ och 1816 $^9/_1$—45 $^{31}/_{12}$. L. 1813 $^9/_1$—$^{26}/_6$; 2 v., O. (eller T.) o. L. 1815 $^5/_1$—$^{30}/_{12}$,1863 $^9/_{12}$ —64 $^{29}/_6$ och $^{28}/_{12}$—66 $^{29}/_{12}$; Ti. o. F. 1864 $^1/_1$—$^{29}/_{12}$; 3 v., Ti., T. o. L. fr. 1867 $^9/_1$ (fortfarande). 8 s. 8:o (13,6 à 12,7×7,3 à 7,3) fr. specie 1786—92 $^5/_{12}$ och 1793 $^{29}/_1$—1804 $^9/_5$; 1 rdr bko 1804 $^{16}/_5$—1813; 1 rdr 8 sk. bko 1814, 15; 1 rdr 24 sk. bko 1816—24; 1 rdr 32 sk. bko 1825—49; 2 rdr bko 1850—58; 3 rdr rmt 1859— 63; 5 rdr rmt 1864; 6 rdr 1865—76 och 7 kr. (o. p.) fr. o. m. 1877.

Lunds Weckoblad började 1775 utgifvas af ett sällskap, i hvilket akad. bibliotekarien, prof. *Gustaf Sommelius* war hufvudpersonen. I dess 1:a nr (1775 $^5/_1$) meddelas en plan öfver tidningens blifvande innehåll, som skulle bestå af:

»1:o. Allehanda Utländska Nyheter. 2:o. Berättelser om märk-värdiga händelser... här i Skåne och de öfriga Södra Provincierna af Giötha Rike: såsom Giftermål och Dödsfall... likaledes Förslag och Befordringar. icke allenast innom Academien och Stiftet utan

*) Flock 10 (1792, 23) i. o. m. 1809 hafva s.k. titelblad: Lunds Weckoskrift Nytt och Gammalt.
**) 1889 (52) $^{7}/_{12}$) har titeln: Lunds Weckoblad Gammalt och Nytt. N:r 1.

äfven till Civile och andra Publique Ämbeten... 3:o. Korta Recen-sioner af alla här i Lund utkommande Disputationer och Böcker. 4:o. Korta Lefvernesbeskrifningar af Ämbetsmän här i nedre Orterne samt andra minnesvärda Personer. 5:o. Korta Vitterhets- och Skaldestycken. 6:o. Allehanda Kongl. Majtts Befallningshafvandes Publicationer ifrån Södra Orterna, Markegångs Taxor, märkvärdiga Processer och Domar. 7:o. Allehanda Konunga Bref och elljest betydeliga underrättelser eller anecdoter, som ifrån äldre tider kunna bidraga till något ljus i Svänska Historien och Genealogien. 8:o. Korta Oeconomiska Rön och Afhand-lingar särdeles angående Svänska Hushållningen. 9:o. Waror, Saker eller Böcker, som någon åstundar och annaler sig vilja köpa eller sälja, skolande äfven torgprisen, åtminstone en gång i månaden blifva införde.»

I första numret finnes ett poem (undertecknadt B. L.) författadt af *Bengt Lidner*, hvilken ofta sedermera såsom student i Lund läm-nade bidrag i Weckobladets äldsta årgångar. I följd utaf tillaggsnå-budet 1785 $^3/_5$ till förordningen angående skrif- och tryckfriheten, var utgifvandet af »Nytt och Gammalt» inställdt från 1785 $^{15}/_6$ till 1786 $^1/_2$, enär hvilken tid det i nämnda påbud för utgifvande af vecko-skrifter föreskrifna privilegiet lunnit anskaffas af boktryckaren *Carl Gustaf Berling*, hvilken 1785 $^{22}/_8$ beviljades privilegium å utgifvande af Nytt och Gammalt. Till åtrydnad af förordningen angående skrif- och tryckfriheten 1798 $^{26}/_3$ sökte och erhöll Berlings son, direk-tören *Christian Fredrik Berling* privilegium å Nytt och Gammalt, som utfärdades 1798 $^{16}/_{10}$ och hvarutinnan bl. a. det villkoret finnes, »at inga andre utländske nyheter däri uptagas än som uti Post-Tidningen äro införda.»

Burleiner, som af fältboktryckaren *P. Sohm* på befallning trycktes.

Lunds Weckoblad redigerades först af juris professor *Lars Johan Colling* († 1786 $^{10}/_5$). Under de första åren af detta århundrade hade bibliotekarien, prof. *Anders Lidbeck* tillsyn vid redaktionen och vid denna tid sågo flere af *Esaias Tegnérs* vittra tillfällighetsstycken häruti först dagen, likson och poemer af *Eleonora Charlotta D'Albe-dyhll* f. *Wrangel*, vanligen signerad: *Ch. Wr.* Akademie boktryckaren m. m. *Carl Fredrik Berling* erhöll 1809 $^3/_5$ privilegium å fortsatt ut-gifvande af Nytt och Gammalt samt 1828 $^{11}/_{11}$ utgifningsbevis å Lunds Weckoblad, Nytt och Gammalt. Hans son, e. o. ama-nuensen vid universitetsbiblioteket, fil d:r *Fredrik Johan Berling* blef härutinnan 1839 $^{18}/_{12}$ af docenten, sedermera bibliotekarien, fil. d:r *Edvard Wilhelm Berling* och 1867 $^6/_8$ af tidningens n. v. redaktör *Adolf Ferdinand Mathson*, hvilken allt ifrån 1865 $^8/_{12}$ haft dess led-ning sig anförtrodt. Dessförinnan hade tidningen likväl ett par år redigerats af *Otto Kleverström* (1862—64?) och *Jacob Flagerström* (1864?—66 $^8/_{12}$). Akad. boktryckaren F. Berling erhöll 1869 $^{10}/_{12}$ utgif-

ANNEX 2

EXAMPLE OF CURRENT BIBLIOGRAPHICAL TARGET: Expressen

EXPRESSEN(1944)   Kungliga biblioteket
STOCKHOLM   Tidningssektionen
                                   1986 09 25 MW/GS

Beskrivningen gäller fr o m/valid from: 1986 02 01--

Titel/title: EXPRESSEN

Utgivningsmönster/publishing pattern

Utgivningsperiod/period of publication: 1944 11 16--

Frekvens/frequency: daglig/daily

Tryckort/place of printing: [Stockholm]
1 ed: ..... [RN,"riks"]
2 ed: .... [RC]
3 ed: ... [F,"förort"]
4 ed: .. [S1,"innerstaden"]
5 ed: . [S2,"sista innerstaden"] [huvudedition/main edition]

Tryckort/place of printing: [Jönköping]
1 ed: R....
2 ed: R..
3 ed: R.
4 ed: R ["Via"]

Bilagor/supplements: SPORT / EXPRESSEN (må/Mon); SPEL / EXPRESSEN
(ti/Thu); PENGARNA & LIVET / EXPRESSEN (on/Wed) [1985 09 18--];
TV / EXPRESSEN (To/Tue); GUIDEN / EXPRESSEN / STOCKHOLMS NÖJESTIDNING
(fre/Fri) [--1986 02 14]; EXPRESSEN / FREDAG / MED / GUIDEN
[1986 02 21--]

Löpsedlar/news bills: flera per utgivningsdag/several every day of
publication

Anmärkningar/notes

Chefredaktör och ansvarig utgivare/chief editor: Bo Strömstedt

Utgivare/publisher: AB Kvällstidningen Expressen, Stockholm

Tryckeri/printing office: Dagens Nyheters Tryckeri, Stockholm;
Expressens Tryckeri, Jönköping

Editionsmönster/pattern of editions: En del av editionerna trycks
inte alla dagar/some editions are not printed every day

Politisk tendens/political tendency: liberal

Upplaga/circulation: vard 580 309, sönd 688 632, helgd 759 150/
weekdays 580 309, Sun 688 632, holidays 759 150 (TS-upplagan första
halvåret 1986)

Satsyta i tryck/type area in print: 25x38 cm
Färg/colour: svart + 3 färger/black + 3 colours

Mikrofilm/microfilm

Tre rullsviter/three series of reels
H: F
E: RN i sin helhet, ändrade sidor av RC, S1 och S2 samt editionerna 1,
2, 3 och Via/RN complete, altered pages of RC, S1 and S2 and the
editions 1, 2, 3 and Via
L: löpsedlar/news bills

Färgsymbol/colour symbol: symbolen används enbart för flerfärgs-
bilder/the symbol is only used for multi-colour pictures

ANNEX 3

EXAMPLE OF RETROSPECTIVE BIBLIOGRAPHICAL TARGET: Dagen

('Ansvarig utgivare' is the person legally responsible for the contents of the newspaper)

DAGEN(1945)   Kungliga biblioteket
STOCKHOLM   Tidningssektionen
                                87 10 29/ÖH JH IK

Beskrivningen gäller/described period: 1945--1978

Titel/title:
DAGEN [1945 11 01--1957 03 30]
DEN KRISTNA RIKSTIDNINGEN / DAGEN [1957 04 01--1968 10 12]
DAGEN / DEN KRISTNA RIKSTIDNINGEN [1968 10 15--1978 12 31]

Utgivningsmönster/publishing pattern

Utgivningsperiod/period of publication: 1945 11 01--fortgår 1987/
continues 1987

Provnummer/specimen issue: 1945 10 01

Frekvens/frequency:
6 i veckan/6 days a week [1945 11 01--1965 06 30]
ti,on,to,fre,lö/Tue,Wed,Thu,Fri,Sat [1965 07 01--1978 07 01]

Periodiska bilagor/periodical supplements: -

Löpsedlar/news bills: normalt 1 per publiceringsdag/normally 1 every
day of publication

Editionsmönster/pattern of editions: editioner med och utan * utgavs
1946 04 01--06 29. 1963--1968 förekommer 1- och 2-stjärniga editioner
På 1960- och 1970-talen förekommer editioner riktade till särskilda
församlingar eller orter, så kallade ortsnummer/editions with and
without * were published 1946 04 01--06 29. During 1963--1968
editions with one and two stars appeared. From 1960 many so called
"local issues" were published for distribution to various parishes
and towns.

Anmärkningar/notes

Provnummer/specimen issue: ett provnummer utkom 1945 10 01
(källa: Sahlberg 1977, sid. 104). Det har ej återfunnits/a specimen
issue was published 1945 10 01. It has not been found.

Redaktör/editor:
1945 11 01 Petrus Lewi Pethrus
1947 01 02 Samuel Teofil [Jack] Hårdstedt
1947 05 02 Lewi Pethrus
1952 01 02 Christer Pierre Backman
1957 08 01 Lewi Pethrus
1974 09 05 Olof Petrus Djurfeldt

Ansvarig utgivare, registreringsdatum:
(för ställföreträdande ansvarig utgivare anges tidsperioden)
1945 07 18 Lewi Pethrus
1946 12 31 Jack Hårdstedt
1947 05 07 Lewi Pethrus
1948 06 21--10 01 Karl Gustav Natanael Ottosson, ställföreträdande
1960 02 18--04 02 Nils Gustav Andersson, ställföreträdande
1967 11 01--1968 05 01 Olof Djurfeldt och Nils Sven Ferdinand
                    Forsberg, ställföreträdande
1970 03 01--05 31 Sverre Larsson, ställföreträdande
1970 11 01--1971 04 30 Olof Djurfeldt, ställföreträdande
1972 01 13--04 30   "   "   "
1973 11 29--1974 02 28 "   "   "
1974 10 25 Per Östlin
(samtliga uppgifter från Patent- och registreringsverket, Periodiska
skrifter)
1977 02 25--11 19 Olof Djurfeldt, ställföreträdande (tidningen)

Utgivare/publisher:
1945 11 01 Tidnings AB Dagen, Stockholm
[i mars 1961 övertog enskilda pingstförsamlingar aktiemajoriteten
i Tidnings AB Dagen från Karl G. Ottoson]

Tryckeri/printing office:
1945 11 01 Klara civiltryckeri AB, Stockholm
1946 04 01 Evangelipress, Örebro
1947 10 23 AB Godvils tryckeri (Evangelipress tryckte samma dag sitt
           sista nummer/the same day Evangelipress printed their last
           issue)
1968 10 15 Tryckcentralen, Örebro
(uppgifterna hämtade ur tidningen)

Editionsmönster/pattern of editions: under andra kvartalet 1946 utkom
två editioner. I editionen utan * har ändrat material befunnits ligga
senare i tiden och lokalt närmare tryckorten, varför den bedöms som
huvudedition. Under april sker ändringar på första och sista sidan,
därefter enligt ett mer oklart mönster. Editionerna 1963--1968
uppvisar mycket små skillnader och det inbördes förhållandet har ej
kunnat fastställas. Enligt en muntlig uppgift från tidningen rörande
1966--1968 betecknar * Stocholmseditionen och ** landsorts-
editionen/1946 04 01--06 29 two editions were published. The edition
without * seems to be the latest printed one and is filmed as the
main edition. The editions 1963--1968 differ only slightly and their
mutual relationship is unknown.

Politisk tendens/political tendency:
opolitisk (TS-boken)
[för en utförlig redogörelse om tidningens politiska inriktning,
se: Sahlberg, C-E: Pingströrelsen och tidningen Dagen. -
Uppsala, 1977]

Upplaga/circulation:

13 600 [1947]	25 900 [1965]
11 100 [1948]	23 400 [1970]
13 000 [1950]	27 400 [1975]
23 800 [1955]	24 600 [1978]
25 700 [1960]	

(Samtliga uppgifter hämtade ur TS-boken)

Satsyta i tryck/type area in print:
50x35 cm [1945]
41x27 cm - 52x36 cm [1946--1947]
51-52x35 cm [1948--1968 10 12]
38-39x25 cm [1968 10 15--1978]

Färg/colour:
svart/black [1945 11 01--1947 02 12]
svart + 1 färg/black + 1 colour [1947 02 13--10 23]
svart/black [1947 10 23--1949 12 15]
svart + 1 färg/black + 1 colour [1949 12 16--1968 10 12]
svart + 1-3 färger/black + 1-3 colours [1968 10 15--1978 12 31]

Litteratur/literature:
Dagen jubileumsnummer: 1955 11 01, 1960 11 01, 1965 10 30,
   1970 10 29, 1975 10 31, 1980 11 01, 1985 11 01.
Larsson, Sverre: I går, i dag, i morgon. - Stockholm, 1980
Sahlberg, C.-E.: Om Herren inte bygger huset... - Stockholm, 1985
Sahlberg, C.-E.: Pingströrelsen och tidningen Dagen. - Uppsala, 1977

Mikrofilm/microfilm

Två rullsviter/two series of rolls:
H: huvudedition/main edition
E: edition med */edition with *
L: löpsedlar/news bills

Editioner/editions: på E-rulle ligger edition med * 1946 04 01-
-06 29; 1946 04 01--04 30 har första och sista sidan filmats,
1946 05 02--06 29 varje sida. I övrigt har ändrade sidor filmats i
anslutning till det ordinarie numret/the edition with *
1946 04 01--06 29 is filmed on the E-roll. 1946 04 01--04 30 the
first and last pages are filmed, and 1946 05 02--06 29 every page is
filmed. Except for that period, altered pages have been filmed in
connection with the regular issue.

Provnummer/specimen issue: provnumret har inte kunnat återfinnas/the
specimen issue has not been found

Löpsedlar/news bills: löpsedlar för nedanstående perioder har
filmats. Övriga har inte kunnat återfinnas/news bills for the periods
below have been filmed. Others have not been found

1945 nov-dec	1964 (ofullständigt/incomplete)
1950 (2 st)	1965--1967
sep 1952-dec 1954	1968 jul-dec
mar 1955-dec 1957	1969 (4 st)
1958 (ofullständigt/incomplete)	1971--1972
1959--1961	1973 apr-dec

Färgsymbol/colour symbol: Fram till 1968 10 12 används symbolen
närhelst färg förekommer, därefter endast för flerfärgsbilder/Up to
1968 10 12 the symbol is used for any appearance of colour. After
that it is used only for multi-colour pictures

Förlaga/copy: Uppsala universitetsbiblioteks ex., kompl med Kungliga
bibliotekets m. fl. Löpsedlarna tillhör Riksarkivet [1945--1958] och
Tidningen Dagen AB [1959--1973]/Uppsala University Library copy,
supplemented by the Royal Library copy and others. The news bills
belong to Riksarkivet [1945--1958] and Tidningen Dagen AB
[1959--1973]

ANNEX 4

EXAMPLE OF 'BIBLIOGRAPHIC' PREPARATION FORM FOR RETROSPECTIVE MICROFILMING

Titel: *(title)*	DAGEN

Artal: *(period)*	1947 10 01 -- 12 31 226(579) - 302(655)

Frekvens:	6/week
Huvudredaktör:	Lewi Pethrus *(editor)*
Ansv. utg.:	— '' — *(legally responsible)*
Utgivare:	
Tryckeri: *(printing office)*	⟨Evangeliipress, Örebro [1947 1001--1023]⟩ ⟨AB Godvils tryckeri, Sthlm [1947 1023-- 12 31]⟩
Upplaga:	
Satsyta: *(type area)* *(in print)*	41x27 cm [1001--1023] 51x36, 51x35 [1023 -- 1231]
Färg: *(colour)*	black + 1 colour (OBS! No colour after change of printing office)
Sid/nr: *(pages/issue)*	8-12 (9)

245	1947 10 23	2 issues nr 245(598) published. (One in format 41x27, 12 pages, pr. in Örebro, one 51x36, 16 pages, pr. in Stockholm) Microfilm according to special note !!
257	1106	misprinted 527
259	1108	- '' — 529
266	1117	- '' — 566
267	1118	- '' — 567
268	1119	Number missing
295	1220	Supplement: DAGENS JULLÄSNING 1947 (8 pages)

ANNEX 5

EXAMPLE FROM Arskatalog for mikrofilm, TK, THE ANNUAL CATALOGUE OF SWEDISH
NEWSPAPERS AND THEIR MICROFILMS

E X P R E S S E N, Stockholm

Sviter: H
E
L

Tryckort Stockholm: Fem ed märkta ` ` ` ` ` - `. [` huvudedition]
Tryckort Jönköping: Fyra ed märkta R` ` ` ` -R.

En del editioner trycks ej varje dag.

H: ` ` ` [F, "förort"]
E: övriga editioner
L: löpsedlar

Svit	Period	Beställnings-nummer	Svit	Period	Beställnings-nummer
H	2-15 jan	MF84/TK 29	E	jan	MF84/TK 42
H	16-31 jan	MF84/TK 30	E	1-15 feb	MF84/TK 43
H	1-15 feb	MF84/TK 31	E	16-29 feb	MF84/TK 44
H	16-29 feb	MF84/TK 32	E	1-15 mar	MF84/TK 277
H	1-15 mar	MF84/TK 165	E	16-31 mar	MF84/TK 278
H	16-31 mar	MF84/TK 166	E	1-15 apr	MF84/TK 343
H	1-15 apr	MF84/TK 167	E	16-30 apr	MF84/TK 344
H	16-30 apr	MF84/TK 168	E	2-15 maj	MF84/TK 431
H	2-15 maj	MF84/TK 383	E	16-31 maj	MF84/TK 432
H	16-31 maj	MF84/TK 384	E	jun	MF84/TK 433
H	1-15 jun	MF84/TK 385	E	jul	MF84/TK 434
H	16-30 jun	MF84/TK 386	E	1-15 aug	MF84/TK 800
H	1-15 jul	MF84/TK 759	E	16-31 aug	MF84/TK 801
H	16-31 jul	MF84/TK 760	E	1-15 sep	MF84/TK 802
H	1-15 aug	MF84/TK 761	E	16-30 sep	MF84/TK 803
H	16-31 aug	MF84/TK 762	E	1-15 okt	MF84/TK 1042
H	1-15 sep	MF84/TK 881	E	16-31 okt	MF84/TK 1043
H	16-30 sep	MF84/TK 882	E	1-15 nov	MF84/TK 1200
H	1-15 okt	MF84/TK 883	E	16-30 nov	MF84/TK 1201
H	16-31 okt	MF84/TK 884	E	1-15 dec	MF84/TK 1202
H	1-15 nov	MF84/TK 1196	E	16-31 dec	MF84/TK 1203
H	16-30 nov	MF84/TK 1197			
H	1-15 dec	MF84/TK 1198	L	jan-jun	MF84/TK 731
H	16-31 dec	MF84/TK 1199	L	jul-dec	MF84/TK 1368

ANNEX 6

EXCERPT FROM AN ENGLISH TRANSLATION OF THE SWEDISH STANDARD SS 622351: 'Micro-filming of newspapers on 35mm unperforated microfilm.' (Swedish proposal 10-15-1984   ISO/TC 171) (Pages 4-12)

8. Arrangement of the newspapers

8.1 Newspapers shall be photographed in chronological order. The divisions between rolls shall be done in a systematic and bibliographically acceptable way. The rolls shall always comprise full units of time (days, months or years) and the roll period shall divide into the next larger unit.

Normally the following periods are used: a third, half or whole month, two, three, four or six months, one year or several years.

Examples of unacceptable roll divisions:

January 1 - February 15
1956-01-01--1957-03-15 (unless publication ceases on this date)

Examples of acceptable roll divisions:

March 1 - 15
January 1 - February 28
1956-01-01--1956-12-31

8.2 Newspapers shall normally be filmed in full including all sections and supplements. In case the newspaper has editions the principal edition shall be filmed in full including all sections and supplements.

Numbered or lettered sections shall be filmed in numerical or alphabetical order followed by unnumbered sections and supplements of different kinds. However, spurious supplement pages, printed with the newspaper itself, are filmed at their original place.

The other editions should preferably be filmed in one or several chronological series. They might also be filmed each day directly after the principal edition. The editions do not need to be filmed in full as they are often best represented by those pages which have been changed compared to other editions.

Placards shall preferably be filmed in a chronological series of their own. They might also be filmed directly before the principal edition each day.

8.3 Newspapers shall be filmed in proper sequence, even if they have been mislabelled or arranged or bound with pages, sections or issues out of sequence. If they are filmed out of sequence for bibliographic or practical reasons, this has to be mentioned in a film target or an annotation target, possibly with a graphic symbol according to SS 62 23 53.

9   Film targets

9.1 Design of targets

9.1.1 A system which allows changes and repeated use is recommended. The contrast between the letters and the background should be at least 0,7.

9.1.2 The parts of the text which are to be legible to the naked eye shall comply with the following requirements:

- clear lettering, for example block lettering
- minimum letter height on the film: 2mm

9.1.3 The language of the targets shall be the language of the newspaper to be microfilmed and one of the ISO official languages i.e. English, French or Russian.

9.1.4 Calendar dates and periods shall be given in accordance with SS 01 02 11.

9.2 Sequence and contents of targets (see figure 2)

9.2.1 "Beginning of roll" symbol (according to SS 62 23 53).

9.2.2 Identification target

The identification target shall contain the following information:

9.2.2.1 Title of the newspaper - legible to the naked eye

This identification title might be shortened and typographically standardized, i.e. hyphens and points are omitted. If needed it is transliterated according to ISO-standards. If required, the first year of publication can be given within brackets directly after the title.

9.2.2.2 Language of the newspaper (optional) - legible to the naked eye

9.2.2.3 Place of publication - legible to the naked eye. If required, the country is added in full or abbreviated according to SS 01 51 10.

9.2.2.4 Series on the roll (if needed) - legible to the naked eye.
The series of editions is indicated by an "E", placards by a "L" and the main edition with an "H".

9.2.2.5 Period on the roll - legible to the naked eye.

9.2.2.6 Name of body responsible for microfilming

9.2.2.7 Year of microfilming.

9.2.2.8 Copyright restrictions (if needed).

9.2.2.9 Roll number (if needed) - legible to the naked eye.

If the data contained in 9.2.2.6 - 9.2.2.9 are too extensive, they can be put on one or more targets close to the identification target.

9.2.3 **Bibliographical target** - not legible to the naked eye

The bibliographical target shall contain the following information, or part of it:

9.2.3.1 Identification

- identification title, including the first year of issue in round brackets
- place of publication
- described period

9.2.3.2 Bibliographical description

- complete title
- title variations (if needed with indication of period)
- complete edition titles
- colophon, i.e. a recording of the imprint

9.2.3.3 Publishing pattern

- period
- frequency
- pattern of editions
- supplements
- placards

9.2.3.4 Annotations

- notes on 9.2.3.2 and 9.2.3.3
- publisher
- printing office
- main editorial office (in case it differs from the place of publication)
- composing office (in case it differs from the printing office)
- editors
- political tendency
- circulation
- type area in print
- colour
- predecessors and successors

9.2.3.5 The microfilming

- division in series and contents of the series
- original (filmed newspaper copy)
- notes concerning the microfilming

Further information can be added if needed.

9.2.4 Technical target

The technical target makes it possible to check that the technical quality fulfils Swedish standard. This target shall contain:

- the reduction ratio used
- a metric reference scale
- ISO test chart No. 1 or No. 2
- grey plates, one with 50% and one with 6% reflection
- SP-number (the registration number of the raw film, given by Swedish National Testing Institute).

9.2.5 List of symbols and their meaning

This target shall contain the relevant symbols from SS 62 23 53. The meaning shall be given in the language of the newspaper and in one of the ISO official languages, i.e. English, French or Russian.

The symbols are used in the film to inform about the filming and about deviations and deficiencies in the original.

9.2.6 Additional targets

Further targets may be used to inform or to ease the use of the microfilm:

9.2.6.1 Film target — not legible to the naked eye

A film target indicates something that only concerns the film in question, for example missing sections, extensive numbering erros, bad quality of the original or accidental deviations in the publishing pattern. The film target is located after the target with symbols.

9.2.6.2 Dividing target — legible to the naked eye

Dividing targets are used to subdivide the contents of the roll, for example in series, years, months or weeks.

9.2.6.3 Annotation target — not legible to the naked eye

Annotation targets are used to make a note within the film at the relevant place. The symbol "missing pages and/or issues" (see SS 62 23 53) for example is used as annotation target to show that some pages or newspaper issues are missing.

9.2.7 The end of the roll

The identification target shall be repeated. If needed, further targets may be repeated and, in this case, in reverse order from the order at the beginning of the film.

9.2.8 "End of roll" symbol (according to SS 62 23 53)

10 Processing the exposed film

Exposed film must be processed to give an essentially black image in conformity with density requirements specified in SS 03 51 22 (=ISO 6200). The residual thiosulphate content of the processed film, as determined by ISO 417, shall be less than 0,7 ug/cm^2.

11 Quality

11.1 Legibility

The legibility of a microfilm is examined with the test chart contained in the technical target according to ISO 446 or ISO 3334. The legibility shall at least reach the values given in table 1.

11.2 Optical density and contrast

The film image shall have sufficient contrast to permit easy reading and reproduction, in accordance with SS 03 51 22. Unless a different background density is required to produce such contrast, the background density of the camera negative as measured by a densitometer shall fall within the range 0,9 to 1.4. The variation within an image shall not exceed 0,2 when the original has the same reflectance overall.

If the variation exceeds 0,2 due to stains or other causes of differential reflectance in the paper, the page shall be photographed twice, at different exposures on successive frames, so that the density requirement shall be satisfied for all text on either one frame or the other.

12 Correcting the processed camera negative

12.1 Pages improperly filmed shall be refilmed, along with enough pages before and after each instance to allow space for splices to eliminate the possibility of defacing the images. The remade film shall be inspected and then spliced into the negative, thus replacing the faulty film.

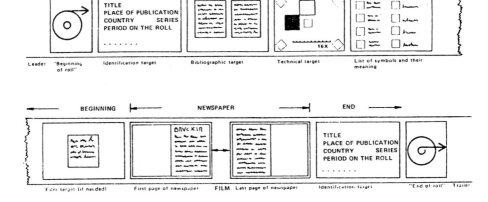

Notes

This standard differs from the International Standard ISO 4087-1979 at the
following points:

7.1 All films shall have leader and trailer. In the ISO-standard this is
outspoken only for distribution copies. In order to facilitate chemical
checking the leaders and trailers of the camera negative shall be unexposed.

8.2 The arrangement, when editions and placards are filmed, is also dealt
with.

9.2 This part, which deals with the sequence and contents of targets, has
been extensively revised.

11.2 The interval of background density is 1,0-1,4 in the ISO standard. This
has been somewhat widened considering the strongly yellowed paper and low
contrasts, which exist among the originals. On the other hand the maximal
variation within an image has been restricted to 0,2 to avoid loss of text
when the original is uneven. The ISO standard allows 0,4.

Nonessential and editorial differences have not been noted.

- division in series and contents of the series
- original (filmed newspaper copy)
- notes concerning the microfilming

Further information can be added if needed.

(This excerpt has been printed with the permission of
Standardiseringskommissionen i Sverige [SIS] Standardiseringsgrupp)

WORKSHOPS

Workshop (ii)

INTERNATIONAL GUIDELINES FOR THE CATALOGUING OF NEWSPAPERS
Draft for Comment

Prepared for the Working Group on Newspapers
by
Hana Komorous with the assistance of Robert Harriman

June 1987

FOREWORD

This draft document was prepared for the IFLA Section on Serial Publications
Working Group on Newspapers following discussions at its meeting in October
1986 in London. The text represents the Working Group's review of the draft
text prepared by Hana Komorous and subsequent comments on the resulting draft
received from members of the IFLA Section on Serial Publications.

The following participated in the work of the Group:

Helmut Bergmann	Universitätsbibliothek-Wien
Ian P Gibb	British Library, London
Robert Harriman	Library of Congress, Washington, D.C.
Willi Hoefig	Staatsbibliothek, Berlin
Eve Johansson	Newspaper Library,
	British Library, London
Hana Komorous	University of Victoria, Victoria
	British Columbia
Johan Mannerheim	Kungliga Bibliotheket, Stockholm
Françoise Perraud	Bibliothèque Nationale, Paris
Wilbert Ubbens	Staats-und Universitätsbibliothek,
	Bremen

The document is being circulated to the members of the Section of Serial
Publications with the intention that it be approved as a provisional document
which will be distributed at the International Symposium on Newspaper
Preservation and Access to be held on August 12-15, 1987 in London.

TABLE OF CONTENTS

1. INTRODUCTORY NOTES

1.1. Scope

These Guidelines specify requirements for item identification, bibliographic description, and location information needed for creation and exchange of newspaper records.

A separate set of data elements is defined for manual and for machine-readable records. Both sets include data needed for the description of newspapers in original and in non-print form.

The Guidelines are intended to identify cataloguing and holdings data necessary for the creation of newspaper records which would fully satisfy needs relating to access and accuracy of description, and which could be used worldwide.

This document does not provide rules and instructions for the creation of newspaper cataloguing records or for coding of UNIMARC records. The original standards from which these Guidelines were developed should be consulted as appropriate.

1.2. Purpose

The purpose of these Guidelines is:

1. To define a set of data elements required for item identification and bibliographic description of newspapers which would facilitate compatible newspaper cataloguing worldwide.

2. To define data elements required for identification of agencies holding newspapers in their collections.

3. To facilitate international exchange of newspaper records in manual and machine-readable form.

1.3. Use

It is anticipated that these Guidelines will be used for:

1. Current and restrospective cataloguing of newspaper collections.

2. Compiling union lists of newspapers.

3. Input of newspaper records into automated data base facilities.

4. International exchange of newspaper bibliographic records.

5. Compiling newspaper bibliographies and specialized listings.

1.4. Definition

The International Organization for Standardization (ISO) defines a newspaper as follows:

'Newspaper: serial publication which contains news on current events of special or general interest. The individual parts are listed chronologically or numerically and appear usually at least once a week.

Note - newspapers usually appear without a cover, with a masthead, are normally larger than A3 (297mm x 420mm) in size.'

It is recognized that within different national contexts there may be variations to this definition, for example special newspapers may be excluded.

1.5. Standards

The set of newspaper data elements for manual records presented in these Guidelines is based on the International Standard Bibliographic Description for Serials (ISBD(S)) [1].

The set of newspaper data elements for machine-readable records is based on UNIMARC [2].

2. CATALOGUING CRITERIA

As the primary purpose of these Guidelines is to define a set of data elements required for the creation of newspaper cataloguing records, specific cataloguing rules and their interpretation are not given. The user should consult ISBD(S) and the appropriate cataloguing code.

However, in order to achieve maximum compatibility of newspaper cataloguing records, the following criteria are recommended for the creation of separate bibliographic records:

1. Editions.
   Separate entries should be made for the following types of editions:
   - Geographic editions;
   - Language editions;
   - Special format editions (e.g., large print, airmail, etc.);
   - Different frequency editions.
   - Various daily editions.

3. Supplements.
   Separate entries should be made only for supplements that are published separately.

4. Microform reproductions.
   Separate entries may be created for newspapers reproduced in microform.

3. LOCATION INFORMATION

For the purposes of these Guidelines, location information should consist of identification of the appropriate national union list (preferably), national library, national bibliography or the information organization or institution where local holdings and location information relating to the item described is maintained.

This location information should consist of the name of the national union list or information organization in coded form when possible. Otherwise, the full name of the union list or organization may be used.

Location information should be provided with the bibliographic description reflecting each appropriate edition and each appropriate format (e.g., newsprint original, microfilm, microfiche) held. If this is unknown, the location information should be provided only with the bibliographic description reflecting the original newsprint format.

4. NEWSPAPER DATA ELEMENTS - MANUAL RECORDS

Codes: M = Mandatory, MA = Mandatory if applicable or available, O = Optional

Description		Req. code
Area 1	Title proper	M
	Parallel title(s)	MA
	Other title information	
	(in specific cases)	O
Area 2	Edition statement	MA
Area 3	Numeric and chronological designations	MA
Area 4	Place of publication	M
	Publisher	MA
Area 5	Extent	O
	Dimensions	O
Area 7	Notes:	
	General note	O
	Frequency	O
	Variant title	O
	Language	MA
	Linking notes*	MA
	Edition note	O
	Reproduction note	O
	No more published note	MA
	Publication details (may include notes on	
	proof numbers, placards, place of	
	publication, publisher and printer)	O
	Geographic coverage	MA
	Item described	O
	Index availability	O
Area 8	ISSN	MA
	Key title	O
Area 9	Location data	MA

*(Linking notes may include: continuations, absorptions, mergers, splits, other editions, translations and changes back to original title.)

5. NEWSPAPER DATA ELEMENTS - UNIMARC RECORDS

As the primary purpose of these Guidelines is to define the set of data elements needed to describe newspapers, UNIMARC data for the Record Label and the Directory are not specified.

Codes: M = Mandatory, MA = Mandatory if applicable, O = Optional
Abbreviations: REP = Repeatable, NR = Not repeatable

0 - IDENTIFICATION BLOCK

Field	Ind. 1	Ind. 2	Data Req.	Sub. Ident.	Subfield	Comment
001 Record Identifier			M		Record Identifier	NR
011 ISSN	ƀ	ƀ	MA		ISSN	REP
				$a	Number	NR
				$z	Erroneous no.	REP

100 - GENERAL PROCESSING DATA

100 General Processing Data			M			NR
	ƀ	ƀ				
1. Date Entered on File			M			Char. pos. 0-7
2. Type of Publication						8
					a - curr. published	
					b - no longer published	
					c - unknown status	
3. Publication Date 1						9-12
4. Publication Date 2						13-16
7. Modif. rec. code			M			21
					0 - unmod. record	
					1 - mod. record	
8. Lang. of Cat.			M		(codes)	22-24
10. Character Set			M			26-29
					01 = ISO 646(IRV)	
					02 = GOST 13052-67	
					03 = ISO ext. Latin	
					04 = ISO ext. Cyrillic	
					05 = ISO Greek	
101 Language of the item			M			NR
	0				Item is in the orig.	
	1				Item is a transl.	
	2				Item contains transl.	
		ƀ				
				$a	Language of text	REP
				$g	Language of title proper	NR
102 Country of publication			M			NR
	ƀ	ƀ				
				$a	Country of publication	REP
				$b	Locality of publication	REP
110 Coded data field: Serials			O			NR
	ƀ	ƀ				
1. Type of serial designator					Char. position	0
2. Frequency of issue						1
3. Regularity						2
111 Coded data field: Serials-physical attributes						
	ƀ	ƀ	O			NR
				$a	Serials-phys. attr.	REP

Char. pos.0: Phys. medium designator
Char. pos.1: Form of reproduction code

Field	Ind. 1	Ind. 2	Data Req.	Sub. Ident.	Subfield	Comment
2 - DESCRIPTIVE INFORMATION BLOCK						
200 Title/statement of responsibility			M			NR
	1				Title is significant	
		ƀ				
				$a	Title proper	NR
				$d	Parallel title	REP
				$e	Other title info.	REP
205 Edition statement	ƀ	ƀ	MA			REP
				$a	Edition	REP
207 Material specific area: serials-numbering			MA			NR
	ƀ					
		0			Formatted	
		1			Not formatted	
				$a	Dates/vol. designations	NR
				$z	Source of numb. info.	NR
210 Publication, distribution, etc.	ƀ	ƀ	M			NR
				$a	Place of publication	REP
				$c	Name of publisher	REP
						NR
215 Physical description	ƀ	ƀ	O			REP
				$a	Extent of item	NR
				$c	Other physical details	NR
				$d	Dimensions	NR
3 - NOTES BLOCK						
300 General note	ƀ	ƀ	O			REP
				$a	Text of note	NR

This field should contain notes on any aspect of the newspaper bibliographic record or a related record which do not fit any category in the Linking Entry Block.

Field	Ind. 1	Ind. 2	Data Req.	Sub. Ident.	Subfield	Comment
321 Availability of indexes	ƀ	ƀ	O			REP
				$a	Text of note	NR
326 Frequency statement note	ƀ	ƀ	O			REP
				$a	Frequency	NR
				$b	Dates of frequency	NR

4 - LINKING ENTRY BLOCK

Ind. 1 = ƀ
Ind. 2 = 0 Do not print a note
        1 Print a note
Data requirement: MA

Fields are repeatable. Structure of 4XX fields is described on p.60, UNIMARC, 2d.ed.

Fields to be included:

430 Continues
431 Continues in part
434 Absorbed
435 Absorbed in part
436 Formed by merger of... and...
440 Continued by
441 Continued in part by
444 Absorbed by
445 Absorbed in part by
446 Split into ... and ...
447 Merged with ...and...
448 Changed back to ...
451 Other ed. in same medium
452 Other ed. in another medium
453 Translated as
454 Translation of

Field	Ind. 1	Ind. 2	Data Req.	Sub. Ident.	Subfield	Comment
510 Parallel title proper			0			REP
	0				Title is not significant	
	1				Title is significant	
		ƀ				
				$a	Title	NR
				$e	Other title info.	REP
				$j	Vol. or dates	NR
				$n	Miscell. info.	NR
515 Running title			0			REP
	0				Title is not significant	
	1				Title is significant	
		ƀ				
				$a	Title	NR
				$j	Vol. or dates	NR
				$n	Miscell. info.	NR
517 Other variant titles			0			REP
	0				Title is not significant	
	1				Title is significant	
		ƀ				
				$a	Title	NR
				$e	Other title info.	REP
				$j	Vol. or dates	NR
				$n	Miscell info.	NR

Field	Ind. 1	Ind. 2	Data Req.	Sub. Ident.	Subfield	Comment
520 Former title			MA			REP
	0				Title is not significant	
	1				Title is significant	
		ƀ				
				$a	Former title proper	NR
				$e	Other title info.	REP
				$n	Misc. info.	NR
				$j	Vol. or dates	NR
				$x	ISSN	NR
530 Key-title			0			REP
	0				Key title is same as title proper	
	1				Key title differs from title proper	
		ƀ				
				$a	Key title	NR
				$b	Qualifier	NR

7 - INTELLECTUAL RESPONSIBILITY BLOCK

Field	Ind. 1	Ind. 2	Data Req.	Sub. Ident.	Subfield	Comment
701 Personal name - alternative intellectual responsibility			0			REP
	ƀ					
		0			Name entered under forename	
		1			Name entered under surname	
				$a	Entry element	NR
				$b	Part of name other than entry	NR
				$c	Addition to name	REP
				$f	Dates	NR
711 Corporate name - alternative intellectual responsibility			0			REP
	0				Corporate name	
	1				Meeting	
		0			Name in inverted form	
		1			Name entered under place or jurisd.	
		2			Name entered under name in direct order	
				$a	Entry element	NR
				$b	Subdivision	REP
				$c	Addition to name or qualifier	NR

8 - INTERNATIONAL USE BLOCK

Field	Ind. 1	Ind. 2	Data Req.	Sub. Ident.	Subfield	Comment
801 Originating source	ƀ		M			REP
				0	Original cat. agency	
				1	Transcribing agency	
				2	Modifying agency	
				3	Issuing agency	
				$a	Country	NR
				$b	Agency	NR
				$c	Date of transaction	REP
805 Holdings data field	ƀ	ƀ	MA			REP
				$a	Reporting agency	REP
				$d	Inclusive dates	NR

MANUAL CATALOGUE RECORDS

1. Newsprint

The Houston Chronicle. -- Vol. 1, no. 1 (Oct. 14, 1901)- .
-- Houston, Tex. : [Houston Chronicle Pub. Co.], 1901- .
-- v. : ill. ; 58 cm.

Daily.
ISSN 1234-567X = The Houston chronicle.
USNP sn84-31354.

The Sun. -- Vol. 96, no. 135 (Apr. 11, 1983)- . -- Vancouver,
B.C.: Pacific Press, 1983- . -- v. : ill. ; 60 cm.
Daily.
Continues: Vancouver sun.
ISSN 0828-1793 = Sun (Vancouver)
(CaBVIUCN)1434.

2. Microform

Chicago tribune [microform]. -- 116th year, no. 48 (Feb. 17, 1963)-
   .-- Chicago, Ill. : Chicago Tribune Co., 1963- . -- v. :
ill. ; 59 cm.

Daily.
Continues: Chicago daily tribune.
Microfilm. Ann Arbor, Mich.: University Microfilms International.
   microfilm reels; 35 mm.
ISSN 3456-789X = Chicago daily tribune.
OCLC 7960181.

Victoria daily times [microform]. -- Vol. 1, no. 1 (June 9, 1884)-
v. 88, no. 126 (Nov. 6, 1971). -- Victoria, B.C.: The Times Publishing Co.,
1884-1971. -- 96 v. : ill. ; 60 cm.

Daily.
Continued by: Victoria times.
Microfilm. Calgary, Alta.: Commonwealth Microfilm Library.
496 microfilm reels; 35 mm.
(CaBVIUCN)1151.

UNIMARC EXAMPLES

1. Newsprint

001		sn84-31354
011		$a1234-567X
100	ƀƀ	$a1987010119019999ƀƀƀ0engy0103ƀƀƀb
101	0ƀ	$aeng
102	ƀƀ	aUSbtx
110	ƀƀ	$acda
111	ƀƀ	$aey
200	1ƀ	$aThe Houston chronicle
207	ƀ0	$aVol. 1, no. 1 (Oct. 14, 1901)-
210	ƀƀ	$aHouston, Tex.$c[Houston Chronicle Pub. Co.]$dOct. 14, 1901-
215	ƀƀ	$av.$cill.$d58 cm
326	ƀƀ	$aDaily
530	0ƀ	$aThe Houston chronicle
801	ƀ0	aUSbDLC$c19750907
805	ƀƀ	$aOCoLC

2. Microfilm

001		7960181
011		$a3456-789X
100	ƀƀ	$a1987010119639999ƀƀƀ0engy0103ƀƀƀb
101	ƀƀ	$a eng
102	ƀƀ	aUSbil
110	ƀƀ	$acda
111	ƀƀ	$aey
200	1ƀ	$aChicago tribune
204	ƀƀ	$amicroform
207	ƀ0	$a116th year, no. 48 (Feb. 17, 1963)-
210	ƀƀ	$aChicago, Ill.$cChicago Tribune Co.$dFeb. 17, 1963-
215	ƀƀ	$av.$cill.$d59 cm
300	ƀƀ	$aMicrofilm. Ann Arbor, Mich. : University Microfilms International, microfilm reels ; 35 mm
326	ƀƀ	$aDaily
430	ƀƀ	$aChicago daily tribune
530	1ƀ	$aChicago tribune$b(Chicago, Ill. 1963)
801	ƀ0	aUSbDLC$c19811130
805	ƀƀ	$aOCoLC

UNIMARC EXAMPLES (continued)

1. Newsprint

```
001        (CaBVIUCN)   1434
011        $a08281793
100 ƀƀ     $a19860101a19839999ƀƀƀƀ0engƀ0103ƀƀƀb
101 ƀƀ     $aeng
102 ƀƀ     $aCA$bbc
110 ƀƀ     $acaa
111 ƀƀ     $aey
200 1ƀ     $aThe Sun
207 ƀ0     $aVol.96,no.135 (Apr.11, 1983)-
210 ƀƀ     $aVancouver, B.C.$cPacific Press$d1983-
215 ƀƀ     $av.$cill.$d60cm
326 ƀƀ     $aDaily
430 ƀ1     $12001ƀ$aVancouver Sun
530 1ƀ     $aSun$b(Vancouver)
801 ƀ0     $aCA$bCaOONL$c19830901
805 ƀƀ     $CaBVIUCN
```

2. Microfilm

```
001        (CaBVIUCN) 1151
100 ƀƀ     $a19860101b18841971ƀƀƀƀ0engƀ0103ƀƀƀb
101 ƀƀ     $aeng
102 ƀƀ     $aCA$bbc
110 ƀƀ     $acaa
111 ƀƀ     $aey
200 1ƀ     $aVictoria daily times
204 ƀƀ     $amicroform
207 ƀ0     $aVol.1, no.1 (June 9, 1884)-v.88, no.126 (Nov.6, 1971)
210 ƀƀ     $aVictoria, B.C.$bThe Times Publishing Co.$d1884-1971
215 ƀƀ     $a96v.$cill.$d60cm
300 ƀƀ     $aMicrofilm. Calgary, Alta: Commonwealth Microfilm
            Library. 496 microfilm reels; 35mm
326 ƀƀ     $aDaily
440 ƀ1     $12001ƀ$aVictoria times
801 ƀ0     $aCA$bCaBVIV$c19750314
805 ƀƀ     $aCaBVIUCN
```

REFERENCES

1   International Federation of Library Associations and Institutions.
     International Standard Bibliographic Description for Serials.
     Second edition [Draft].

2   International Federation of Library Associations and Institutions,
     Working group on Content Designators. "UNIMARC: universal MARC format."
     2nd ed. rev., London, IFLA International Office for UBC, 1980.

WORKSHOP REPORT
by
Hana KOMOROUS
University of Victoria, Canada

The International guidelines for the cataloguing of newspapers which were
prepared as part of the programme of the Working Group on Newspapers were
introduced, their scope, their purpose and their proposed use were described
as the basis for the workshop. We decided to conduct the workshop in a very
informal way, where we could just exchange opinions, rather than lecture on
the guidelines or on the principles of cataloguing serials, and that format
proved to be very successful. The discussion included opinions, questions and
concerns of the users of bibliographic and locating tools for newspapers, as
well as opinions, concerns and answers of librarians who have been, who are,
or who will be creating newspaper records in their respective countries.

Let me now summarise the topics of the discussion. First the "Guidelines".
The document was very favourably received by the participants and the guidelines were welcomed as a tool for basic principles for the description of
newspapers, which will eventually facilitate the international exchange of
newspaper records.

Secondly, the level of description. A detailed and lengthy discussion on the
level of description for newspapers resulted actually in a consensus that
despite our desire to provide a full bibliographic record for newspapers, a
basic bibliographic record, sufficient to identify the newspaper, describe it
and link it to related records, is preferable (and economically viable). The
"Guidelines" will eventually be very helpful in determining what the level of
description should be.

Thirdly, one of the main topics was location information on newspapers. It
was agreed that at an International level, identification of the cataloguing
agency and the reporting agency for each country, are preferable to the inclusion of holdings statements from a variety of sources. The reporting agency,
be it an institution, a consortium, a union list or a database will provide
more detailed information on holdings and locations. The workshop participants
felt that the user prefers having location information to more titles, rather
than having detailed information for fewer titles. In other words the consensus was that it is more important to locate a title than to have it described
in detail.

The fourth topic was machine-readable records for newspapers. The discussion
revealed that in general machine-readable records for newspapers in European
collections are not yet available, especially records for retrospective newspaper files. This is not the case in North America, where the bibliographic
databases of newspapers are growing. This is, however, changing and the participants from European countries expressed their desire and their readiness to
create machine-readable records for newspapers. They see that, and quite
correctly so, as a means for the international exchange of newspaper records.

The session ended on a positive note, recognising the need for further
exchange of information and further co-operation.

Workshop (iii)

THE USER'S VIEWPOINT

Dr Jeremy BLACK

Lecturer, University of Durham, Department of History, UK

The most dramatic recent change in the availability of newspapers has been the spread of microform programmes. This has varied chronologically and geographically, and the following reflections arise from the personal research of one scholar devoted in general to the eighteenth-century British press. However, the spread of microforms is so general that it is likely that the issue will soon be of significance in whatever fields it has not yet reached.

Newspapers as a source are distinct from manuscript holdings and should be treated in a different fashion. They were intended for what were, by the standards of the age, distribution and mass production. There was never any sense that they would end up in one location and that they have often done so is a historical accident. In this they clearly differ from manuscript holdings. Furthermore, the location of newspaper material is often a matter of chance. Though national collecting policies now exist they are a very recent development and in the eighteenth century there was no official attempt to collect newspapers. In this respect, Britain, with its lapsing of pre-publication censorship in 1695 and the rapid development of newspaper forms and content that owed nothing to the official newspaper, the Gazette, followed a liberal path that was not necessarily beneficial to future historians.

Without official national collection the survival of newspapers was necessarily random and episodic, largely a matter of the private initiative of individual collectors. A prominent reason for this was the nature of the newspaper industry, dominated by a number of small firms, usually individual printers or consortia of booksellers, that were often of distinctly limited durability. In 1733 the London weekly the Hyp-Doctor, produced by the maverick 'Orator' Henley, claimed that 'the life of a paper is as uncertain as his, who gives life to it.' Furthermore, the nature of the business was such that it was relatively easy to end newspapers. At least initially nearly all newspapers were part of a general printing business. It was therefore relatively simple for printers to test a market by setting up a newspaper, and, if it failed, they could concentrate on their other activities. This lack of specialisation, and, in particular, the relatively low investment required by a printer when founding a paper, helps to explain the large number of titles launched and abandoned. The relatively low level of necessary investment also encouraged the launching of new papers thus engendering additional competitiveness and departures from the market, a contrast with the more expensive system two centuries later. In sum these factors led to newspapers that in general had short runs produced by small scale publishers, not a propitious background for the survival of eighteenth-century newspapers in the offices of their twentieth-century counterparts, though the Stamford Mercury is an obvious exception.

Individual collection was inevitably incomplete and this poses major problems for the modern user of eighteenth-century newspapers. The holdings of even the major libraries are often patchy, and newspapers lack the serried regularity of state papers. A comparison of the collection of papers built up by Dr Charles Burney and held in the British Library with the diplomatic correspondence from the same century held in the same building that was accumulated by the Duke of Newcastle makes this point clearly.

Microfilming is the only answer to the patchy nature of existing holdings and the sole means by which the intention of eighteenth-century printers, namely the provision of a large number of copies of the same item and their distribution in several locations, can be realised. With regard to the first point there is therefore a clear distinction between the microfilming of an existing archive, which simply serves to multiply the number of such holdings, and the microfilming of all copies of an existing paper, which is of far more value for the scholar. The latter is being attempted in the Harvester microfilm edition of eighteenth-century English provincial papers, which has brought together copies of papers held in a number of archives in order to produce as complete a run as is possible. A significant advantage for the scholar and librarian is that it is easier and cheaper to make copies from microfilms than from the originals.

There are essentially two ways in which newspapers can be organised. They can be arranged in a chronological sequence in which the titles are mixed together to form a single, continuous record. This is the method favoured for the Bodleian Library's collection of newspapers compiled by John Nichols. In contrast the principal holding of eighteenth-century newspapers held in the British Library, that accumulated by Dr Charles Burney, is organised by title.

Both methods are of advantage to the scholar, and it is necessary to make clear that there is no single user's point of view, nor any generally accepted optimum method. The political historian concerned to assess the different ways in which various papers assessed a particular crisis is seeking a different organization from the scholar concerned to study the development of a particular title or group of titles. Thus the microfilm company seeking in its market research to establish the nature of existing and potential demand will necessarily receive contradictory advice. As anyway libraries are not going to disbind volumes for the convenience of copiers, it is understandable that microfilming reflects the nature of current holdings, and is, consequently, variable in its organization. Thus, series that seek for completeness by adding material from several holdings commonly do so by adding material out of sequence rather than interspersing it in chronological order. This is understandable, and provided that a clear note is placed at the beginning of each reel, need cause no particular difficulty. However, in time it is to be hoped that material will be produced in order.

In light of current research interests of most scholars it is probably best if material is presented as in the Burney collection. The mixing of titles makes it difficult to study particular papers, particularly if runs are incomplete, and it is fair to say that most scholars wish to study either individual papers or, if they are considering all papers in a given period, find it easiest to do so by a process of accumulating studies of individual titles.

If organization is a problem, indexing is another. The potential and need for indexing clearly varies greatly. If individual scholars obviously seek different information, it is equally apparent that the potential for indexing varies by title. Thus, one of the most helpful forms of indexing can be by author, but whereas this is quite possible for twentieth-century newspapers, it is a very different situation two centuries earlier, when articles were commonly anonymous or pseudonymous. The attempt to decipher the latter and to identify authorship has, in general, proved unsuccessful. Literary scholars have exhausted forests in the case of British newspapers, and their political counterparts have not done much better seeking to identify such authors as Junius. An authorship indexing system cannot therefore be proposed with any confidence for other than modern papers.

With regard to subject-indexes, clear problems of cost arise. To film a newspaper is less expensive at present than to index one, and though intelligent machine-reading systems are being developed it is likely that for a while at least they will not be offered with newspaper microfilms. However, it is at this point that it is best to conclude by noting that it is difficult to predict future developments. Film made possible the duplication of image, thus easing the burden on the scholar forced to take copious notes. Indexing systems will revolutionize content analysis, one of the most interesting areas of newspaper research.

There are disadvantages entailed in microfilming. These include inadequate reading facilities, the possibility that libraries resort to microfilm to too great an extent, to the detriment of the user, the inappropriate location of collections from the point of view of the user and the difficulty of obtaining microfilm on inter-library loan. There is often inadequate information about the location of holdings though the rapidly expanding nature of microfilm poses difficulties in this sphere. With different user and library interests a creative tension clearly exists in the field of microfilming.

WORKSHOP REPORT
by
Jeffery FIELD
National Endowment for the Humanities, USA

In our workshop we discussed collection development policies, and we concerned ourselves with the adequacy of documentation of such policies. Most national libraries collect according to deposit laws, which require the deposit of newspapers. However, we found that the deposit varies from country to country and while the major national dailies are deposited and kept by all the National Libraries, many regional papers and local papers are not necessarily kept by all the National Libraries.

In India those papers become the responsibility of regional institutions and the problem then is a link between the collection development desires of the national library, and what can be achieved working through regional libraries.

In Yugoslavia while the holdings of research and national libraries are well documented, holdings of public libraries are not adequately recorded. There is a problem of adequacy of documentation of local and regional newspapers.

We also discussed adequacy of collections of foreign holdings and while many national libraries attempt to collect newspapers from neighbouring countries, the means of acquiring those newspapers are uncertain. For some institutions it is a problem of lack of equality in the costs of producing items, again an example from India. It is about a tenth the cost to produce a copy in India because of labour costs and other costs as it is in the United States, and so you have a disparity in an exchange programme, if in fact you would like to build your collection through foreign exchange programmes.

We pointed then to a number of problems that libraries face in developing collections, including lack of funds for purchases, and, as mentioned, the inadequacy of both bibliographic and monetary exchange programmes. The lack of complete runs and the lack of information on how to acquire missing issues and again the lack of policies or practices to collect or preserve papers that are held in regional and local areas. We pointed to the fact that many national libraries have no control over local collection developement policies, no legal control, nor control perhaps for preservation standards. We also looked at the interaction between scholars and libraries and ways in which scholars influence collection development activities by national libraries. Some national libraries poll academic departments to determine what their specific teaching or research needs are and attempt to develop programmes that way. Other national libraries depend upon their in-house selection or bibliographic experts to tell them what new purchases to make.

We ended our discussion with some speculation about the way in which technologies of the future might begin to affect collection development policies, particularly as news, the content of newspapers, is transmitted more and more through electronic media. That was however, quite speculative, and we were left then with a list of some problems that we need to solve and hope that discussions tomorrow will give us the means of approaching some of those inadequacies of documentation.

Workshop (iv)

MICROFILM: HARDWARE, STORAGE, STANDARDS AND TECHNICAL ASPECTS

T ILBURY

Reprographic Operations Manager, British Library

1. ORGANISATION OF MICROFILMING UNIT

Microfilming began at the British Library in 1950 with a gift from the Rocke-feller Foundation. The gift came in the form of 4 cameras, 2 microfilm readers, a silver positive duplicator and a film processor. After about 10 years it became apparent that we would need to enlarge on our microfilm act-ivities. This was to satisfy the Library's increased demand for a larger archival and space saving programme, and at the same time to accommodate the ever increasing requests from other national libraries, public libraries and universities at home and abroad.

In 1971 we moved into our purpose built microfilm unit. Here we have a camera force of 27, all 35mm planetary type. These have been divided up into bays, 3 cameras to each bay, designed to get away from a "factory type" of production line. It is far better for a working environment to have small units within a large area instead of long rows of cameras up and down the room. Also when film needs to be changed it is advisable that this is carried out in subdued light, which in effect means only two other cameras need to turn off their lights enabling all other cameras to remain unaffected and to continue working.

In order to keep production flowing it has been necessary to engage 6 support staff ("paperkeepers") for the preparation of newspapers prior to filming. This is primarily for the archival programme where most of the material for filming is in parcels. These are newspapers of which some have been folded for as long as 70-80 years and all need to be carefully ironed out. This saves valuable time as far as the camera operator is concerned leaving him to devote all his time to the job of filming. The paperkeepers also collate, look for any issues missing, pages missing and so on and record this infor-mation for the camera operator to enable him to film an appropriate "board" to inform the user of the microfilm.

After processing all film passes through to our quality control section. We have found it sufficient to have 18 checkers, a ratio of one checker to app-roximately one and a half cameras. A one to one ratio is, I feel, a little too generous as it is always quicker to check a roll of film than it is to create it.

The checking section is divided into individual checking cubicles; this again breaks up the production line effect and personalises the work more with the staff, which I feel is very important when one bears in mind the repetitive nature of the work. As most of this type of work is carried out in subdued artificial light we have tried to enhance the working conditions by using various colours of laminates on the cubicles.

2. QUALITY

Now what is our aim? Or what are we aiming for after we have reduced a very large newspaper onto miniature film? First and foremost it must be of good quality for the reader to be able to read it without any difficulty. It must be of uniform density throughout, even illumination, good resolution and carry sufficient bibliographical information for the reader.

The background density is all important. We would recommend a density reading for most newspapers of 1.2 to 1.4. (What I mean by background density is really the contrast. If you can imagine that the text or information area on the negative are the clear areas that are controlled by the background density, if you therefore allow that density to become as high as 4.4 or 5.4 and so on it will have an overall effect of dulling the clear areas thereby losing contrast). If this is achieved throughout the roll it will enable the subsequent making of the reference copy a comparatively easy task. To obtain a high quality film to archival standards is the all important factor, and this in turn will go some way to eliminating the resistance towards reading microfilms. It is a fairly easy task to record background density by means of a densitometer; most of them record the negative density by means of a digital display readout. Now how is this background density achieved? It is a combination of camera exposure and film processing. The first is variable and the other, film processing, cannot under any circumstances be allowed any variance; it must be controlled at all times. I cannot stress just how important it is. Correct film processing is the key to running a successful microfilm unit.

Most microfilm cameras have a fixed shutter speed so the way to compensate for differing originals is by increasing or decreasing the illumination by the variac control. Now onto film processing. The important points are that all chemicals must be kept at a constant temperature, activity must be balanced at all times, the more film throughput the more replenishment you will require. Cleanliness is also very important. If processing racks are cleaned regularly this will help to eliminate any chance of scratching. It is recommended that film should be processed as soon as possible after exposure and checked initially to detect any malfunction associated with the camera as faults do occur from time to time. Every page should be individually inspected in order to ensure that you have a true and accurate copy of the original file, any pages improperly filmed must be re-filmed along with enough pages before and after the mistake to allow space for splicing. Every effort should be made to keep the number of splices to a minimum, and these should only be made in the master negative; on no account should splices be made in the reference copy.

3. SETTING UP AND MAINTAINING MICROGRAPHICS UNITS

3.1. Planning

First, assess the quality and nature of material to be filmed i.e.
   a) document sizes
   b) quantity to be filmed
   c) whether one or both sides need to be filmed
   d) are they valuable documents that need special handling?
      Must be protected from theft?
   e) expected use of microfilm copies, including required speed of retrieval

3.2. Equipment

a) cameras
b) processors
c) readers, reader/printers
d) duplicators, silver or diazo
e) quality control equipment and refrigerators for pre-exposed process control strips
f) splicers
g) storage equipment
h) silver recovery equipment
i) safes, fire proof/theft proof

3.3. Maintenance

Before purchasing any item of equipment, the guarantee of the supplier to undertake an efficient and effective after-sales service is essential. If no such guarantees are forthcoming, try to get another supplier who can provide them. Equipment will not function or indeed last long if maintenance cannot be assured. All equipment will at some time need attention.

A preventive maintenance programme with the addition of emergency calls is usually the norm. On average the cost per annum is around 10% of the purchase price. If equipment can be purchased and operated in the country of manufacture the problems associated with the supply of spare parts are minimised. If however you have to purchase equipment abroad it is advisable to be sure that the supplier holds a sufficient amount of spare parts and has the expertise to service the equipment.

3.4. Processing

A quantitative test for thiosulphate and certain other chemicals remaining in the processed film should be used to appraise the adequacy of washing. All film destined for archival performance should meet these recommendations. The accepted criterion for adequate washing is the Methylene Blue Method as determined by ISO 417 is not more than 0.7 micrograms per sq. cm. of residual sodium thiosulphate ($Na_2S_2O_35H_2O$) on the film.

3.5. Standards

Standards are essential. Points such as filming procedures, arrangement of the file, film targets, optical density and contrast are all invaluable information for departments whose experience may be limited in microfilming techniques. All film currently made in the British Library Newspaper Library is produced to the recommendations of BS 5847, the "Specification for 35mm. microcopying of newspapers for archival purposes". Standards guarantee that projects such as the Newspaper Library's NEWSPLAN will be successful as far as the quality of the microfilm is concerned, and will be compatible with an ongoing in-house filming programme.

3.6. Storage of microfilm

The archival performance of photographic records depends on the chemical stability of the film, how the film is processed and the conditions under which the processed records are stored.

It is desirable to have properly controlled air-conditioning of the storage area and the correct relative humidity and temperature. It is considered that a R/H of 40% (+5%) and a temperature of 68 deg. F is sufficient for archival storage.

Film should be stored in containers. They can be either a closed non-airtight container or a sealed airtight container. If all air is filtered to remove dust, purified from noxious gases and the R/H is maintained at 40% the closed non-airtight container can be used. If these cannot be quaranteed the sealed airtight container should be used.

The potential life of the film depends largely on atmospheric conditions, temperature, humidity, cleanliness and the manner in which the film is used.

Inspection of an adequate number of properly selected samples should be made at regular intervals.

3.7. Site and service

Vibration often produces serious loss of definition in microforms. Most other drawbacks can be overcome but it is rarely possible to stop vibration. Sites that are over or near a railway, motorway or other roads carrying heavy traffic should therefore be avoided.

Access should be checked before the site is chosen. If rooms are above ground level it is important to check that stairs and lift doors are large enough to allow equipment in.

Floor loading should be checked that it can suppport the weight of the equipment.

Because planetary cameras have to be high above the camera table, a ceiling height of at least 3m. should be allowed if 35mm. microfilm is to be used. Otherwise 2.4m. will suffice.

3.8. Dust

Dust is the commonest cause of films scratching. Dusty slides should be avoided, and rooms where film is exposed and processed should be provided with dust extractors.

3.9. Ventilation

Rooms where film is exposed and processed should be well ventilated as the equipment used will emit some heat and fumes. Ducting may be required for their extraction.

3.10. Lighting

Tungsten lamps should be used for the rooms and there should be an even distribution of light. Fluorescent lighting should not be used directly over the camera, nor should the camera be positioned so that it will be affected by other lights switched on and off during the day.

Cameras should be positioned so that direct sunlight does not fall on the copyboard.

3.11. Readers

Readers should not face windows and should be positioned to avoid reflections on their screens.

3.12. Work stations

These should provide the operator with some privacy while allowing adequate supervision. They should be designed so that the size and number of pieces of equipment can be varied to meet the changes in demand.

3.13. Warning notice

Notices warning of any hazards should be prominently displayed on the equipment concerned.

WORKSHOP REPORT 1
by
Tom BOURKE
New York Public Library

Johan Mannerheim of the Kungliga Biblioteket, Stockholm, was the leader of our discussion. A great deal of what he said was based upon his earlier paper.

We started off discussing the priorities for selection of which there are two major ones. Chronological, which was not recommended, means doing a given time period. The procedure which was recommended was a title by title approach where you simply take a given title and film it in its entirety from beginning to end so at least you get a given title done at a time. We had a brief discussion of format and it was pretty much unanimous that a 35mm roll microfilm format for newspapers still predominates.

There was a discussion of standards which was based on ISO 4087, which was last issued in 1979 and is still pretty much a valid document though there have been some revisions made to a proposed density specification which will change the acceptable ranges which at present run from 1.0 to 1.4 to run from There is something called maximum and minimum density and the change reduces the difference between these from 0.4 to .02, which means you would have less variety of densities within a given reel.

The reduction ratios were discussed and those run fairly standard from 14.1 to 22.1. There was a brief discussion of some miscellaneous matters such as image placement, film arrangement and targetting. We did mention briefly other things such as quality control, the ability to correct a microfilm after it has been processed, which usually involves a sort of splicing. There was a description of the micrographic symbols which are now being used. There was also some discussion on the processing of microfilms, involving the bathing to remove the residual hypo, which can damage the microfilm, problems of legibility, density, contrast, use of splices when retakes are necessary. Some discussion took place of the duplicates that can be made from the archival film and the printing masters. There was a discussion of some of the storage requirements, such as using underground vaults with humidity controls, sealed bags, which it was pointed out by some that should not contain polyvinyl chloride which is not a good thing to have around microfilm. Brief discussion followed on the film types that are being used: silver, which is the camera film and which is also available as a distribution film, and diazo which is a dye process and is considered to be sensitive to light though there has been talk lately that some of the new diazos are less sensitive to light. Reversal processing and the advantages and disadvantages of it was the next topic. Reversal processing means that you can make a direct image negative directly from your camera negative, so if you are going to make a third or subsequent generation copies for distribution you can either go negative to negative to positive, or negative to positive to positive: Johan Mannerheim did not recommend a negative to positive to positive. He claims that his experience has shown that has produced film which have suffered a great loss in tone and loss of contrast.

There was a discussion of the advantages and the disadvantages of retention of the originals. Those of us from America, I think, pretty much tend to take the point of view that the originals should be discarded after filming unless there is a real need to keep them. I think that some of us have found it as somewhat of a revelation that our colleagues in Europe and the rest of the world tend to put more emphasis on retention of the originals. The procedure which is currently being used in Stockholm is that multiple copies of the newspaper are being received, the one copy used for filming is discarded and an additional physical copy is retained and that restricted access to the originals is a matter of policy unless there is a bona fide reason for still consulting the originals which usually involves the use of colour.

WORKSHOP REPORT 2
by
Susan BOYDE
Royal Institute of International Affairs, London

This group benefitted from the very detailed outlines provided by both Johan Mannerheim and its leader, Terry Ilbury, of the procedures and planning needed to undertake a major microfilming project.

The questions discussed were very practical, and concentrated mainly on equipment and machinery. Terry Ilbury took us through the British Library experience in choice of cameras, processing equipment, checking machines, readers and reader printers, and the design of working space.

A proposal was made that the IFLA Newspaper Group could perhaps form a consortium from amongst its members for the purchasing of cameras. This would allow institutes who could only afford 1 or 2 cameras to acquire the West German equipment which the BL would recommend - but which could only be ordered in minimum batches of 8 or 9.

It was also suggested by several participants that the IFLA Newspaper Group should produce an agreed common specification for 35mm roll film readers that were sufficiently robust and well-designed to survive normal library use and encourage users to like the microfilm medium; this should then be put out to tender to manufacturers to enable a good machine to be available at a reasonable price.

Reader printers were also discussed; and whether it was really necessary to choose a machine that would copy whole pages of newsprint or whether A4 sheets were not acceptable.

Other topics dicussed were the kind of staff required for large microfilm projects, and ways of improving their productivity; the space problem now posed by the large and growing quantity of microfilm material; the need to find new storage space and possible solutions such as caves; and film quality and care. With the latter more than one library commented on the need to replace the silver halide working copies of their most heavily used titles. The development of film coating techniques to protect the emulsion from wear was mentioned; and discussion of diazo v. silver halide for working copies produced some positive support for modern diazo.

The group also discussed whether optical disk technology had answers for some of these problems; but sadly concluded that whatever its advantages, librarians were stuck with the practical problems of microfilming, equipment, storage and care for some decades to come.

Workshop (v)

INDEXING, PRESS CUTTINGS AND ON-LINE DATA-BASES

Frank DUNN

Chief Librarian, Today, London

Access has to be via some form of indexing. It is a pointer to the information potentially required. With the advent of the full text data-base
allowing multiple access the index is no longer seen to be an alphabetically
arranged listing, thus disconnecting the physical filing order from the retrieval process. A post-co-ordinate system.

Press cuttings highlight the confusion between indexing and classification.
Cuttings are arranged under subject headings. Often cross referenced by the
simple expedient of posting multiple copies under potentially required headings. A pre-co-ordinate system. Thus published newspaper and other media
indexes often reflect the organisations news library's subject headings schedule. Such schedules have been enhanced and are, in reality, thesauri. Thesauri held on computer are dynamic and offer greater flexibility in access than
a simple alphabetic subject classification.

On-line data-bases can be viewed as those that hold a full text file of the
source and those that do not. The latter, usually bibliographic, tend to be
more structured than the former. Structured not just in their multiplicity of
elements, fields, etc but also in their formality of indexing. Successful
retrieval in either type of data-base can be problematical. In the full text
this is usually due to the fact it is the full text of the source. And thus
reflects the house style (as regards proper names) and linguistic style the
newspaper uses: which invariable reflects its position in the market. Whilst
the bibliographic data-base may not necessarily index nor the classification
reflect the sought after term(s). And any residual style will be that of the
individual indexer/abstracter and the data-base host.

As more newspapers appear in the form of full text files there will be an
increasing pressure for more systematic indexing. A significant pressure
group will be the primary users, the source newspapers themselves. Enhancing
the full text file by using the keyterms from a thesaurus is a possible
answer. And perhaps the solutions achieved in this implementation will ease
the future indexing problems that digital optical disc storage will bring.

WORKSHOP REPORT
by
Dawn OLNEY
Cataloguer, British Library Newspaper Library,

The leader of this session was Frank Dunn, who is the Chief Librarian of the
Today newspaper, and the discussion basically centred on experiences of Frank
as a completely automated newspaper library, which uses World Reporter as its
host.

With the newspaper industry changing so rapidly the Today newspaper library
takes the information direct from the database and once the story has been
input into the system it is electronically available, which then raises the
question if electronic editions of newspapers are different from the hard
copies. There might be a situation in the future where electronic files are
the only way to access newspapers.

We spent some time discussing the problems of online retrieval. Today has a
full text retrieval system which is available on World Reporter, but it does
have certain problems as regards subject access, different spellings particularly between the United States and Great Britain, and also the fact that on
World Reporter you cannot allow synonym control. As World Reporter as a host
has developed, it now has papers on, like the Economist, Financial Times, the
Guardian, the Telegraph, and the Sunday Times and Times to come soon. They
all get their information on to the electronic file in different ways. This
does mean that as most resources do not have a direct imput system, words can
get scrambled and garbled. If you have a very large database it means that a
lot of characters can be misread.

Today library aims to feed their text into World Reporter within 24 hours of
the hard copy being available. The record apparently is 5 hours.

On the question of scanning all different editions, Today like many newspapers
is editorially produced in London but has various print sites around the country. This means that there can be as many as nine different editions. At the
Today library, their solution is to standardise on the last London edition,
and then pull out any stories that have been dropped from that edition so that
they can amalgamate them into one file. Every word is indexed with the exception of 'the' 'an' articles. They are all indexed before the text is ready to
go on the World Reporter, but it does mean that when it actually comes to
searching, it is normally best if you are searching for small articles, rather
than large ones of say 3,000 words or more. It does mean that you can get too
many false drops. How the system actually works at Today newspaper library,
is that on the editorial computer the library staff search the programmes for
the texts and these are then edited at the terminal. Once it is in the format
of the four fields which are used for World Reporter it is then transmitted.
The actual editing is done at the terminal linked to the editorial computer,
which is archived on World Reporter. The library does not clip anything that
is available online such as the Guardian, which is available on World Reporter
as well, but it does keep a clippings file of other newspaper which are not
available, so it does combine both.

Another problem that Today has experienced using online databases as a press
cuttings library is that they cannot file (because they are not cutting their
own paper) the clipping of photographs which does create a problem. They do
therefore have to make a record and they are inputting online that there is a
photograph of that particular article. What they also find is that journalists prefer to actually have clues as to how the story was treated which you
just do not get online; there is no mention of how the story actually appeared
or on what page, which can be quite important. There are no abstracts on
World Reporter; it is full text or nothing, about which again there was a lot
of discussion on whether there could be some possibility of using abstracts.

The reporters at the Today library, on the whole, do not do the searching
themselves, it is left to the library staff. It is probably one of the few
national papers where all the staff are professional librarians. They do use
online databases but also the standard reference tools as well. They have
decided to write their own thesaurus, which does not exist at the moment which

will be for their own use, but hopefully will eventually go onto <u>World</u> <u>Reporter</u>.

Questions were asked about whether they saw any local papers actually going onto <u>World Reporter</u>. The problem there is that for a lot of provincial papers it is not probably worth their time and effort to actually go online. If they have to change their own data quite a bit (and since they will not get too many royalties from it), it is not worth their while.

Finally, Frank Dunn was asked whether <u>Today</u> journalists actually like using online databases for researches, or whether they would prefer the clippings files. As with most things the younger journalists are quite happy to use online databases, the older ones will actually take some prodding.

Workshop (vi)

PRESERVATION STRATEGIES: POLICY, PLANNING AND BUDGETING
Preserving newspapers by microfilming: the role of the Bibliothèque
Nationale

Françoise PERRAUD

Conservateur, Département des Périodiques, Chef de service des dons,
acquisitions et microfilm des périodiques, Bibliothèque Nationale,
Paris

The Periodicals Department of the Bibliothèque Nationale holds all the daily
newspapers published since 1880 and all periodical publications from 1960
onwards in its Paris stacks. Eighteenth century newspapers and other periodical publications up to 1959 are kept in the Department of Printed Books.
Regional, professional and specialised publications of any date are kept in
the Bibliothèque Nationale's annexe at Versailles.

As early as the 1950s, the Periodicals Department was concerned by the particular problems of conservation, storage and access posed by newspapers and
had envisaged microfilming as a solution. Lack of funds, space and staff
meant, however, that the Bibliothèque Nationale's photographic service could
not undertake such an ambitious project then. In 1958, the Director of the
Periodicals Department, Jean Prinet, initiated the creation of a private company to preserve and microfilm the French press, the A.C.R.P.P. (Association
pour la conservation et la reproduction photographique de la presse, B.P.21,
Marne la Vallée, Cedex 2. Tel. (1) 60.17.68.10.)

The chairman of the A.C.R.P.P. is, by tradition, the Director General of the
Bibliothèque Nationale and the Secretary General a curator. There is also a
manager to organise the administration and finance.

Other organisations apart from the Bibliothèque Nationale are represented on
the company's board of directors, such as the various journalists' unions,
both regional and national, the Centre National de Recherches Scientifiques
(C.N.R.S.) and Documentation Française. The A.C.R.P.P.'s aim is to produce
microfilms of the French press which are as complete as possible and of high
quality according to both French and international standards for archival
microfilms. These microfilms are made from items in the Bibliothèque
Nationale's collections. Where gaps occur other collections are borrowed by
the A.C.R.P.P.

The Association markets the microfilms and publishes a catalogue. The latest
issue, which came out in 1985, lists about 3,000 titles. Between 1958, when
it was founded, and 1986 the A.C.R.P.P. produced about 38,300,000 original
negative images, 26,000,000 of which are of old newspapers.

The Association produces about 1,800,000 original negative images a year. At
present, half of these are of current newspapers. About 15,000,000 duplicate
images are made every year.

In 1986 the Periodicals Department acquired 1,400,000 new images from the
A.C.R.P.P.. A <u>Preservation Plan</u> for the Bibliothèque Nationale's collections
was worked out between 1978 and 1980 and funded by a large grant from the
French government (10,000,000 francs a year from 1981 onwards). This then

made it possible to double the microfilm acquisitions budget, to appoint a
temporary member of staff to check the films and to buy high quality microfilm
readers. It is important to point out that, for the time being, microfilm is
still the most suitable technique for reproducing newspapers until the new
digitised media are further developed.

Since the beginning, the Department's priority in its microfilming policy has
been the preservation of the most fragile and most frequently used collections, that is, **the collections of national daily papers from the 19th and
20th centuries which are kept in Paris.** Of 1,800 Parisian daily newspapers
listed in the card-index, 308 of the most important exemplars of the French
press have been microfilmed in the entirety. It has thus been possible to
transfer 10,700 volumes to Provins where they are kept in optimum conditions:
stored flat and in acid-free envelopes where the volumes have been disbound
for microfilming. Once microfilmed, papers are no longer issued to readers,
only the microfilm may be consulted.

In addition to these efforts to preserve **old national papers**, the Department
is taking preventive measures by buying microfilms of 10 **current national
papers**, for example, La Croix, Le Figaro, l'Humanité, Libération, from the
A.C.R.P.P. and the microfilm of Le Monde from Research Publications, the firm
which produces it.

Microfilming has also proved to be a satisfactory solution to the problem of
conserving **local editions of regional daily papers.** Due to a lack of space
and of staff only the main edition of regional papers with multiple editions
used to be kept by the Bibliothèque Nationale. Since 1975, the Department has
been systematically microfilming or acquiring these newspapers in order to
cover all the local editions published in France.

The A.C.R.P.P. microfilms 30 regional dailies, 23 of which are filmed at the
request of the Bibliothèque Nationale. These 23 papers with their 121 local
editions are microfilmed in the A.C.R.P.P.'s studios installed in the Bibliothèque Nationale's premises in Provins. The reproductions of the main
editions are followed by reproductions of the pages specific to each local
edition. The Bibliothèque Nationale's staff at Provins are responsible for
making up the "fascicles", consisting of each day's main edition and the differing pages from the local editions, following a very strict matrix. At the
moment, nine people are employed to do this; in 1986 they made up 6,221
"fascicles".

13 regional daily papers produce their own microfilms or have their various
editions microfilmed by local firms. The Bibliothèque Nationale buys negative
copies of these microfilms from 11 newspapers and borrows the original negatives from two others to be copied by the A.C.R.P.P.

These negative copies, on silver film, or, occasionally, on diazo film, are
used as archival microfilms by the Department. 5,230 reels are thus stored in
Provins at a temperature of $14^{\circ}C$ and a relative humidity of 35%. Positive
copies will be made in Provins for the reader's use.

We will be entering into negotiations with two regional daily papers whose
microfilms we have not yet been able to obtain. We thus hope to achieve our
goal of holding all the local editions on microfilm. It must, however, be
added that the quality of the microfilms sold by the papers is variable as is
the way in which the local editions are filmed.

In the particular case of local editions, the microfilm is not seen as a way

of protecting the originals from use in order to preserve them more effectively, but as a substitute for the document itself.

However, very few of the old regional papers held in Versailles were microfilmed, in spite of the poor state of preservation or the rarety of certain
local papers. The Bibliothèque Nationale has therefore decided to take part
in the action to preserve old regional papers held in municipal libraries
which is being taken by the Direction du Livre et de la Lecture (D.L.L.).
Since 1982 this intervention has taken various forms:

- The allocation of grants for setting up studios in municipal libraries
  or in regional associations for interlibrary co-operation, and for
  concluding deals with private firms.

- Meeting the cost of the microfilming according to the agreement made
  between the D.L.L. and the A.C.R.P.P. in 1983.

The Bibliothèque Nationale only plays a direct part in the microfilming
carried out by the A.C.R.P.P.

In this way the Library has acquired newspapers from 6 French departments:
Aube, Charente-Maritime, Cher, Gironde, Puy-de-Dôme, Saône-et-Loire.

The collections of the municipal libraries concerned are microfilmed in
Provins. The A.C.R.P.P. borrows any missing issues, or those which are in too
poor a condition to be filmed, from the Bibliothèque Nationale. Thus, the
Versaille Annexe lent 24,414 issued and 50 volumes of newspapers in 1986.
Before microfilming, 17,829 pages of these newspapers were restored in
Provins. The Bibliothèque Nationale bought 2,522 30 metre reels from 1983 to
1986, this represents 130 old regional newspapers.

The Bibliothèque Nationale has, exceptionally, lent its own collections to
projects in which it is not involved and has answered bibliographic enquiries
or requests for information about reading and reprographic equipment. The
library has emphasised the importance of reproducing the newspapers published
in the departments which have been covered by one of the volumes of the
"Bibliographie de la press française politique et d'information générale des
origines à 1944". Any microfilming project should be preceded by a detailed
bibliographical study to locate the various collections, to establish the
condition and completeness of the sets of newspapers to be reproduced and to
check which microfilms already exist.

Other microfilming projects for the press are at present being carried out on
the initiative of the D.L.L., as mentioned above.

For example, an association of libraries in the Loire Region (A.R.C.O.B.) has
been given financial aid by the D.L.L. and the Regional Council to set up a
studio in the Bibliothèque Nationale's premises at Sablé. In exchange for
this space the Library will receive copies of the microfilms.

The volume of newspapers to be reproduced for conservation purposes, the frequent gaps in the collections and the cost of microfilming are factors which
have obliged all libraries, including the Bibliothèque Nationale, to co-
operate with each other and sometimes with press organisations and depart-
mental archives. To be effective, a newspaper preservation policy must be
carried out on a national scale and with the collaboration of the libraries
and archives which hold the press collections and of the press organisations.

The efforts of the Periodicals Department are directed towards both old and current newspapers and both the regional and the national press. But every day about 6,000 issues are received by legal deposit. These publications present immediate storage problems (since the stacks in Paris and in Versailles are full) and in the long term will present the same conservation problems as the older collections, given the quality of the paper.

One of the solutions which will most probably be adopted is to buy foreign newspapers only on microfilm to save space. But we do not have the capacity to deacidify and microfilm all the French papers received by legal deposit which it is our duty to keep and make available to the public. The solution of microfilming certain advertising papers and destroying the originals to save space and because "in any case, we can't keep them in good condition" is at present only a hypothesis. We do not have the means to microfilm them. The development of the regional press's own microfilming projects therefore seems to be a good thing, naturally on condition that there is some co-ordination of the various projects and that the microfilms produced are of high quality. The Direction du Livre et de la Lecture has taken on this role of co-ordinator and adviser to the municipal libraries with good results. The Bibliothèque Nationale will take part in some of these projects and will thus be able to continue its action to preserve the newspapers published in Paris and in the ex-overseas territories.

The other aspects of a microfilming policy are preserving the microfilm, its quality, the number of copies to be made, the conservation of archival negatives and access to the positive copies. The microfilms produced by the A.C.R.P.P. comply with the technical specifications laid down by the AFNOR and ISO standards for archival microfilms. The Association uses silver emulsion film on polyester base, 35mm and unperforated. The A.C.R.P.P. is responsible for the quality of the microfilms it produces. The Periodicals Department only checks the legibility of one third of the reels received through the A.C.R.P.P. and of all the reels bought from the regional papers. The latter are also checked by the Bibliothèque Nationale's photographic service. In 1986, 1,670 of the 2,572 reels received were viewed.

The Library always buys the archival negative and two copies of all the micro-films produced by the A.C.R.P.P.:
- The first generation, or archival, negative is not used and is kept in a special store in Paris.

- The second generation, or master, negative, paid for by the Library, is kept by the A.C.R.P.P. to provide duplicates for its customers.

- The positive or distribution copy is used by the readers.

As far as concerns the microfilming projects carried out with the D.L.L., since the D.L.L. made the contract, it is the owner of the archival negative, and the municipal library concerned receives two copies: a master negative and a positive copy. The Bibliothèque Nationale buys one positive copy and shares the cost of the master negative deposited at the A.C.R.P.P. with the D.L.L.

When the municipal library or the co-operative association carries out the microfilming, it owns the three generations: it can then entrust the D.L.L. with the original negative which is kept with the D.L.L.'s own negatives in the Photographic Archives (Fort de Saint-Cyr).

In order to gather together all the information about the microfilms financed by the Ministry, the Direction du Livre et de la Lecture asked the Centre

National de Coopération des Bibliothèques Publiques in Massy to create a com-
puterised catalogue of newspapers on microfilm which would allow the master
negatives and distribution copies to be located. This catalogue will be published at the end of 1987. The shelfmarks for microfilms will also be given
in entries in the C.C.N. (National Union Catalogue).

One of the most pressing problems is still that of storing archival negatives
made by the Bibliothèque Nationale and by the municipal libraries in optimum
conditions for security. Five hundred trays each holding 300m of microfilm
are in temporary storage in Paris and cannot be transferred to Provins where
the collections of originals are kept. The project for a national conservat-
ory, where the original microforms made by French libraries would be kept,
should be revived soon.

The microfilms are consulted in the Periodicals Department's reading room.
There are 27 Bell and Howell Mark II microfilm readers with 18x lenses for
this purpose. This equipment was chosen for its durability, for the size of
the screen (457 x 609 mm) and for the positioning of the screen which is
horizontal and slightly sloped so that the whole page can be read naturally.
This last consideration is vital for readers undertaking long research.

Two Regma AR3 and Fuji 30 AU reader-printers operated by the Library staff
provide prints on paper. Higher quality prints can be made by the Photographic Service within the limitations of the law of March 11th 1957 on literary
and artistic property. The A.C.R.P.P. markets the microfilms.

The microfilm readers are set out in rows one beside the other, shaded from
the light by small cabins made of flame-proof cloth and surrounded by an ever-
increasing labyrinth of filing cabinets containing over 27,000 positive reels.

Given the expansion of the collections on microfilm in the medium term and
even in the short term, we would like two projects to be carried out:

- The creation of a central store to keep the original negatives safe.

- A reading room for microfilms in the Periodicals Department.

The task of conserving and providing access to microfilms could then be
accomplished in the best conditions.

WORKSHOP REPORT
by
Françoise PERRAUD

As a curator of the Bibliothèque Nationale in France I spoke particularly
about the preservation policies in the National Library since 1958. Our experience is different from that of many other national libraries bacause we do
not have any microfilming studios in the periodicals department. We have
entrusted this to a private company called the French Association for the
Preservation of Newspapers. We discussed the criterion for choosing titles to
be restored and microfilmed and the difficulty, even the impossibility, of
carrying out the two tasks at the same time, given the enormous mass of documents to be restored and to be microfilmed and given the cost of the technical
processes of restoration and the microfilm programme. The need to restore and
to keep the microfilmed newspapers did not meet with unanimous approval. The
ideas of our American colleagues are different from those of European librarians, and we have therefore discussed with the working group the following
subjects, should we keep original collections when they have been microfilmed?

Workshop (vii)

PROBLEMS OF MASS CONSERVATION OF NEWSPRINT IN LIBRARIES

Dr Gerhard BANIK

Director, Institut für Restaurierung, Österreichische
Nationalbibliothek

1. INTRODUCTION

On 29 March 1987 The New York Times published an article headed: "Millions of
Books are Turned to Dust - Can They Be Saved?" As an introduction a short
part of this article shall be quoted here [1]:
'Imagine the New York Public Library's 88 miles of bookshelves, and then
imagine 35 miles worth of those books crumbling between their covers.
Library of Congress officials estimate that 77,000 books among their 13
million enter the endangered category each year. At least 40 percent
of the books in major research collections in the United States will
soon be too fragile to handle.

Research is under way, here and in Europe, on methods of repairing and
strengthening damaged paper, but progress is slow. Expensive chemical
treatments can remove acid from book paper and arrest deterioration,
but such measures make sense only for books that have some physical
strength left. The fact remains that about 25 percent of the books in
libraries are beyond hope of ever being used again. They must either
be reproduced in some way or left untouched.'
This statement is an exact description of the actual situation in libraries
and archives in North America and in Europe as far as modern paper qualities
are concerned.

The most important influence on paper permanence from application of modern
technology is due to the introduction of acid agents into the paper. Acid
catalyzed deterioration causes 80-90% of paper decay in libraries and archives
[2]. Especially modern papers are endangered as they are internally sized
mostly be means of aluminium sulphate rosin. Aluminium sulphate is sensitive
to humidity and undergoes hydrolysis if the paper is stored under unsuitable
conditions. The sulphuric acid generated from the hydrolysis reaction of the
aluminium sulphate decomposes the cellulose molecule by breaking the β-gluc-
osidic bonds. This chain-shortening leads to a corresponding decline of the
mechanical strength of the cellulose fibre and the paper respectively. Furthermore paper can be affected by absorbance of acidic compounds from the air,
i.e. atmospheric pollutants like SO_2 or NO_x. Experimental tests on the
absorption of SO_2 were carried out by Hudson and Millner [3] and some recent
experiments have been reported by Sobotka [4] on the occasion of the last
IARIGAI conference.

Newsprint is characterized by its content of short wood fibres and lignin. It
is generally made from acidic pulp that contains a number of impurities and it
has a low surface finish. In order to increase the strength 10-20% cellulosic
fibres - normally sulphite pulp - are added. The resulting paper is of low
permanence and is produced as a "throw-away" product. Research and central
libraries are expected to preserve even these holdings as important historic
records - if possible eternally.

2. CONSERVATION TECHNOLOGIES OF NEWSPRINT

The problem of acidic destruction of paper has been recognized for nearly a hundred years. The first attempt to stabilize paper permanence by a deacidification treatment was undertaken by Sir Arthur Church in 1891 using a solution of barium hydroxide in methanol to deacidify backings of Raphael cartoons. In 1936 Schierholtz was granted a patent for the application of alkaline earth bicarbonates for deacidification of paper [5]. Several alkaline earth compounds have been proposed and serve as neutralizing agents in routine treatments in practical conservation [6]. Deacidification procedures are undertaken by individual conservators treating single items or books of high value. Recently it has been realized that treatment of library holdings in order to extend the useful life of printed books and newspapers is beyond the scope of traditional conservation procedures. This led to the development of several mass conservation technologies in North America and Europe. The basis of all mass conservation technologies is neutralization of acid paper and the deposition of so-called alkaline reserve in the paper web to inhibit its further deterioration by acidic compounds.

In a mass deacidification process the paper has to be neutralized uniformly and buffered at a pH of 7 to 8. This means that books and papers must be penetrated completely in short time by a neutralizing agent that simultaneously is deposited in the paper to build up the alkaline reserve. Naturally the chemicals used should not harm the object in any way. For treatment of library and archival stocks non-toxic chemicals that additionally do not leave an odour in the treated items are required. Mass conservation technologies developed so far include vapour phase and liquid phase processes. For liquid phase techniques aqueous and non-aqueous systems are applied. Table 1 shows the most important technologies of mass conservation already in practical application or in use in pilot plants.

It can be stated that none of the technologies offered meets all requirements of libraries and archives. Mass deacidification is only a part of a complete mass preservation program that is needed by central libraries and archives in order to extend the lifetime and usability of their holdings. Although deacidification of paper is a very important step in order to inhibit its further deterioration, restrengthening of embrittled stocks is necessary as well as protection against detrimental oxidizing and biological attacks. A detailed discussion of advantages and disadvantages of the technologies listed up in Table 1 is given by Smith [7], Kelly [8] and Cunha [9].

It must be mentioned here that the two technologies developed in the US, the diethyl zinc process and the methyl magnesium carbonate process, lead only to deacidification and the treatments do not include any restrengthening of the paper. The application therefore is useful for non-affected or moderately weakened items. The three other processes shown in the table combine deacidification and restrengthening of the paper. The technique developed at the Austrian National Library which is described below is applicable for embrittled items showing no or moderate physical damage. The approach of the British Library prefers strengthening by means of deposition of a polymer within the paper web to deacidification. Simultaneous deacidification is possible by adding an amine compound to the strengthening agent (10). Only the technology practised in the German Democratic Republic offers a solution for mass conservation of heavily mechanically destroyed paper. This technique includes the introduction of a new paper carrier to the treated item leading to an increase

of paper thickness. From a technological aspect this is an excellent solution
for longterm restrengthening, but as the original character of the item is
changed, the technique is not generally accepted in conservation.

Although libraries and archives are expected to preserve the original, the use
of photocopies, microfilm, optical discs and magnetic media should be considered as a final solution to replace unusable items. According to ageing
tests, archive quality microfilms have a lifetime of several hundred years
(11). The other substitution techniques mentioned so far are not tested carefully enough to estimate the longterm stability of the materials.

3. THE VIENNESE METHOD

The preservation procedure for the treatment of newsprint developed at the
Austrian National Library is based on an aqueous infiltration treatment. The
process involves deacidification and restrengthening of embrittled newsprint.
Like the diethyl zinc process and the methyl magnesium carbonate process, the
Viennese method depends on the use of a vacuum chamber to introduce the deacidifying and restrengthening chemicals into the paper. The simultaneous deacidification and strengthening of the paper have the advantage that besides the
deacidification and buffering the sizing agent will retard the further degradation of the paper due to the influence of oxidizing agents. It is known that
even diluted vegetable sizes retard the yellowing of newsprint which is the
consequence of the oxidation of lignin being present in the wood pulp.

As a strengthening agent a methylcellulose of low viscosity and as neutralizing agent calcium hydroxyde were chosen after previous testing. After impregnation the items are shock frozen at -40°C in order to avoid formation of
large crystals that can cause decay of the paper web. The final step is
freeze drying of the frozen block to prevent individual sheets from sticking
together during the drying process. The technique has been described in
detail by Wächter on the occasion of the IFLA meeting in Vienna 1986 [12].

In general the process is designed for the treatment of complete book-blocks
after removal of the book cover. The most important problem of the technique
is connected with the penetration behaviour of the deacidifying and restrengthening solution. A book block acts like a filter, similar to absorbing
layers in thin-layer chromatography. That means that the solvent – which is
water – is penetrating more easily through the material than the dissolved
neutralizing and restrengthening chemicals. To overcome this disadvantage the
thickness of the spine must be limited to 4 cm. To handle thicker volumes,
the blocks are divided in such a way that the remainder of the binding stays
in the block in order to prevent movement of the individual sheets during
treatment. For further improvement of the penetration behaviour a restrengthening agent of low viscosity like MC 40 has to be used. MC 40 shows to a
small extent a weaker strengthening effect than products of higher viscosity,
e.g. MC 400, but the material envelopes the fibres more uniformly and therefore provides a sufficient mechanical support for the treated paper.

Due to the aqueous impregnation the book-block swells extensively to about
twice its normal thickness. The swelling can be reduced to a quarter by
pressing out excess liquid. This in addition leads to a reduction of the
drying time in the freeze dryer. The treatment does not cause significant
change in the dimension of the treated papers or book-blocks. The original
book cover therefore can be used again.

In our opinion an aqueous treatment has some additional advantages. Firstly acidic compounds being present in the paper and discolouration products from the oxidation of lignin and cellulose are at least partly washed out. Secondly printing inks and stamping inks according to our experience have proved not to be sensitive to the treatment. This is an advantage especially in comparison with non-aqueous liquid infiltration procedures on the basis of alcohol solutions, where stamping inks and coloured illustrations have to be masked in order to avoid bleeding and offsetting [13].

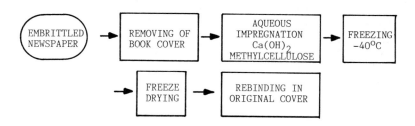

4. TESTING PROGRAM FOR INVESTIGATION OF PAPER IMPROVEMENT

To evaluate the performance of the deacidification and strengthening process used, several tests were chosen which are mainly designed for industrial paper testing. Unfortunately industrial test procedures do not meet the specific requirements of archives and libraries as far as the improvement of usability and permanence of the treated items is concerned. Therefore a testing program had to be established involving mechanical, chemical and optical test procedures. For the initial part of the investigations the following procedures were considered the most important.

- Folding endurance
  The measurement of the folding endurance is the most widely used testing procedure for the investigation of the mechanical properties of paper during ageing. This test procedure evaluates the fibre - fibre bonds in the paper and its results can only be taken as approximate values of the flexibility of the paper which mainly influences its longterm usability.

- pH measurements
  As already mentioned the presence of acidity in the paper has a detrimental effect on its durability. The success of any mass preservation program therefore is connected with a uniform neutralization and buffering of the paper due to the treatment. The measurement of the internal acidity gives information on penetration and deposition of the neutralizing agent into the paper web and can be measured either by extraction procedures according to the DIN Standard Proposal 53.124 or on the surface according to the procedure proposed by Merck [14] if the integrity of the object is important. Both methods have been used and approximately lead to the same results.

- Ink-resistance
  Ink-resistance-tests are normally used to investigate the wettability of paper. In case the method could be successfully applied to test the change in wetting behaviour due to the conservation treatment. A normal quality of newsprint absorbs water. In the course of its natural ageing the mat-

erial becomes more and more hydrophobic. This is probably due to the fact that the most porous particles in the paper formed by the grinding operation which are responsible for the sheet flexibility and wettability undergo accelerated decomposition during natural ageing.

All tests were carried out with non-treated, treated and artificially aged paper. For artificial ageing a large variety of conditions have been proposed so far. Temperatures of 105°C, and 85°C are used to age in dry atmosphere and 85°C and 60°C at 68% RH for artificial ageing in moist atmosphere. According to investigations by Graminski et al. [15] temperatures below 70°C cause accelerated degradation of paper similar to natural ageing processes that occur at room temperature. The climate conditions used for this test program are evaluated from a research program executed by Sobotka at the GLY (16). According to this result the samples were aged in a climate chamber for 240 hours at 60°C and 80% RH.

5. RESULTS

5.1. Folding endurance

The measurements of folding endurance have clearly shown an improvement of the mechanical strength of the treated paper. The values of untreated naturally aged newsprint are between 0 and 5 double folds. The improvement in the folding endurance is reasonable but in terms of absolute folding endurance units remain still poor. To a certain extent the requirements of a library are fulfilled as the conclusion can be drawn that the increase in mechanical strength will increase the usability of the items. By means of the artificial ageing tests it could be proved that the improvement in mechanical strength is stable to the applied ageing procedure.

5.2. pH Measurements

The results of the pH measurements by surface and extraction methods have shown that book-blocks are penetrated by the solutions in the vacuum chamber. The books are sufficiently deacidified and the measured pH range between 9 and 5.7 according to the penetration direction. The deacidification can be further improved by spreading up the book-block during the soaking proceau_re or raising the concentration of calcium hydroxide in the solution. The results shown in the appendix respresent the deviation of the different measuring points on the sheet from pH7.

5.3. Ink resistance

The results of the test program are shown in the graphics in the appendix. It can be seen that the aged newsprint is receptive to ink penetration only to a very small extent. In addition the results show that in the middle of the text-block where the individual leaves are protected from oxidizing attacks and from absorbance of acid pollutants, the ink resistance is lower. Due to the treatment the paper becomes hydrophylic and the ink resistance is similar to the behaviour of unaged newsprint. The wettability is reduced to a small extent due to artificial ageing. The results can be taken as an indirect proof for a homogenous penetration of the polar methyl cellulose into the book-block.

6. CONCLUSION

The conservation technique recently developed and installed at the Austrian National Library allows the treatment of 56 volumes of newspapers per week. The process is certainly unable to treat such a large amount of books as it is planned for the DEZ process for the Library of Congress which is designed for treatment of 15,000 volumes of printed books per week. The system is flexible in its application and offers simultaneous neutralization and restrengthening of the paper within one operation. The results achieved so far from testing the improvement of the treated items make it evident that the technology is a suitable approach to newsprint conservation.

REFERENCES

1   Stange, E, 'Millions of books are turning to dust – can they be saved?' in: The New York Times Book Review, 29 March 1987, p.3.

2   Smith, R D, 'The History and use of magnesium alkoxides in the nonaqueous deacidification of books, documents and works of art on paper', Paper presented at the 1983 Annual Meeting of Internationale Arbeitsgemeinschaft der Archiv-, Bibliothek- und Graphikrestauratoren (IADA), The Hague, Netherlands, 13 Sept. 1983.

3   Hudson, F L, and Milner W D, 'The permanence of paper', in: Paper Technology, Vol.2, 1961, p.155.

4   Kobotka, W, 'The effect of atmospheric pollution on printed paper and pollution by burning off paper'; in: W H Bank, (editor) 'Advances in Printing Science and Technology'. London, Pentech Press, 1986, p.52.

5   Smith, R D, 'Nonaqueous deacidification: its philosophies, origin and status', in: 'Proceedings of New Directions in Paper Conservation, 10th Annual Conference of The Institute of Paper Conservation'. Oxford, in press.

6   Daniels, V, 'Aqueous deacidification of paper', in: Petherbridge, G, (editor) 'Conservation of Library and Archival Materials and the Graphic Arts'. London, Butterworths, 1987, p.109.

7   Smith, R D, 'Mass deacidification: the wei to understanding', in: C & RL News, January 1987, p.2.

8   Kelly, G, 'Non-aqueous deacidification of books and paper', in: Petherbridge, G, (editor) 'Conservation of Library and Archive Materials and the Graphic Arts'. London, Butterworths, 1987, p.117.

9   Cunha, G M, 'Mass deacidification systems available to librarians', in: 'Proceedings of New Directions in Paper Conservation, 10th Annual Conference of the Institute of Paper Conservation'. Oxford, in press.

10 Clements, D W, 'Emerging technologies – paper strengthening', in: 'Proceedings of the Conference on Preservation of Library Materials, sponsored by the Conference of Directors of National Libraries, 7-10 April 1986'. Vienna, Austria, in press.

11 'Newsprint and its preservation'. Library of Congress Preservation Office, Preservation Leaflet No. 5, November 1981.

12 Wächter, O, 'Paper strengthening - mass conservation of unbound and bound newspapers', in: 'Proceedings of the Conference on Preservation of Library Materials, sponsored by the Conference of Directors of National Libraries, 7-10 April 1986'. Vienna, Austria, in press.

13 Scott, M, 'Mass deacidification at the National Library of Canada', in: 'Proceedings of the Conference of Preservation of Library Materials, sponsored by the Conference of Directors of National Libaries, 7-10 April 1986'. Vienna, Austria, in press.

14 'Aquamerck, Wasserlabor für den Offsetdrucker'. Darmstadt, E Merck, n.y.

15 Graminski, E L, Parks, E J, and Toth, E E, (a) 'The effects of temperature and moisture on the accelerated ageing of paper'. NBS Report 78 - 1443, March 1978. (b) 'The effects of temperature and moisture on the accelerated ageing of paper', in: Eby, A K, (editor), 'Durability of Macromolecular Materials'. ACS Symposium Series No. 95, p.341.

16 Sobotka, W, 'Simulierung von normaler Älterung von Papier durch Klima-schrankversuche', in: Das österreichische Papier, No.6, 1983. p.27.

WORKSHOP REPORT
by
Merrily SMITH
Library of Congress, USA

The general consensus in this group was that at least one copy of each news-paper title must be saved in the original format, by somebody, somewhere, somehow. And not only that but that the newspaper title must be accessible. Therefore microfilming and mass treatment are both needed. The only presently operating possibilities for the mass treatment of newspapers to deacidify them, that is to stabilise them chemically and to strengthen them physically, are in Austria at the National Library and in the German Democratic Republic in Leipzig. The Austrian process is an aqueous process of deacidification and impregnation to strengthen the paper and the process in Leipzig is a process aqueous also, of deacidifying the paper and strengthening it by splitting it and reinforcing it from the inside with another sheet of very thin paper.

Other systems exist or are in development for the mass deacidification of paper-based materials and for their strengthening. For example at the public archives in Canada, at the Library of Congress, and at the Bibliothèque Natio-nale. But these systems are either not planned for use in the treatment of newspapers, or it is not technologically feasible at the moment to use them for newspaper treatment.

We identified in our session the need to develop national and international policies for newspaper preservation, and to integrate those policies with the overall preservation policies of the library. We also agreed that it was important to work co-operatively in newspaper preservation both at the nat-ional and international levels. In discussion points were made that the lib-rarian must take the responsibility for selecting materials for treatment and for filming, and not abdicate and give that responsibility to the conservation staff. The point was also raised that more published information is needed about technological strategies for mass conservation treatment, including information about costs.

To summarise our session the need was identified to conserve originals, the options available for doing that at a mass level were identified and the biggest question of all was raised but not answered, which is who will pay for it all.

APPENDIX

FIGURE 1. Surface pH measurements, newsprint from 1934 before treatment.

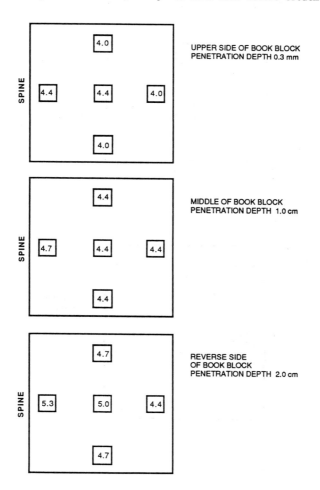

FIGURE 2. Surface pH measurements, newsprint from 1934 after treatment.
Solution: o.8% Calciumhydroxide, 1% MC 400

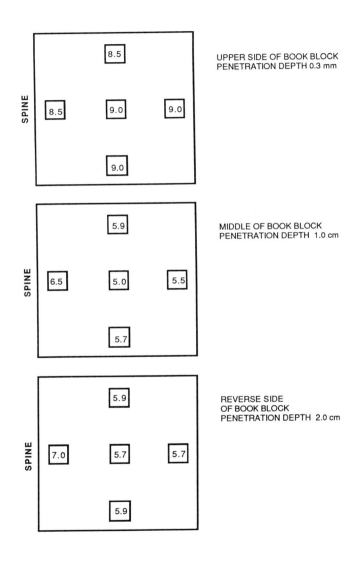

UPPER SIDE OF BOOK BLOCK
PENETRATION DEPTH 0.3 mm

MIDDLE OF BOOK BLOCK
PENETRATION DEPTH 1.0 cm

REVERSE SIDE
OF BOOK BLOCK
PENETRATION DEPTH 2.0 cm

FIGURE 3.   Ink resistance, newsprint from 1934, same treatment as described in Figure 2.

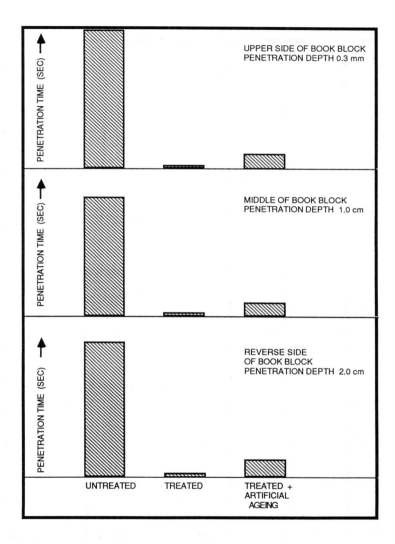

FIGURE 4. Conservation processes.

TECHNOLOGY	PROCESS	AGENT	USER
CHEMICAL DEACIDIFICATION NO PAPER STRENGTHENING	NON AQUEOUS LIQUID PHASE IMPREGNATION	METHOXY-MAGNESIUM METHYLCARBONATE IN FREON + METHANOL	PUBLIC ARCHIVES AND NATIONAL LIBRARY OF CANADA, OTTOWA SINCE 1981 BIBLIOTHEQUE NATIONALE PARIS, SINCE 1986
	VAPOUR PHASE IMPREGNATION	DIETHYLZINC (DEZ)	LIBRARY OF CONGRESS, WASHINGTON, PILOT FACILITY REGULAR OPERATION 1990 EXPECTED
CHEMICAL DEACIDIFICATION CHEMICAL PAPER STRENGTHENING	AQUEOUS LIQUID PHASE IMPREGNATION FREEZE DRYING	CALCIUMHYDROXIDE + METHYLCELLULOSE	OSTERREICHISCHE NATIONAL-BIBLIOTHEK, WIEN SINCE 1986
	NON AQUEOUS LIQUID PHASE IMPREGNATION EXPOSURE TO X RAYS	METHYL METHACRYLATE ETHYLACRYLATE DIMETHYLAMINOETHYL METHACRYLATE	BRITISH LIBRARY, LONDON IN DEVELOPMENT
CHEMICAL DEACIDIFICATION MECHANICAL PAPER STRENGTHENING	PAPER SPLITTING INTRODUCTION OF A NEW CARRIER AQUEOUS LIQUID PHASE IMPREGNATION	CALCIUMHYDROXIDE + COTTON LINTERS AS NEW CARRIER	DEUTSCHE BUCHEREI, LEIPZIG, SINCE 1980

Workshop (viii)

OPTICAL DISCS AND NEWSPAPER PRESERVATION

Bernard WILLIAMS

Director, Centre for Information Media and Technology (Cimtech)
Hatfield Polytechnic, UK [1]

1. INTRODUCTION

Changes in technology since the 1950's are beginning to supplement and sometimes to replace print. Changes in the technology for producing printed publications have implicationsfor preservation - a rapidly increasing proportion
of publications is prepared in machine readable form on computers, word-
processors or photo-composers, and optical discs can store information originally published in print or on microfilm. To varying extents the new media
all pose problems for the preservation of knowledge. Librarians and archivists should take the lead in identifying and solving these problems.

2. OPTICAL DISCS AND CD(ROM) DISCS

Optical discs and CD(ROM) discs store data (which may be in the form of encod-
ed characters or document images) written on to the discs by high power
lasers. The contents are read by low power lasers and may be displayed on
high resolution terminals, printed out, transferred to magnetic media or
transmitted to remote locations. Both types of media are new. Optical discs
are closely related to parrallel developments in video discs and typically
originate from the same manufacturers. Compact ROM discs are direct deriv-
atives of the compact audio discs which, since 1982, have become an established addition to the record market.

Optical discs are currently coming into use in a number of specialised applic-
ations. Current discs are either read-only (i.e. the data is recorded on the
disc by the supplier and cannot be removed or amended by the user) or direct-
read-after-write (i.e. user organisations can record their own data on the
discs but cannot subsequently erase or amend it - these discs in a cumbersome
but explicit phrase are also known as 'Write-once-read-many-times' discs).
Developments are taking place to produce erasable, re-writable discs but these
have not yet reached the market. Potentially optical discs can be used for
the archiving of computer or word-processing data, for the supply of software
and for the dissemination of bibliographic databases and publications. Manufacturers generally claim a ten-year storage like for read-only or direct-
read-after-write discs, but the technology is too young for the claims to be
validated. Standards are lacking, and continuity and technological obsolescence pose major problems.

Like optical discs, CD(ROM) discs can potentially be used for the archiving of
computer or word-proscessing data, for the supply of software and so on.
Physical standards are firmly established (all CD(ROM) discs are 12cm in dia-
meter) but there are no standards for internal formats (i.e. the way the
information is formatted on the disc). Technological obsolescence is less of
a problem: manufacturers' claims for storage life with digital data are ten

years. As with magnetic media, extended lifetimes could be achieved at a cost by transferring the data via a magnetic disc to a new optical disc.

3. THE PROBLEMS POSED BY NON-PRINT MEDIA

To date our preservation and publishing systems have been built up on the assumptions of print media. For non-print media we need a completely different infrastructure. The following are the major issues:

3.1. Legal deposit

There are no depository arrangements or equivalent for material held on magnetic media, published through on-line services or supplied on optical disc. We have undoubtedly lost for all time some information which appeared on such services. There are formidable problems in extending legal deposit to non-print media.

3.2. Obsolescence

The technology of magnetic discs is highly volatile and subject to rapid change. Optical discs are currently in an even more volatile stage of their development and to forecast which discs (if any) might be in use in, say, twenty years' time would be pure speculation. First there is the problem of media and format standards - discs vary in size and internal formatting. The equipment needed to read magnetic and optical disc media is high technology equipment which is both costly to maintain in use indefinitely and impractical to re-build when needed. There are associated software problems: costs of re-formatting are high.

3.3. Integrity

We have no assurance with machine-readable information that changes can be detected or that data have not been corrupted accidentally or deliberately. Obviously there are secutiry measures but these are invariably vulnerable to the skilled 'hacker'. In British government departments I understand that it is now official policy that no information which has been processed in machine readable form is regarded as legally valid. Of the non-print media, only microforms can demonstrate an integrity comparable to that of printed media. The situation is summarised in the table below.

	Archival life	Format standards	Legal	Obsolescence	Integrity
Microforms	Indefinite*	Good	None	Very good	Good
Magnetic media	1 year	Poor	None	Poor	Poor
On-line	None	N/A	None	N/A	Poor
Optical discs	10 years**	Poor	None	Poor	Fair
CD(ROM)	10 years	Fair	None	Fair	Fair
Print media	Indefinite***	Good	Good	Excellent	Excellent

*   Silver-halide film only
**   Read-only or direct-read-after-write only
*** Good quality rag-based paper only

FIGURE 1
Summary of the problems posed by non-print media

REFERENCE

1   This paper is based on an introductory article originally published in
     Information media and technology, the journal of the Centre for Inform-
     ation Media and Technology, No.1, Winter 1985/6. pp.13-15.

WORKSHOP REPORT
by
Graham CRANFIELD
British Library Newspaper Library

In the first part of the session, Dennis Griffiths gave an introductory talk
on recent developments in the transmission of newspaper papers by satellite,
both internationally and within a single country, and on the implications of
local and regional editions being printed at remote sites by this means.

A number of issues arose in the following discussion. What for instance
should we deem to be the place of publication of a newspaper editorially produced initially at one central site, and produced in variant local editions at
several remote sites? This might happen within one country, with five different local variants of the Toronto Globe and Mail or in several countries or
regions as in the case of the Financial Times and Wall Street Journal. Also
the development and the technology, and the decreasing cost of production will
have various other implications, for instance there are plans for in-house
newspapers in airlines and certainly ships. What are librarians to do with
those? More newspapers with smaller circulations will be viable and there are
plans in the UK for a magazine printed at 30 remote sites, at each of which
there is a possibility that there will be a separate local insert, probably
mainly carrying advertising material with possibly editorial material as such.
Again what problems does that pose for the librarian?

A major problem arose from the discussion, namely who is responsible for en-
suring that local editions of newspapers produced, in the way that is described above, are preserved. There was a discussion that librarians in the area
covered by the local edition had primary responsibility but there was a need
for co-operation within that country or between countries to ensure that nothing slips through the net.

In the other part of the workshop Bernard Williams in his introductory paper
discussed the relative advantages of the different storage media and the problems posed by each. Print and microfilm are established media with no new
problems likely to crop up. CD-ROMs and optical discs offer far greater storage density but there are problems regarding the archival permanence of the
physical media and in particular the instability of the technologies, the
likelihood that any given standard or format would rapidly become obsolescent.
In the discussion that followed it was clear that there was considerable interest in the potential of optical discs, in spite of the problems cited by
Bernard Williams. The dense storage capacity of the discs was clearly attractive as was the fact that the discs are not physically degraded by use and
that a single disc can be accessed at multiple sites. It was recognised however that the economics of this new technology are likely to create problems,
because of the cost of the equipment needed to create and access the discs.
The possiblity was raised that newspaper publishers might at some point prod-

uce copies on optical discs for CD-ROMs. One speaker suggested that the main error had been made in the 19th century where there was a change from rag paper to wood pulp and hoped that we might reverse that trend. However, Dennis Griffiths was not optimistic that the economics of most newspaper production would allow a reversion to rag paper, even at the request of librarians! However, he suggested that perhaps the normal newsprint could be sprayed by some suitable chemical on arrival in the library.

Another advantage of optical discs and CD-ROMs was searchability, although only machine-readable text is easily searchable. This led to a discussion on the two different aspects of the whole problem, i.e. the preservation of the content and the preservation of the physical form. Clearly the library is responsible for keeping a copy of the newspaper itself in the original and/ or in microfilm. However thought needs to be given also to how far the librarian can and should enable readers to access the content of newspapers in terms of searchable optical discs or CD-ROMs or online databases.

INTERNATIONAL FEDERATION
OF LIBRARY ASSOCIATIONS
AND INSTITUTIONS
Series IFLA Publications
Edited by Willem R.H. Koops

**16 Library Service for the Blind
and Physically Handicapped:
An International Approach.**
Key Papers presented at the
IFLA Conference, Štrbské Pleso,
CSSR, 1978.
Edited by Frank Kurt Cylke.
1979. 106 p. Bd. DM 30.00,
IFLA members DM 22.50
ISBN 3-598-20377-2

**17 Guide to the Availability
of Theses.**
Compiled by the Section of
University Libraries and other
General Research Libraries.
Edited by D.H. Borchardt
and J.D. Thawley.
1981. 443 p. Bd. DM 68.00,
IFLA members DM 51.00
ISBN 3-598-20378-0

**18 Studies on the International
Exchange of Publications.**
Edited by P. Genzel.
1981. 125 p. Bd. DM 32.00,
IFLA members DM 24.00
ISBN 3-598-20379-9

19 Public Library Policy.
Proceedings of the IFLA/Unesco
presession Seminar, Lund,
Sweden, 1979.
Edited by K.C. Harrison.
1981. 152 p. Bd. DM 36.00,
IFLA members DM 27.00
ISBN 3-598-20380-2

**20 Library Education Programmes
in Developing Countries with
Special Reference to Asia.**
Proceedings of the Unesco/
IFLA preconference Seminar,
Manila, Philippines, 1980.
Edited by Russell Bowden.
1982. 211 p. Bd. DM 68.00,
IFLA members DM 51.00
ISBN 3-598-20387-7

**21 Françoise Hébert
and Wanda Noël:
Copyright and Library Materials
for the Handicapped.** A study
prepared for the International
Federation of Library
Associations and Institutions.
1982. 111 p. Bd. DM 36.00,
IFLA members DM 27.00
ISBN 3-598-20381-0

K·G·Saur München·London·New York·Paris
K·G·Saur Verlag · Postfach 71 10 09 · 8000 München 71 · Tel. (0 89) 7 91 04-0

INTERNATIONAL FEDERATION
OF LIBRARY ASSOCIATIONS
AND INSTITUTIONS
Series IFLA Publications
Edited by Willem R.H. Koops

K·G·Saur München·London·New York·Paris
K·G·Saur Verlag · Postfach 71 10 09 · 8000 München 71 · Tel. (0 89) 7 91 04-0

	DATE DUE	